Lyric Wonder

Rhetoric & Society

General Editor: Wayne A. Rebhorn

Lyric Wonder

*Rhetoric and Wit in
Renaissance English Poetry*

JAMES BIESTER

CORNELL UNIVERSITY PRESS

ITHACA AND LONDON

Publication of this book was made possible, in part, by a grant
from Loyola University of Chicago.

First published 1997 by Cornell University Press.

Printed in the United States of America

Library of Congress Cataloging-in-Publication Data

Biester, James.
    Lyric wonder : rhetoric and wit in Renaissance English poetry / James
Biester.
        p.   cm. — (Rhetoric and society)
    Includes bibliographical references and index.
    ISBN 0-8014-3313-4 (cloth : alk. paper)
    1. English poetry—Early modern, 1500–1700—History and criticism. 2. English
language—Early modern, 1500–1700—Rhetoric. 3. English wit and humor—History
and criticism. 4. Rhetoric—History—16th century. 5. Rhetoric—History—17th
century. 6. Renaissance—England. I. Title. II. Series: Rhetoric & society.
PR411.B54   1997
811'.309—dc20   96-35473

This book is printed on Lyons Falls Turin Book, a paper that
is totally chlorine-free and acid-free.

Cloth printing   10   9   8   7   6   5   4   3   2   1

For Elaine

Contents

Foreword

Stated simply, the purpose of this series is to study rhetoric in all the varied forms it has taken in human civilizations by situating it in the social and political contexts to which it is inextricably bound. The series Rhetoric and Society rests on the assumption that rhetoric is both an important intellectual discipline and a necessary cultural practice and that it is profoundly implicated in a large array of other disciplines and practices, from politics to literature to religion. Interdisciplinary by definition and unrestricted in range either historically or geographically, the series investigates a wide variety of questions; among them, how rhetoric constitutes a response to historical developments in a given society, how it crystallizes cultural tensions and conflicts and defines key concepts, and how it affects and shapes the social order in its turn. The series includes books that approach rhetoric as a form of signification, as a discipline that makes meaning out of other cultural practices, and as a central and defining intellectual and social activity deeply rooted in its milieu. In essence, the books in the series seek to demonstrate just how important rhetoric really is to human beings in society.

James Biester's *Lyric Wonder: Rhetoric and Wit in Renaissance English Poetry* offers a compelling account of the rise and decline in the late sixteenth and early seventeenth centuries of what he calls the "admirable style," a style that is traditionally referred to as "metaphysical" and whose most prestigious practitioner was the poet John Donne. The appearance of this style, Biester argues in his introduction and first chapter, is due to a confluence of social and political as well as aesthetic developments. Living

in an aristocratic, highly competitive culture, aspiring courtiers and writers
in late Elizabethan England sought to distinguish themselves from others
by employing a verbal style that produced a sense of marvel. This admirable style had already been defined by continental Renaissance theorists of
the lyric, who, relying on ancient rhetoric, and particularly on Aristotle and
other Greek writers such as Demetrius and Hermogenes, had pronounced
deinotēs, or the marvelous, the chief end of poetry. The marvelous actually
included a wide range of meanings from forceful and overpowering, through
strange and terrifying, down to clever and witty. To produce it, the poet
was to employ a variety of techniques such as obscurity, roughness, brevity,
and wittiness, precisely the techniques Donne and the other metaphysicals
employed as they wrote their poetry and sought to advance their social and
political careers. Having thus established a fundamental connection between style and social aspiration, Biester broadens his analysis in his second and third chapters, explicating the close relationship between the use
of the admirable style in epigrams and satires and the poet's adoption of the
persona of the melancholic, a persona that was the focus of quite ambivalent responses in Renaissance culture. These chapters also offer subtle readings of Donne's first and fourth *Satyres*, showing how the poems not only
illustrate features of the admirable style, but also thematize the issues, especially the political issues, associated with it. Biester's fourth chapter goes
on to link the religious to the political, showing how Renaissance English
Christianity, like the monarch who was its head, was centrally concerned
with the wonder generated by paradox, mystery, and miracle, and how
writers of religious lyrics consequently produced enigmatic works in the
admirable style in order to elicit a response of wonder in their readers.
Biester's fifth and final chapter seeks to account for the decline of the admirable style in the seventeenth century, a decline that is acknowledged to
have had multiple causes and to have proceeded at a much faster pace in
secular than in religious writing. Here he argues that the neoclassicism of
James's court, his absolutist claim to be the sole object worthy of wonder,
and his easing of the restrictions Elizabeth had placed on courtly advancement all served to make it less necessary for courtiers and poets to "show
off" by employing the admirable style. Finally, Biester points out that neoclassical authors in the seventeenth century, embracing Longinus's notion
of the sublime, continued to see wonder as a legitimate end for poetry, even
as they were dismissing Donne and his version of the admirable style. In
fact, they resuscitated a criticism of that style that went back to the Greek
rhetorical tradition, rejecting it as extreme and sophistical, as creating monsters rather than genuine works of art.

WAYNE A. REBHORN

Acknowledgments

Much of Chapter 1 and a portion of Chapter 3 originally appeared in "Admirable Wit: *Deinotēs* and the Rise and Fall of Lyric Wonder," *Rhetorica* 14.3 (Summer 1996); these portions are reprinted by permission of the International Society for the History of Rhetoric. A brief section of Chapter 3 appeared in "Gender and Style in Seventeenth-Century Commendatory Verse," *SEL Studies in English Literature 1500–1900* 33.3 (Summer 1993), and is reprinted by permission of *SEL Studies in English Literature 1500–1900* 33.3 (Summer 1993). I thank the staffs of the libraries at Loyola University Chicago, the Newberry Library, Columbia University, and the University of Pennsylvania for their assistance. I am also grateful to the Loyola Endowment for the Humanities for a summer research stipend.

Edward W. Tayler and Kathy Eden offered invaluable assistance with the early stages of this project, and I have benefited from the advice and encouragement of James A. Coulter, James V. Mirollo, James Shapiro, Ernest W. Sullivan II, and my colleagues Allen J. Frantzen, Suzanne Gossett, Steven E. Jones, Thomas Kaminski, and Christopher Kendrick. My debt to Wesley Trimpi, who introduced me to the study of rhetoric and its cultural significance, is incalculable. Wayne A. Rebhorn, the series editor, has provided the ideal mixture of challenge and support, and I am grateful to him for both. The manuscript had the good fortune to receive thankfully pointed criticism from Bernhard Kendler, and to be edited by Kristina Kelsey with the assistance of Patty Peltekos. Finally, I am most grateful to my children, for renewing my appreciation of wonder, and to my wife, to whom this book is dedicated, for everything.

J. B.

Note on Transcriptions and Citations

I have modernized spelling by changing *i* to *j* and *u* to *v* (and vice versa), but have otherwise retained original spelling and punctuation in all material quoted, unless specified. Passages of Latin and transliterated Greek omit internal accents. All references to classical texts, with the exception of Hermogenes' *On Types of Style*, are to section numbers rather than page numbers.

Shortened book titles appear in the source citations and footnotes.

Introduction

In act 5 of *A Midsummer Night's Dream*, Hippolyta describes as "strange and admirable" the young lovers' convincing account of their inexplicable adventures overnight in the forest near Athens (5.1.27).[1] Immediately afterward, while considering how to entertain the marriage party, Theseus comes across the abstract that hails the play Bottom and company hope to present as "A Tedious brief scene of young Pyramus / And his love Thisbe, very tragical mirth" (5.1.56–57). Although this description proves all too accurate, it amazes him (5.1.58–60):

> Merry and tragical? Tedious and brief?
> That is hot ice and wondrous strange snow!
> How shall we find the concord of this discord?

In its paradoxes, the brief for the mechanicals' play exhibits *discordia concors*, the unresolved juxtaposition of opposites.[2] The wonder The-

---

[1] All references to *MND* are to William Shakespeare, *A Midsummer Night's Dream*, *The New Cambridge Shakespeare*, ed. R. A. Foakes (1984). References to all other plays by Shakespeare are to *The Riverside Shakespeare*, ed. G. Blakemore Evans et al. (1974). Theseus expresses similar surprise when the hunting party first meets the lovers (4.1.139–42).

[2] On *discordia concors*, see Edward W. Tayler, *Milton's Poetry* (1979), 102–3, 200–204, and 246n20; and Melissa C. Wanamaker, *Discordia Concors* (1975). On paradox, see Rosalie L. Colie, *Paradoxia Epidemica* (1966); and A. E. Malloch, "The Techniques and Function of the Renaissance Paradox," *Studies in Philology* 53 (1956): 191–203.

seus registers is the textbook reaction to paradox, or *synoeceosis*, which John Hoskyns presents in *Directions for Speech and Style* (c. 1599) as "a fine course to stirr admiracion in the hearer," because the audience will "thinke it a strange harmonie which must bee exprest in such discords." Hoskyns, writing in 1595 or 1596, deems it a "figure nowe in fashion not like ever to be soe usuall."[3] The paradoxes "tedious brief" and "tragical mirth" stir the same kind of admiration in Theseus—if not to the same degree—as the wonders in the lovers' tale stir in Hippolyta: the "wondrous strange" style of the announcement is analogous in miniature to the lovers' "strange and admirable" tale of how they found concord after discord.

The verbal parallel between "strange and admirable" and "wondrous strange" should be obvious to Renaissance scholars, yet textual editors have frequently overlooked or undervalued it, proposing to demolish it by emending line 59: "That is hot ice and wondrous strange snow." Eager to make "wondrous strange snow" into a paradox balancing "hot ice," they reject "strange," which in itself poses no more or less than the average challenge to interpretation. In *The Riverside Shakespeare*, for example, G. Blakemore Evans suggests that "strange" is "perhaps an error, replacing some word which with *snow* would produce a 'discord' similar to *hot ice*" (242).[4] Theseus, though, offers "hot ice" not as a paradox parallel to some other paradox which we can recover by emending "strange," but as a wondrously strange method of describing snow.

Here again Hoskyns comes in handy, defining *synoeceosis* as "a composicion of contraries" that "by both wordes intymateth the meaning of neyther precisely but a moderacion & mediocrity of both."[5] In line 59, then, Theseus is not trying to devise his own pair of paradoxes (he is no poet); by noting that snow is not wondrous strange, but that describing it as "hot ice" *is*, he demonstrates that he recognizes *synoeceosis* when he sees it. Warmer than ice, yet frozen, snow is in Hoskyns's terms "a moderacion & mediocrity" of the contraries heat and ice. Only when we

---

[3] John Hoskyns, *Directions for Speech and Style*, in *The Life, Letters, and Writings of John Hoskyns 1566–1638*, ed. Louise Brown Osborn (1973), 150; I have removed Osborn's brackets around letters in Hoskyns's shorthand. Hoskyns's examples, from Sidney's *Arcadia*, include "wanton modestie," "mourning pleasure," "delightfull sorrow," and "wittie ignorance."

[4] Evans is the textual editor, but it is possible that the gloss should be attributed to Lloyd E. Berry or Marie Edel, who also contribute to the explanatory notes. Cf. the gloss on "strange" by Alfred Harbage: "probably an error, since an oxymoron like *hot ice* is wanted; suggested emendations: scorching, scalding, seething, flaming, fiery, sable, sooty, swarthy" (*The Complete Pelican Shakespeare: The Comedies and the Romances*, rev. ed., Alfred Harbage, general editor [1981], 126).

[5] Hoskyns, *Life, Letters*, 150.

hear it described as "hot ice," however, will we be stirred to admiration and forced to convert discord to concord; the word "snow" does not prompt us to consider the paradoxical nature of what it signifies, or to marvel at the author's insight into such mysteries.

Banish poor "strange," then, and we banish Theseus's analysis of paradox as well as Shakespeare's parallel between the wondrously phrased abstract and the lovers' admirable tale. One moral my own already tedious brief tale might point is that overzealous emendation kills the letter and the spirit, but I want to use it in two other ways. First, it warns against the danger of overly confident reading, against taking wonders for signs.[6] The urge to emend "strange" arises not from indiscriminate application of editorial principles, but from a failure to appreciate the force of historical change even, or perhaps especially, on words with which we think we are familiar. In this case, editors have failed to recognize—or forgotten—that the adjectives "wondrous" and "admirable," however distinct they have become, were once much closer. The zeal to expunge "strange" arises not out of ignorance, exactly, but out of arrogance: we think we know too much.

Whatever is strange, Aristotle observes, startles us into attention; the familiar is a tranquilizer, which is why it breeds contempt rather than reverence. We treat a familiar word in early modern literature the way we might treat a buoy in murky and unfamiliar waters, lazily latching onto it as a stable signpost, forgetting that it too may be adrift. Relaxing our attention, we take our sense of the word as always already in force. Paradoxically, the word that seems most transparent can therefore remain most opaque, because by failing to estrange it we miss both its local meanings and the network of associations it derives from other contemporary universes of discourse. "Wonder" and "admiration" remain in the English lexicon, but their modern meanings obscure their crucial force in poetic theory and in Renaissance culture generally. Misreading them means misreading the appeal of the marvelous within the cultural poetics of late Renaissance England.

These changes in the lexicon have kept us from understanding why poets in the late sixteenth and early seventeenth centuries adopted witty, difficult, rough, and obscure styles, and from recognizing the kinds of forces that precipitated this change. By resuscitating the various meanings of "wonder," "admiration," and their cognates, I hope to situate this phenomenon within its cultural context, as more than a merely aesthetic development or chapter in literary history. Because we

[6] On the general risk of distorting Renaissance texts by effacing their obscurity, see Stephen Orgel, "The Poetics of Incomprehensibility," *Shakespeare Quarterly* 42 (1991): 431-37.

have few explicit statements of motive by these poets themselves, recovering what they took to be the purposes of this shift is especially
difficult. But as Jacques Le Goff insists when musing on the lexicograph-
ical and cultural meanings of "the marvelous" in the Middle Ages, the
words must come first: "The history of words is history itself. When
terms appear or disappear or change their meaning, the movement of
history stands revealed."[7] The frequency with which critics connected
obscure wit to "admiration" or wonder reinforces the importance of reconstructing both what these poets understood "admiration" to mean
and why they considered the production of it so crucial to their activity
as poets and as courtiers.

The second lesson I want to draw from Shakespeare's pairing of the
lovers' narrative with the clowns' paradoxes is that contemporaries of
the poets writing in strong lines recognized style as an alternative
source of the "admiration" produced by marvelous tales. In a letter from
William Drummond of Hawthornden to Dr. Arthur Johnston (the only
contemporary text that describes this poetry of wonder as metaphysical,
or filled with "*Metaphysical* Idea's [sic], and *Scholastical* Quiddities"),
Drummond twice specifies the effect of such poetry as "Admiration."[8]
In his *Life of Cowley*, similarly, Samuel Johnson attributes the obscurity
and other "faults" of the "metaphysical poets" to "their desire of exciting admiration." He defines the essence of their poetry as "wit," or "a
kind of *discordia concors*; a combination of dissimilar images, or discovery of occult resemblances in things apparently unlike." According to
Johnson the result of their efforts is that the reader "sometimes ad-
mires" such poems, but "is rarely pleased" by them. Here and in other
references to witty or strong-lined poetry and prose, the effect of obscurity, roughness, and compression is equivalent to the effect of miracles:
wonder, awe, or admiration.[9]

---

[7] Jacques Le Goff, *The Medieval Imagination*, trans. Arthur Goldhammer (1988),
12. On the challenges involved in pursuing the historical reconstruction of words and
texts, see J. G. A. Pocock, "Texts as Events: Reflections on the History of Political
Thought," in Kevin Sharpe and Steven N. Zwicker, eds., *Politics of Discourse: The
Literature and History of Seventeenth-Century England* (1987), 21–34.

[8] In *Literary Criticism of Seventeenth-Century England*, ed. Edward W. Tayler
(1967), 216. For background to Drummond's identification of the kind of admiration
which such poetry causes with that caused by monsters, see Quintilian, *Institutio
Oratoria* 8.Pr.32–33, and Horace, *Art of Poetry* 1–13. Cf. *Literary Criticism*, ed. Tayler, 16, and J. V. Cunningham, *Woe or Wonder: The Emotional Effect of Shakespearean Tragedy* (1951), reprinted in *The Collected Essays of J. V. Cunningham*
(1976), 68.

[9] Samuel Johnson, *Lives of the English Poets*, ed. George Birkbeck Hill (1905), 1:18–
35. For similar statements about the effect of strong lines or "metaphysical conceits,"
see chapter 3 below. Joseph Addison opens *Spectator* no. 58, the first in his influential

However unfavorable Johnston's and Johnson's statements may be, their consistency with each other and with Theseus's response to the mechanicals' abstract shows that, in employing strong lines and "metaphysical" conceits, poets of the late sixteenth and early seventeenth centuries were deliberately seeking to provoke wonder. Such writers were willing to sacrifice clarity and vividness, qualities that authorities on rhetoric and poetry strongly urged them to pursue, in order to achieve this goal. My intention throughout this study is to reconstruct the route by which they were led to pursue wonder regardless of the consequences. The first step is to recognize the raw power of admiration as an emotion in the Renaissance.

Johnson's accusation that "metaphysical" poets produce occasional admiration but precious little delight should put us on alert, because we usually admire with pleasure whatever we think deserves to be approved or imitated. Something quite different provoked the reaction cited in the *O.E.D.* for sense 1.a of "admire": "This would make you admire, your haire stand an [sic] end, and bloud congeale in your veynes" (1.166). In 1626, when that sentence was written, "admiration" could be the dread that turns one to stone, and we had better not forget it. Milder but just as telling evidence of the distance between early modern and current definitions of "admire" appears in Ben Jonson's reputed comment that Marlowe's mighty line was fitter for admiration than imitation.[10]

The realm of the "wonderful" is also a small world now, having collapsed into that which is strongly agreeable or pleasant, but the *O.E.D.* cites from 1632 the sentence, "They made a wonderfull massacre of poore afflicted Christians" (20.495). (This shift seems to have been more recent than that for "admirable": Oz and its wizard pack more terror than Disneyland). "Awful" has been corralled too, moving from the now rare senses of "terrible, dreadful, appalling" and "sublimely majestic" to the more frequent current usage, still designated as slang by the *O.E.D.*, "as a mere intensive deriving its sense from the context" (1.833). That which is "awful" is usually "exceedingly bad" or distressing. Once roughly synonymous with "admirable" and "wonderful" as a term to describe whatever makes one marvel, it has become their opposite. In the halving of their force, these words have all undergone a ra-

---

series of essays on true, false, and "mixt" wit, with the sentence "Nothing is so much admired and so little understood as wit" (*The Spectator*, ed. Donald F. Bond [1965], 1:244).

[10] William Bolesworth is the source: see *Ben Jonson*, ed. C. H. Herford, Percy and Evelyn Simpson (1925–52), 11:45; in the *Life of Milton* Samuel Johnson warns that "like other heroes," Milton "is to be admired rather than imitated" (*Lives*, 1:194).

tionalizing process similar to that which Freud describes as characteristic of the "primal words" studied by Karl Abel.[11] In losing their range of meaning, they have been flattened from expressions of the powerfully ambivalent response to "strange harmonie" into univocal expressions registering differentiated responses to uniform phenomena: they are Leviathan gutted and filleted. "Hence it is," says Lafew, "that we make trifles of terrors, ensconcing ourselves into seeming knowledge, when we should submit ourselves to an unknown fear" (*All's Well That Ends Well* 2.3.3–6).

Along with "marvelous," "miraculous," "astonied," "astonishing," and "amazing," these words belong to the family of terms that includes the Greek *thauma, thaumaston, deinos, deinotēs,* and *ekplēxis;* the Latin *admiratio, admirabilis, mirum, miraculum, mirabilis,* and *mirandus;* and the French and Italian *admirer, merveille,* and *meraviglia* or *maraviglia.* The Latin adjective *admirabilis* and the Greek *deinos* register especially strongly the sense of a response to something that is powerfully affective either positively or negatively, something that so repulses or attracts, or repulses *and* attracts, that it renders the soul incapable of normal operation. *Deinos* has an enormous and fascinating range of meanings, including fearful, terrible, terrifying, terrific, mighty, powerful, wonderful, marvelous, strange, able, and, notably, clever. The weaker modern senses of "admirable" and "wonderful" have obscured the family relationship between these terms, preventing us from understanding both how and how strongly Renaissance poetics, rhetorical theory, and conduct manuals encouraged courtier-poets to astonish their audiences.[12] As Daniel Javitch, Frank Whigham, and Richard Helgerson

[11] *Standard Edition of the Complete Psychological Works of Sigmund Freud,* trans. James Strachey et al. (1957), 11:158–59.

[12] In studying the rise and fall of admirable style from the late sixteenth to the mid-eighteenth centuries, I have relied especially on Cunningham, *Woe or Wonder,* in *Collected Essays,* 1–129; Samuel H. Monk, *The Sublime* (1935); and Baxter Hathaway, *Marvels and Commonplaces* (1968). Anyone hoping to understand conceptions of wonder in the Renaissance owes a substantial debt to Cunningham's work in particular, as Stephen Greenblatt acknowledges in his fascinating analysis of how the discourse of the marvelous informs European accounts of the Americas, *Marvelous Possessions* (1991), 176n79. Although the connection between wonder and the forms of wit that became popular at the end of the sixteenth century has rarely been recognized, valuable exceptions include James V. Mirollo, *Poet of the Marvelous* (1963); Dennis Quinn, "Donne and the Wane of Wonder" *ELH* 36 (1969): 626–47; and, more recently, John L. Klause, "Donne and the Wonderful" *ELR* 17 (1987): 41–66. On the importance of *meraviglia* to the Italian "baroque" theorists, see Joseph A. Mazzeo, *Renaissance and Seventeenth-Century Studies* (1964), 29–59; J. W. Van Hook, "'Concupiscence of Witt': The Metaphysical Conceit in Baroque Poetics," *Modern Philology* 84 (1986): 24–38; and Peter G. Platt, "'Not before either known or dreamt of': Francesco Patrizi and the Power of Wonder in Renaissance Poetics," *Review of*

have shown, these categories of texts and arts dissolve in the practice of courtiers, whose amateur poetry was always at least in part rhetorical performance.[13] Describing these performances thickly, gauging their nature, purpose, and significance within the culture, requires awareness of how poetic and rhetorical wonder resemble wonderful conduct, and how the techniques and principles of one art accord with those of another.

Because we have had close to a century of analysis of the obscurity of Donne and other seventeenth-century poets, of often brilliant transformations of Donne's and Marvell's hot ice into snow, I will focus far less on demonstrating that their poetry was marvelously obscure than on considering their motives for pursuing wonder through style. (Skeptical readers are invited to reread Donne's "Valediction: Of My Name in the Window.") I hope to complement the wealth of close readings by showing with greater scope and intensity what this cloaking action signified, what it meant within Renaissance culture to be marvelous. By recapturing the meanings of "wonder" and a sense of its place in this extensive network of terms in Renaissance critical theory, however, we inevitably gain insight into practice. As Quentin Skinner has argued in reference to Renaissance political theory, "in recovering the terms of the normative vocabulary available to any given agent for the description of his . . . behaviour, we are at the same time indicating one of the constraints upon his behaviour itself."[14] By identifying with precision both the effect of wonder that authors hoped to create and the methods that authorities on rhetoric and poetry specified as means to this end, we will be able to make more sense of their style. We will, that is, be able to place more firmly in context or describe more thickly their choice of style that creates wonder.

"Choice," of course, is a loaded term, and I do not mean to suggest that the mechanism by which authors in the late sixteenth century adopted a style was simple, fully conscious, or uniform. On the contrary, I hope to show that the pursuit of wonder through style in lyric poetry was an overdetermined phenomenon in Jacobean and late Elizabethan England. If choice is defined as full autonomy, then of course these authors no more had it than I do: their practice was circumscribed by the social, linguistic, aesthetic, political, economic, and religious sys-

---

English Studies, N.S. 43 (1992): 387–94; and his forthcoming *Reason Diminished: Shakespeare and the Marvelous*. For earlier conceptions of the marvelous, see part one of Le Goff, *Medieval Imagination*.

[13] See Daniel Javitch, *Poetry and Courtliness in Renaissance England* (1978); Frank Whigham, *Ambition and Privilege* (1984); and Richard Helgerson, *Self-Crowned Laureates* (1983).

[14] Quentin Skinner, *Foundations of Modern Political Thought* (1978), 1:xiii.

tems and codes in which their work was produced. Yet these poets had been explicitly advised to be self-conscious about their verbal acts, to consider the rhetorical impact of their modes of self-presentation in activities ranging from telling a joke to advising a prince. They had cultivated flexibility in moving not merely from Latin or Greek to English, but from style to style as the demands of *occasio* shifted. J. G. A. Pocock suggests that we can fairly ascribe some degree of intentionality to an action when there is evidence that an agent "can be said to have had before him a number of possible actions, giving effect to a variety of intentions, and that the act he did perform, and the intentions to which he did give effect, may have differed from some other act he could have performed and may even have meditated performing."[15] Few records of what these poets thought they were doing (much less what they were meditating doing) survive, but there can be no doubt that they knew other styles and stylistic techniques were available to them: Renaissance poets learned about style above all from manuals of rhetoric, and these manuals repeatedly stress the value of clarity and vividness. The road not taken by these poets was the broad way: the way encouraged as most conducive to communication, and the way that seemed to many authors before and after this era to be most effective given then-standard epistemology and psychology. What I hope to trace, then, is not the obscure process by which a single author decided to choose a style likely to astonish readers, but the obscure network of motives for departing from the broad way available to lyric poets in the late sixteenth and early seventeenth centuries.

Neither their motives for pursuing wonder through style nor the value of understanding this shift can be dismissed as merely formal or formalist: the adoption of a new mode of presentation is a significant episode in the development of English Renaissance culture. Poetic theory and instruction did not provide the sole encouragement to produce wonder, and wonder hardly took on value in an exclusively literary or aesthetic context: wonder both acquired and retained prestige during the Renaissance in a dazzling array of interrelated cultural practices, which together generated its appeal. My analysis, by focusing for clarity's sake on how particular disciplines and sites encouraged the production of wonder, necessarily distorts their synergy. Just as, in Samuel Johnson's famous description of metaphysical wit, one "who dissects a sun-beam with a prism" cannot "exhibit the wide effulgence of a summer noon," so in gathering the remains of wonder's prestige from disparate texts and

---

[15] J. G. A. Pocock, *Virtue, Commerce, and History* (1985), 4.

spheres, I can only hint at its living power in the 1590s, well before its sun had set.

This prestige extends throughout Europe, in disciplines and activities ranging from rhetoric and poetry to philosophy and theology, from outward colonial enterprise to internal competition for power and patronage. Wonder, the anamorphic combination of fear and thrill, was the response generated by that which is beyond or other—by those events, actions, and objects outside the Europeans' experience and expectations. As Stephen Greenblatt has argued in *Marvelous Possessions*, wonder in its multiplicity of senses both fueled the European conquest of the New World and established its dimensions. Greenblatt shows that the marvelous served as a kind of Kantian category through which Europeans invariably filtered their encounters with the geography, flora and fauna, artifacts, and especially the people and customs of the Americas. In the century and a half after Columbus began his imperial venture, Europeans continued to demonstrate their enormous thirst for wonder by seeking out and collecting strange objects and creatures for display in wonder cabinets or *Wunderkammern*.[16] Monsters—understood as prodigies, deviations from nature—provoked similar wonder and study: Bacon, for example, in the *New Organon* calls for "a collection or natural history of all prodigies and monstrous births of nature; of everything in short that is in nature new, rare, and unusual."[17]

Wonder or the marvelous, Greenblatt observes, "is a central feature . . . in the whole complex system of representation, verbal and visual, philosophical and aesthetic, intellectual and emotional, through which people in the late Middle Ages and the Renaissance apprehended, and thence possessed or discarded, the unfamiliar, the alien, the terrible, the desirable, and the hateful."[18] Wonder signified that unstable mixture of repulsion and attraction that characterized many Europeans' response to the New World, the sense of something strange and admirable that pre-

---

[16] On the *Wunderkammern* and European interest in curiosities and prodigies, see Steven Mullaney, "Strange Things, Gross Termes, and Curious Customs: The Rehearsal of Cultures in the Late Renaissance," in *Representing the English Renaissance*, ed. Stephen Greenblatt (1988), 65–92, and *Place of the Stage*, (1988); Katherine Park and Lorraine J. Daston, "Unnatural Conceptions: The Study of Monsters in Sixteenth- and Seventeenth-Century France and England," *Past and Present* 92 (1981): 20–54; and Joy Kenseth, ed., *Age of the Marvelous* (1991).

[17] Francis Bacon, *Works of Francis Bacon*, ed. James Spedding et al. (1857–74; 1963), 2:29. Park and Daston, who cite this passage, describe the gradual shift in attitude toward anomalies as a shift "from monsters as prodigies to monsters as examples of medical pathology" ("Unnatural Conceptions," 20).

[18] Greenblatt, *Marvelous Possessions*, 22.

sented both challenge and opportunity; the experience of seeking, appro-
priating, and possessing the New World, that is, resembled the Kantian
sublime, in which "since the mind is not simply attracted by the object,
but is also alternately repelled thereby, the delight . . . does not so much
involve positive pleasure as admiration (*Bewunderung*) or respect."[19]
Just as for Kant the sublime, unlike the beautiful, induces mental movement, so the Europeans' wonder was both cause and effect of their physical voyages. Of course the violent process of possessing the New World
and making it familiar hardly demonstrated respect, but the energy European nations put into exploration testifies not only to their acquis-
itiveness but to the power of their experience of wonder.

Europeans did not, however, reserve wonder exclusively for the Other.
It conditioned, established, and maintained internal political and social
relations as well, which might be thought of as a series of levels or
mirrors of wonder. At the summit of power, the miraculous divine ex-
acts all love and fear; the monarch's reflected but dread majesty similarly depends on the ability to astonish; and the courtier attempts to
produce the same kind, if not the same degree, of astonishment. Here
again wonder wears two faces, captured in Sir Thomas Elyot's description of majesty's rhetorical effect as "a pleasant and terrible reverence."[20]
Within the fierce competition at court, ability to provoke such reverence serves to mark courtiers off both from those beneath them on the
social scale and from those within their own rank, as Castiglione observes. In the *Book of the Courtier* Federico Fregoso sums up his advice
to prospective courtiers by identifying the common goal of all their activities: the courtier must always strive to have "all men wonder at

---

[19] Kant, *Critique of Judgment*, trans. James Creed Meredith (1957), 91; the German
text consulted is *Kritik der Urteilskraft* (1968). Cf. *On the Sublime*, 29.1 and 35,
where "Longinus" presents sublime wonder as poised between repulsion and attraction, comparing it to the response to powerful, destructive natural phenomena; and
part four of Edmund Burke, *A Philosophical Enquiry into the Origin of Our Ideas of
the Sublime and Beautiful*, ed. James T. Boulton (1968). David Hume's analysis of
"greatness" (*A Treatise of Human Nature*, 2.3.8) also illuminates how the New
World functioned as an attractive challenge to Europeans: "Compliance, by rendering
our strength useless, makes us insensible of it; but opposition awakens and employs
it." Human power is recognized—and therefore in a sense created—only by overcoming such resistance: "In collecting our force to overcome the opposition, we invigo-
rate the soul, and give it an elevation with which otherwise it would never have been
acquainted" (*Treatise of Human Nature*, ed. L. A. Selby-Bigge, rev. Ph. H. Nidditch
(1978), 433). The specific kind of "opposition" Hume refers to is intellectual rather
than physical: the distance of concepts or objects of knowledge from us in time or
space.
[20] Sir Thomas Elyot, *The Book Named the Governor* (1531), ed. S. E. Lehmberg
(1962), 99. See Frank Whigham, *Ambition and Privilege*, 65–67.

him, and hee at no man."[21] Castiglione's widely read injunction recognizes the rhetorical nature of the courtier's actions and discourse, representing the dancing, riding, or speaking courtier as always on stage before an audience of fellow courtiers.[22]

But of all courtly opportunities for amazing, those most likely to prove one fit to wield power were verbal. Of all the ways in which Renaissance poetics—its procedures and its products—have been praised and blamed for being sophistic, this parallel carries the most cultural significance. Just as in fifth-century Athens to be *deinos legein*, or marvelously clever in speaking and interpreting, meant to be *deinos*, or simply marvelous, so the power to speak and write eloquently in the Renaissance was supposed to mean power. Thomas Wilson, writing in 1553, makes the point, although with his characteristic emphasis on the value of clarity:

> Now then who is he, at whom all men wonder, and stande in a mase, at the viewe of his wit and whose doynges are best estemed and who[m] do we moste reverence, and compt halfe a God emong men: Even suche a one assuredly, that can plainly, distinctly, plentifully, and aptly utter both wordes and matter.[23]

In a culture that at least claims to measure one's ability to govern by the mark of eloquence, the ability to astound through words becomes invaluable.

Questions of style are especially significant because courtiers provoke wonder not only through the kinds of actions they perform, but through their manner of performing them. Key to their ability to astound is the *sprezzatura* that conceals the effort required.[24] In Castiglione as translated by Hoby (1561), this association between *sprezzatura* and wonder is explicit: the effect of "readiness" in "rare matters" where "every man

[21] Baldassare Castiglione, *The Book of the Courtier*, trans. Sir Thomas Hoby (1561; 1975), 129. Wayne A. Rebhorn notes that Machiavelli encourages readers of the *Discourses* "in general not to marvel (*non si maraviglieranno*) at the world, especially as they read the analyses he provides to dispel its mysteries (*Disc.*, I,i,125)" (*Foxes and Lions* [1988], 201).

[22] On the role of the courtly audience in affirming the worth of the courtier, and on the individual courtier's status as both performer and audience, see Wayne A. Rebhorn, *Courtly Performances* (1978), 11–51; Frank Whigham, "Interpretation at Court: Courtesy and the Performer-Audience Dialectic," *New Literary History* 14 (1983): 623–39; and Heinrich F. Plett, "Aesthetic Constituents in the Courtly Culture of Renaissance England," *New Literary History* 14 (1983): 597–621.

[23] Thomas Wilson, *Art of Rhetorique* (1553), 182.

[24] See Javitch, *Poetry and Courtliness*; Rebhorn, *Courtly Performances*, 32–41; and Whigham, "Interpretation at Court."

knoweth the hardness of them" is "great wonder."²⁵ Just as unusual natural phenomena astound both by being rare and by seeming to have no
cause, so courtiers astound by mystifying the source of their rare skills.
The apparent causelessness of these wonderful human actions parallels
the apparent causelessness of miraculous events.

Whether conceived of as miracles referable only to God as prime
mover, or as natural questions requiring investigation, strange natural
phenomena evoke terror, awe, wonder: "because we understand not the
true causes, all accidents seeme terrible unto us, and because they happen very seldome, we are thereby affrighted the more" (Seneca, *Natural
Questions* 6.3 [1614]).²⁶ "When else, then," Augustine asks, "does marveling (*admiratio*) arise, or what is the source of this defect, but something unusual and apart from the evident order of its causes?"²⁷ Miracles
for Augustine and heavenly aberrations (*sublimia*) for Seneca of course
have a different order of value from artistic products, but both authors
use examples from the ancient stage to demonstrate how an audience's
inability to understand or duplicate what it sees leads to wonder. "In the
theatre, men wonder (*mirantur*) at the rope-dancer," Augustine insists,
because "the difficulty of the act rouses awe" (*Letters* 120.5).²⁸ In *Epistle*
88 Seneca observes that "The eye of the inexperienced is struck with
amazement by these things [stagecraft, spectacle]; for such persons marvel at everything that takes place without warning, because they do not
know the causes" (88.22–23). Events without perceptible causes are miraculous; seemingly effortless actions that cannot be duplicated, similarly wonderful, become the mark of aristocracy.

As Frank Whigham notes, the emphasis Castiglione places on "readiness" in "rare matters"—*sprezzatura*—is "designed to imply the natural
or given character of one's social identity, and to deny any earnedness,
any labor or arrival from a social elsewhere."²⁹ Castiglione, significantly,
follows Aristotle and Cicero in identifying the capacity for metaphor—
wit—as natural, unlearnable in precisely this sense, which sheds con-
siderable light on why he devotes so much space to witty jests—much

²⁵ Castiglione, *Book of the Courtier*, 46.
²⁶ Seneca, *The Workes of Lucius Annaeus Seneca, Both Moral and Naturall*, trans.
Thomas Lodge (1614); cf. 4.13, 6.29, 7.1, 7.29–32, and *Epistulae Morales* 114.10.
²⁷ Quoted in Kathy Eden, *Poetic and Legal Fiction* (1986), 164n68. As Eden makes
clear, lack of knowledge about causes is equivalent for Aristotle to lack of knowledge.
It is no coincidence that the emotional climax of *King Lear*, the greatest of the Renaissance tragedies written to provoke "woe or wonder," produces Cordelia's line
"No cause, no cause" (4.7.74).
²⁸ Aurelius Augustine, *Letters*, vol. 2, trans. Sister Wilfrid Parsons (1953); for the
Latin text see *Epistulae*, ed. A. Goldbacher (1895; 1970).
²⁹ Whigham, "Interpretation at Court," 626.

more, proportionally, than Cicero does in *De Oratore*. Johnson accuses Cowley and the usual metaphysical suspects of using wit to display their learning, but when we understand their wittiness as one of a number of available strategies for representing themselves as worthy of awe, their pose seems designed to display what they would claim to possess by nature, not by art.

Europeans' responses to works of art and works of artful self-representation were thus tinged by terror, awe, and astonishment of the kind evoked by people foreign and inexplicable to them, by those whose skills rendered them dazzling, and even by events they considered miraculous or supernatural. That wonder was recognized as overpowering when imposed from without, but empowering when possessed, endowed it with rare value; its development into a telos of lyric poetry, however, seems to have occurred not because of the weight of texts, traditions, and disciplines encouraging wonder, but because the peculiar variety of ways in which wonder was conceived enabled it to mimic the three functions poetry had borrowed from rhetoric: moving, teaching, and delighting the audience. The multiple conceptions of wonder available in the Renaissance provided poets with a kind of immunity from the charge that by provoking wonder they were neglecting any one of these duties.

This point is crucial, since although the Renaissance was an age of impressive experiment in literary practice, it was also an age that yearned to coordinate its activities with classical tenets and procedures, even defining itself by contrasting its faithfulness to these tenets and procedures with Medieval divergence from them. "Early modern" may be an easier term for us to justify than "Renaissance," but the older name has the virtue of reminding us how conservative the culture could remain during volcanic shifts in the episteme. For poets and theorists to have devised a new function of poetry that had no resemblance to its functions as classically defined was simply inconceivable, so the protean capacity of wonder to appear in various guises, to lay claim to so many different and even incompatible attributes, was invaluable.

If charged with failing to move, defenders of wonder could cite the Greek rhetorical tradition, where wonder or rapture is the powerful emotional effect of the forceful grand style. Or, for graphic effect, Albertus Magnus's description: "Now, wonder is defined as a constriction and suspension of the heart caused by amazement at the sensible appearance of something so portentous, great, and unusual, that the heart suffers a systole."[30] Even Descartes, no friend of wonder, presents "*ad-*

---

[30] *In I Met.*, Tr. 2, ch. 6; quoted in and trans. Cunningham, *Collected Essays*, 70.

miration" as "the first of all the passions" of the soul, and one of the six primary passions (*Passions of the Soul* Art. 53).[31] A claim to teach? Wonder had been identified by Plato in the *Theaetetus* and Aristotle in the *Metaphysics* as the source of all philosophizing, and St. Augustine had repeatedly insisted that obscure, admirable style provokes inquiry and exercises the soul. Finally, the stress laid by Aristotle on the power of the unexpected and the strange to please, a point consistently repeated by Italian and English critics, offered a potential response to the claim that poetry designed to produce wonder fails to delight.[32]

As examples of the strong lines lyric poets produced in response to the demand for wonder, and of how they are designed to operate, John Donne's epigrams "Hero and Leander" and "Pyramus and Thisbe" and Milton's early "An Epitaph on the Admirable Dramatic Poet W. Shakespear. 1630," are ideal, even if not spectacularly "metaphysical." Among them, these three epitaphs show the range of stylistic techniques deemed admirable. Both "Hero and Leander" and "Pyramus and Thisbe" were originally far more impenetrable than they are in our texts; appearing in some manuscripts without titles, they seem to have been cast as riddles of the "What am I?" (or "Who are we?") variety, offering the kind of challenge laid down for Oedipus by the Sphinx. The wit of the first epitaph lies in its overall brevity, its tightly compressed paradoxes, and its ability to squeeze the whole world—in the form of the four elements— into its microcosm (as in the more famous Holy Sonnet V.):

> Both rob'd of aire, we both lye in one ground,
> Both whom one fire had burnt, one water drowned.

These paradoxes seem less than astounding when we know beforehand that Donne is referring to Hero and Leander, but in the absence of the title they serve as hints or goads rather than as strangely accurate descriptions of the lovers' fate. In a sense the puzzle departs from the usual implied order of the reader's response to a far-fetched conceit: encountering Donne's infamous comparison of compasses to his persona and his beloved in "A Valediction: Forbidding Mourning," the reader seems to be expected to show surprise first at the oddness of the com-

---

[31] René Descartes, *Passions of the Soul*, trans. Stephen Voss (1989), part 2, art. 53.

[32] I will explain why each of these defenses appealed to late Renaissance poets, but the argument can only be hypothetical given the nature of the evidence: it is not empirically demonstrable. The indictments, however, were real enough: from Drummond of Hawthornden's critique of "scholasticall quiddities" as too thorny to be instructive, to Dryden's attack on Donne's love poetry for failing to woo female readers, to Johnson's charge that "the metaphysicals" neglected to please, poet-critics beat admirable style to death for its failure to teach, move, or delight.

parison, and then at its unexpected aptness. The riddle, however, first taxes the reader's own ability to discover aptness, to find the solution that resolves the apparent discord into harmony, making snow out of hot ice.

If not interesting for their manipulations of logic or their metaphoric brilliance, the riddling epitaphs share one crucial quality with more ambitious examples of wit: they offer readers the opportunity to test their own wit. Those who pass the test congratulate both themselves and the author; those who fail seem to be expected to blame only themselves, rather than risk the exclusionary ridicule accruing to those who fail to get the joke. "Pyramus and Thisbe" provides the same kind of test, but its strangeness lies especially in the disruption of metrical and syntactical expectations. By delaying the verb until the second line, Donne renders the first line initially incomprehensible:

> Two, by themselves, each other, love and feare
> Slaine, cruell friends, by parting have joyn'd here.

Shattered by commas that dam its flow and sense, and by the abrupt initial trochee, the first line is the quintessence of what Donne's contemporaries called strong: until reaching the second line the reader cannot possibly know the grammatical function of the phrase "by themselves," or whether the cold contraries "love and feare" are nouns or verbs. Densely paradoxical, "Pyramus and Thisbe" astounds, briefly, both by knotting assorted discords (including the *synoeceosis* of "cruell friends") and by allowing the reader, finally, to pull the string that loosens the knot. The first line, piling indeterminate element on indeterminate element, creates the kind (if not the degree) of frustration, suspense, and eagerness for resolution provided by the complication of a dramatic plot (and perhaps more wonder than Bottom's company produces in their version of the story). The second line, after another metrical jolt supplied by the headless first foot and the near-spondee of the second, resolves into pacifying regularity, ushering the reader out quietly.[33] The enigmatic poem as a whole supplies the challenge of a puzzle and the satisfaction of a puzzle solved. Neither poem has the grandeur that narrative development might provide, or the passion of dramatic action—qualities that later critics would demand as prerequisites for true wonder or sublimity—but both poems attempt to do wittily what

---

[33] Although "cruell" could be read as a disyllable, reading it as a monosyllable throws the emphasis properly onto "Slaine," and poises "cruell friends" more appropriately.

the brief for the mechanicals' Pyramus and Thisbe does only unwittingly: convey the strange wonder of a tale through resources of style.

As a rule Milton and Shakespeare provoked wonder in the more standard way, through epic and tragedy, but when the young Milton wrote Shakespeare's epitaph he praised him through the methods of admirable lyric style. At least part of Milton's agenda, writing his first poem to be published, is to represent himself as "Admirable Lyric Poet" comparable to the dead "Admirable Dramatic Poet" he celebrates.[34] "The king is dead, . . ." Shakespeare, he says, needs no monument of stone because "Thou in our wonder and astonishment / Hast built thyself a livelong Monument" (7–8). Having "astonished" his audience—in the common pseudo-etymological sense of having turned them to stone—Shakespeare can do without further memorial. According to Milton, Shakespeare has astonied "us" by doing precisely what strong lines do—he has provoked our inferences, stimulated our powers of wit. When we as readers have taken Shakespeare's "Delphic lines with deep impression" to heart, "Then thou our fancy of itself bereaving, / Dost make us marble with too much conceiving" (13–14). Shakespeare's Delphic obscurity impregnates our wit, but by leaving us continually "conceiving"—in the senses of both "thinking" and "begetting"—it kills: astonished, we turn to stone, and, in young Milton's even more outrageous pun, marveling makes us marble. Shakespeare's lines are "still-breeding" in the punning sense of Richard II's prison extemporizing, his failed metaphysical conceit of the prison and the world (5.5.1–9):

> I have been studying how I may compare
> This prison where I live unto the world;
> And for because the world is populous,
> And here is not a creature but myself,
> I cannot do it; yet I'll hammer it out.
> My brain I'll prove the female to my soul,
> My soul the father, and these two beget
> A generation of still-breeding thoughts;
> And these same thoughts people this little world. . . .

Despite his intermittent enthusiasm, Richard's effort to find the concord of the discord between his solitary cell and the wide world is iron-

---

[34] John Milton, *Complete Poems and Major Prose*, ed. Merritt Y. Hughes (1957), 63. I arrived at this reading independently of Paul Stevens's "Subversion and Wonder in Milton's Epitaph 'On Shakespeare,'" *ELR* 19 (1989): 375–88, but some of our conclusions are similar. Shakespeare's most notable excursion into lyric wonder is "The Phoenix and the Turtle."

ically "still-born" or "still-bred": he wants thoughts that breed "still" in the sense of "continually," but what he gets are thoughts that quickly die, reminding him of his discontent. Milton switches the scale of values and the cast of characters: Shakespeare the literally dead father lives on in our miraculously impregnated souls or hearts, but metaphorically these hearts have suffered no *petit mort* but the big one, the "systole" described by Albertus Magnus. Milton himself, of course, is implicitly not incapacitated by Shakespeare's Delphic lines, which inspire the poem's central conceit and its attendant puns: in hammering out the poem he is, like Shakespeare, working in marble, a marbler.

Milton would seem, however, to be laying claim to two thrones at once, one of which may still have been occupied: that of John Donne, Monarch of Wit. Milton gives the poem the date of 1630, the year before Donne's death, but it was not printed until 1632 and Merritt Y. Hughes judges the date to be "questionable."[35] First, although the "living monument" theme derives ultimately from Horace and appears frequently in Shakespeare, Milton's formulation of it echoes Donne's "A Funeral Elegy," especially its concluding lines:

> Here needs no marble Tombe, since hee is gone,
> He, and about him, his, are turn'd to stone.[36]

In addition, Donne's favorite pun—that on "dying" as achieving orgasm—is submerged in Milton's pun on "conceiving" in line 14, and the elegy's concluding lines point even more sharply to Donne as its second father (15–16):

> And so sepulchred in such pomp dost lie,
> That kings for such a tomb would wish to die.

Like the miniature tomb or "well-wrought urne" of "The Canonization" that "becomes / The greatest ashes" as well as "half-acre tombes" would, Shakespeare's small but ever-living monument in our hearts is suitably regal.[37] If Milton's play with the elements of "masculine perswasive force" seems forced, his conceit a catachresis, it nevertheless

---

[35] Milton, *Complete Poems*, 63. By supplying an elegy for the Second Folio, Milton is implicitly entering the lists against the elegist of the First Folio, Ben Jonson: on the poem's handling of Jonson, see James Shapiro, *Rival Playwrights* (1991), 193n52.

[36] In John Donne, *The Elegies and the Songs and Sonnets*, ed. Helen Gardner (1965).

[37] John Dryden's first published poem, the metaphysical (some would say grotesque) elegy "Upon the Death of the Lord Hastings," first published in *Lachrymae Musarum* (1649), rings yet another change on this motif, identifying Hastings' "*Virgin-Widow*" as his monument, and urging her to wed Hastings in her soul and to mother images of

demonstrates that he recognized wonder as the mark of praise, and that he viewed an "admirable" lyric device to be the appropriate method of praising an Admirable Dramatic Poet. Milton's meter is more regular here than Donne's in the brief epitaphs, as roughness was the first quality of strong lines to go out of fashion, but Milton shares with Donne the goal of rendering the poetic subject, the poem, and the poet marvelous, and a willingness to do so with style.

In the first chapter I examine how Aristotle's insistence that tragic and epic plots should contain "the marvelous (*to thaumaston*)" expands in the Renaissance into a demand that all poetry create wonder, why this demand leads to a focus on style, and how the Greek rhetorical tradition in particular focuses on wonderful style. After the recovery of the *Poetics*, Italian critics included wonder with fear and pity among the emotions that tragedy seeks to produce, but like ancient critics they largely ignored lyric poetry.[38] There has been very little study of how this absence of lyric theory might have affected lyric practice, of how lyric poets stole what they needed from treatments of epic and, especially, tragedy. Working in a genre that was by definition not narrative, lyric poets could not frustrate the audience's expectations through marvelous scenes of recognition and reversal or through fabulous episodes. Instead, they turned to style, to epigrammatic statement, puns, proverbs, hyperbole, and especially to metaphor: these were the means of endowing language with wonderful strangeness that Aristotle had specified in the *Poetics* and *Rhetoric*. By adopting roughness, obscure brevity, and far-fetched metaphors, they upset their readers' expectations and duplicated, even if in miniature, the astonishing effect of marvelous tales.

For guidance on style Renaissance poets turned to rhetoric, and in the Greek rhetorical tradition after Aristotle these qualities became hallmarks of the most powerful style. Demetrius, Dionysius of Halicarnassus, "Longinus," and Hermogenes were even more explicit than Aristotle in connecting these qualities of style to wonder, or *deinotēs*. For these authors, whose neglected influence during the Renaissance has been uncovered by Debora Kuller Shuger, John Monfasani, and Annabel Patterson, admirable style tends to fall into two categories, in a split that reflects the historical development of the term *deinos* itself: speech

---

his virtue (in *The Works of John Dryden*, vol. 1, ed. E. N. Hooker and H. T. Swedenborg, Jr. [1956]).

[38] See W. R. Johnson's chapter "On the Absence of Ancient Lyric Theory," in *The Idea of Lyric* (1982), 76–95.

may be marvelously clever and polished, like that of Gorgias and other sophists, or marvelously forceful, agonistic, obscure, and concise. These two kinds of *deinotēs* or wonderful style are not always entirely separated either in antiquity or in the Renaissance, but tend to coincide with the two Greek versions of grand style: one artistically embellished and garnished, one raw.

Rough rhythms and bold metaphors are coordinate means of making style *deinos* in Greek rhetoric, but fascinatingly they are also the two qualities that Samuel Johnson finds characteristic of the cult of admiration: he locates its English origin in the "ruggedness" of Ben Jonson's lines as well as the obscurity of Donne's (*Lives*, 1.22). Gregory T. Dime has recently argued that "metaphysical poetry," which scholars "associate . . . principally with conceptual metaphors," should be kept distinct from the poetry of "strong lines," the term used in the early seventeenth century for poetry featuring "metrical irregularity, syntactic condensation, and abstruse ideas." Dime demonstrates that seventeenth-century readers focused less exclusively on far-fetched "conceits" than twentieth-century scholars have, but from at least one angle he creates a distinction without a difference: as Johnson knew, the recognized effect of both compressed syntax and dissimilar images was wonder.[39] The Greek rhetorics that coordinated the methods of wonder Donne and Milton employ—roughness and bold metaphors—were available in the late sixteenth century through translations into Latin, commentaries, and continental rhetorical treatises, but also through alternative channels such as the discussions of amplification in English rhetorical manuals and of jests or witticisms in such works as Hoby's translation of Castiglione's *Book of the Courtier*.

My second chapter examines the lines connecting wit and wonder, and explores the danger involved in posing as a wit in the social context of literary production in the Elizabethan and Jacobean courts. During the later years of Elizabeth's reign, when competition for both political and literary patronage was fierce, any means of distinguishing oneself was potentially useful. Yet the political stature of those who create wonder through wit is difficult to untangle, especially because a quick wit was a traditional characteristic of those afflicted with melancholy, a condition itself regarded with ambivalence because defined both as debilitating madness and inspired genius. Melancholy, in its benign mani-

---

[39] Gregory T. Dime, "The Difference between 'Strong Lines' and 'Metaphysical Poetry,'" *Studies in English Literature* 26 (1986): 47–57. Dime mentions Johnson's inclusion of "strong-lined" features within "metaphysical poetry," but argues that Johnson gives these features little emphasis (54). See also George Williamson's indispensable essay "Strong Lines," in *Seventeenth Century Contexts* (1960), 120–31.

festations, had been associated by Plato, and in the pseudo-Aristotelian *Problem* 30.1, with the height of genius and inspiration. Theseus's famous speech in *A Midsummer Night's Dream* on "the lunatic, the lover, and the poet" has kept that confederation alive (5.1.4–8), but Theseus fails to mention that authoritative texts also identify melancholy as the source of greatness in the *political* sphere. Unlike the cool-headed Duke, Shakespeare's contemporaries—most notably Puttenham in *The Arte of English Poesie* (1589)—regularly included the governor among inspired melancholics. Emerging out of this maze of conflicting evaluations of wit, melancholy, and associated behavior is Donne's *Satyre I*, an Inns-of-Court poem that steers a dangerous course between announcing its poet as satirist and satirizing the satirist's claim to moral superiority.

The third chapter explores a further complication involved in any reading of the melancholy pose: the frequent identification of melancholic satirists as dangerous malcontents and Machiavellians. The curiosity, clipped oral and written style, and skill in dissimulation attributed to melancholics were traits also associated both with tyrants and with historians of questionable repute, particularly Tacitus and Machiavelli. In promoting themselves as witty, then, these poets seem to have been playing a most dangerous game, with enormous risks as well as benefits. The paradox of their unorthodoxy is that it can itself be seen as proof of their capacity to play the modern game of politics: by demonstrating skill in verbal dissimulation, they were displaying themselves as able, like Shakespeare's Hal, to gauge others while remaining themselves the source of constant surprise, wonder. Through sidelong glances at the *arcana imperii*, Tacitus and Machiavelli provided in the political realm what Bacon provided in natural philosophy. They analyzed causes, specifying what means led to what ends, without concern for the moral or prudential perspective on those means. Prime patron of the curious, of those translating, studying, and imitating Tacitus—the so-called *prince de tenèbres*—was the most powerful melancholic at the end of the century, Essex.

Those cloaked in the aura of policy were regarded as suspicious, and they played the part, adopting a verbal style employing what in Roman rhetoric were designated *suspiciones*: obscure phrases offering the audience a chance to display their own wit, to the credit both of themselves and the author. This was precisely what the contemporaries of "miraculous Donne" found most astounding about his poetry, that in Jasper Mayne's phrase "wee are thought wits, when 'tis understood." Combining satire of courtly eccentricity with its own heretical allusions, Donne's *Satyre IV* plays out in a more public setting the strategy of simultaneously distancing and embracing unsanctioned behavior rehearsed in the first satire. Both poems are performances designed to arouse wonder, but the first is sheltered in the near-holiday world of the Inns of Court while the fourth walks abroad in the everyday world of the court. Folly reigns there too, as the poem shows, but the stakes for the poet in satirizing the court are higher.

Given both the strong association of wonders with miracles and the tendency to see even the most explicitly political forms of wonder as modeled on divine awe, the action of adopting an admirable style cannot be understood in isolation from religious and philosophical conceptions of wonder. In my fourth chapter, "Powerful Insinuations: Obscurity as Catalyst and Veil," I investigate how these traditions encourage forms of expression that increase the audience's awareness of human limitations and the limitlessness of the divine. The importance placed by Plato in the *Theaetetus* and Aristotle in the *Metaphysics* on recognizing our ignorance provides a foundation for the Christian emphasis on paradox, mystery, and miracle, and lends further weight to Augustine's powerful defense of scriptural obscurity. To emphasize the incomprehensibility of God, poets such as Donne, Herbert, Crashaw, Vaughan, and Traherne frequently drew comparisons from objects and areas of experience usually considered least divine, cherishing the hieroglyph and enigma as the most appropriate because most awe-inspiring symbols for an unknowable God. In adopting obscurity as a means of self-representation, they also implicitly sought to cloak themselves in the reflected aura of the divine. Christian rationales for obscurity show acute insight into the psychology of wonder, its twin functions of repelling and attracting, and played up the value of preserving reverence and awe. Donne frequently displays his deep awareness of these investigations, and in his Fourth Prebend sermon acknowledges the secular power that accrues to those who deliver knowledge obscurely, through "powerfull insinuations."

The unique matrix of circumstances that drove poets to such extremes of invention did not endure, and my final chapter examines its erratic decay. By the middle of the seventeenth century, wonderful lyric wit, like the wonder cabinet, had lost its appeal, and I conclude by examining the decline of admirable style in light of changes within various spheres of Stuart culture. Although the proliferation of titles under James and the classicizing tenor of the court of Charles and Henrietta Maria made desperate displays of wit less imperative, the continuing circulation of poetry by Donne and other wits kept some features of the movement alive. The banning of satire in 1599, the increased paranoia generated by the Gunpowder Plot, and the Stuart kings' attempts to arrogate all wonder to themselves contributed to the eclipse of quick wit, but in religious verse paradox and mystery established a new orbit, and the sun never completely set on courtly hyperbole.

The new, royally sponsored modes of scientific investigation, designed (to adapt Herbert's phrase) to "rest in Nature, not the God of Nature," were clearly at odds with the metaphysical habit of glimpsing divinity asquint, in the least likely places. The new, complementary Cartesian insistence on clear and distinct ideas combined with the traditional Aristotelian insistence on the psychological importance of the image to make suggestive obscurity seem ineffective in either teaching or moving an audience. Paradoxically, the legacy of Aristotle had made the rise of lyric wonder possible, but it also contributed to its fall, since the antimimetic epistemological premises underpinning strong-lined style were eventually recognized as inimical with the importance placed on the power of the visual image in Aristotelian psychology, rhetoric, and poetics. Stranger still, critics rejected wonderful style at the same time that translation and discussion of the rhetorical treatise *On the Sublime* was raising the general status of wonder. Often wielding comparisons between poetry and painting that, like those of Horace and "Longinus," are grounded in rhetorical principles, these critics treated "metaphysical" pyrotechnics as mere firecrackers compared to the sublime's big bang.[40]

[40] A final irony, beyond the scope of this study, is that the debate over marvelous creations and marvelous style helped to produce the Kantian isolation of the aesthetic sphere, which in turn has encouraged this century's academic treatment of "metaphysical" poems as aesthetic objects separable from their historical, social context, thus in turn obscuring how the style emerged and what, in a cultural sense, it signified: its "rhetoric," in the modern sense. My intention will be to reconstruct this broader context without flattening the aesthetic dimension of wonder.

1 Strange and Admirable Methods

Renaissance theorists concocted various recipes for wonder, but they almost all shopped at the same store, the texts of Aristotle.[1] Theologians may have sanctioned the miraculous to a greater degree, and other authorities on rhetoric were more specific about how to astound, but no one was more responsible for making wonder the primary function of poetry. (The irony here is that later critics of admirable style found many of their ingredients in Aristotle too.) Italian theorists repeatedly invoked Aristotle's specific assertions about wonder as an effect of poetry, and even when they elaborated on these assertions they were often twisting together strands gathered from the *Poetics* and the *Rhetoric*.

Their most significant innovation was in extending to all genres Aristotle's requirement of wonder in tragedy and epic. To explain how other, less prestigious genres should astound, they creatively adapted Aristotle's analyses of epic and tragic plots. Even if lyric poets could not produce wonder in exactly the same ways that tragedians and epic poets did—since by definition they were working in forms that were not narrative—they could still produce the required effect through a similar process, through similar manipulations of logic and psychology. The features of lyric through which poets could best imitate narrative wonder were features of style, and they were identified, conveniently enough, by Aristotle himself.

[1] For an account of the anti-Aristotelian current, see Platt, "'Not before either known or dreamt of.'"

Imitation, Plot, and Style

Although emphasizing that wonder is an effect of epic and tragedy in particular, Aristotle nevertheless associates wonder with all forms of poetry, all forms of imitation. Through imitation poetry teaches, creating pleasant wonder: "Learning things and wondering at things are also pleasant for the most part; wondering implies the desire of learning, so that the object of wonder is an object of desire" (*Rhetoric*, 1.11; 1371a31–b10; cf. *Poetics*, 4; 1448b12–17).[2] Aristotle, unlike Horace and Plutarch, does not see learning and pleasure as merely coordinate effects of poetry. Poetry is not *dulce* and *utile*, pleasant and instructive, but pleasant *because* instructive: "it is not the object itself which . . . gives delight; the spectator draws inferences ('That is a so-and-so') and thus learns something fresh." All poetry, as a species of imitation, causes wonder by sparking inferences, but because tragedy and epic also present actions that are wonderful in themselves, such as "dramatic turns of fortune and hairbreadth escapes," Aristotle focuses on how these forms astonish; he requires them to be marvelous, a demand he does not explicitly make of other forms.

For Aristotle wonder is coordinate with the tragic effects of pity and fear, especially fear, which was at the core of Greek conceptions of wonder. His association of wonder, pity, and fear with tragedy and epic was largely traditional; in the *Ion*, for example, Plato's ingenuous rhapsode describes the emotions he feels when performing Homer: "I will tell you frankly that whenever I recite a tale of pity, my eyes are filled with tears, and when it is one of horror or dismay, my hair stands up on end with fear and my heart goes leaping." Ion also claims that through him Homer sparks the same feelings in the audience: "As I look down from the stage above, I see them, every time, weeping, casting terrible glances (*Deinon emblepontas*), stricken with amazement at the deeds recounted" (535C–E).[3] Aristotle's innovation in the *Poetics* was less in specifying the effects of tragedy and epic than in analyzing how they achieved these effects, and his analysis is our best guide to the later association of wonder with stylistic features of lyric poetry.

Whereas Ion associates poetic effects with particular kinds of stories—tales of pity or horror—Aristotle emphasizes plotting, the struc-

---

[2] Unless otherwise noted, all quotations of Aristotle in translation are from *Complete Works*, ed. Jonathan Barnes, (1984).

[3] All translations of Plato are from *Collected Dialogues*, ed. Edith Hamilton and Huntington Cairns (1963). See also Gorgias, "Encomium of Helen," 9, in Kathleen Freeman, *Ancilla to the Pre-Socratic Philosophers* (1948); and Isocrates, *To Nicocles* 48–49, in *Isocrates*, trans. George Norlin (1928–45).

ture of the action, especially in his treatment of tragedy.[4] Tragic incidents, "incidents arousing pity and fear,"

> have the very greatest effect on the mind when they occur unexpectedly and at the same time in consequence of one another; there is more of the marvelous (*thaumaston*) in them than if they happened of themselves or by mere chance. Even matters of chance seem most marvelous (*thaumasiōtata*) if there is an appearance of design as it were in them; as for instance the statue of Mitys at Argos killed the author of Mitys' death by falling down on him when he was looking at it. . . . (*Poetics* 9; 1452a2–9)

Tragic plots work best, amaze most, by exhibiting surprises that on reflection seem logical, by presenting weird hot ice that we eventually recognize as snow. Poets who ignore the logical continuity of their plots, then, fail to take full advantage of the potential for creating wonder that a particular action, however bizarre, may contain. Surprise won't get it, since Aristotle has almost no use for the random.

Even though a discovery or a reversal alone can produce wonder enough, he prefers plays where they intertwine, such as *Oedipus* (1452a32), and as he evaluates plots he treats the logic of their design as crucial to their ability to produce catharsis. Tragic plots are worst when one "with full knowledge" is about to commit the tragic act but does not: no discovery, no suffering, no tragedy, no wonder. Somewhat better is when the character knowingly commits the tragic act, but better still "is for the deed to be done in ignorance, and the relationship discovered afterwards, since . . . the discovery will serve to astound us (*anagnōrisis ekplēktikon*)" (1454a2–4). Later Aristotle notes that "The best of all discoveries, however, is that arising from the incidents themselves, when the great surprise (*ekplēkseōs*) comes about through a probable incident, like that in the *Oedipus* of Sophocles" (1455a16–18).[5] As J. V. Cunningham puts it, the tragic event "is not what we expected, but what, as

---

[4] In epic, wonder results from unbelievable episodes, which are less likely to be recognized as impossible when read or heard than when seen. Although epic therefore "affords more opening for the improbable" than tragedy, it also perhaps offers less opening for the poet's manipulation of the audience's expectations: its marvelous episodes are improbable under any circumstances, whereas the marvelous scenes in tragedy are unexpected within the structure of the plot (*Poetics* 24; 1460a12–18).

[5] For thorough analysis of both the logic and psychology of tragic fiction, see Eden, *Poetic and Legal Fiction*, 32–61. Aristotle suggests how the unexpected can be probable when he explains why tragic poets use traditional stories and names: "what convinces is the possible; now whereas we are not yet sure as to the possibility of that which has not happened, that which has happened is manifestly possible, otherwise it

soon as we see it, we realize that we should have expected": it is unexpected but somehow probable.[6] Tragic plots astound not through improbability, but through the display of probable events that we might not even have considered possible until they had occurred; once they have occurred, they are convincing.[7]

Substitute "perceptions" for "events," and this analysis fits the metaphor as neatly as the tragic plot: metaphors astound but also convince. Although Aristotle does not explicitly compare the operation of tragic plots to the operation of metaphor, his analyses of style in chapters 21 and 22 of the *Poetics* and Book 3 of the *Rhetoric* made such a comparison possible. Since Aristotle, like other ancient critics, devoted little attention to lyric poetry, his comments on style became especially important for later lyric poets who wanted to comply with his authority by following his prescriptions: in style, at least, they could.[8] Through style they could even imitate the effect of tragedy and epic, because he stresses that distinctive language evokes wonder.

Jolting the audience into attention, unusual language stranges the speaker and the speech pleasantly, insuring that neither will be taken for granted:

> People do not feel towards strangers as they do towards their own countrymen, and the same thing is true of their feeling for language. It is therefore well to give everyday speech an unfamiliar air: wonder is a characteristic of things off the beaten track, and the wonderful is pleasant (*thaumastai gar tōn apontōn eisin, hēdu de to thaumaston*). In verse such effects are common, and there they are fitting: the per-

---

would not have happened" (1451b16–19). As Eden discusses (ibid., 22), Aristotle is inconsistent in his ranking of discoveries; compare *Poetics* 13.6–10 to 14.18–19.

[6] Cunningham, *Collected Essays*, 69.

[7] In *The Advancement of Learning*, Bacon chides "the levity and unconstancy of men's judgements, which, till a matter be done, wonder that it can be done, and as soon as it is done, wonder again that it was not sooner done"; such nonchalance marks the response to Alexander's conquests, Columbus's voyages, and intellectual discoveries such as "the propositions of Euclid, which till they be demonstrate . . . seem strange to our assent, but being demonstrate, our mind accepteth of them by a kind of relation (as the lawyers speak) as if we had known them before" (*Works*, 3:291; Bacon uses "relation" in the *O.E.D.*'s sense 4.b: "Reference or application *to* an earlier date").

[8] On the neglect of lyric by ancient critics, and in particular their lack of interest in specifying its function, see W. R. Johnson, *Idea of Lyric*, 76–95; Albin Lesky, *A History of Greek Literature*, trans. James Willis and Cornelis de Heer (1966), 107–9; and J. W. H. Atkins, *Literary Criticism in Antiquity* (1961), 1:75, 2:44, and 2:288–89.

sons and things there spoken of are comparatively remote from ordinary life. (*Rhetoric*, 3.2; 1404b8–15).[9]

Unfamiliar diction, especially appropriate in poetry, creates wonder and pleasure. As in the *Poetics*, Aristotle goes on to recommend metaphor, for which one must have an innate talent, as the primary means of achieving distinction without sacrificing clarity: "Metaphor gives style clearness, charm, and distinction as nothing else can; and it is not a thing whose use can be taught by one man to another . . ." (1405a7–9; cf. *Poetics*, 22; 1459a3–11). In addition to providing wonder by making speech or verse distinctive, however, metaphor also performs in miniature the wonderful function of imitation in general and of tragic plots in particular.

Like poetic imitation, metaphor teaches pleasantly. Its power to teach and to be simultaneously distinctive and clear have the same source: metaphor introduces and explains the unknown through comparison with the known. Like mimesis, metaphor introduces us to something new, a new object of wonder: "words express ideas, and therefore those words are the most agreeable that enable us to get hold of new ideas. Now strange words simply puzzle us; ordinary words convey only what we know already; it is from metaphor that we can best get hold of something fresh" (3.10; 1410b10–14).

The metaphor also has the quality Aristotle designates as *enargeia* or *energeia*: it places things before our eyes (*pro ommatōn*).[10] This vividness, which it shares with the tragic fiction, makes metaphor forceful and convincing: it captivates, or, more precisely, activates the mind. It also startles: "Liveliness (*asteia*) is specially conveyed by metaphor, and by the further power of surprising the hearer; because the hearer expected something different, his acquisition of the new idea impresses him all the more. His mind seems to say, 'Yes, to be sure; I never thought of that'" (3.11; 1412a17–21). Like the tragic fiction, the metaphor produces wonder by surprising us with what we later realize we should have expected all along: our initial surprise at the unexpected gets compounded when we kick ourselves for not having foreseen the connection. All kinds of distinctive language, according to Aristotle,

[9] I have used Cunningham's altered translation (*Collected Essays*, 63) of the part of the second sentence for which I have supplied the Greek; Roberts offers: "people like what strikes them, and are struck by what is out of the way."
[10] On the distinction between *energeia* and *enargeia*, see Eden, *Poetic and Legal Fiction*, esp. 71, and the studies cited there.

create wonder, but the metaphor uniquely achieves this effect in a manner comparable to the methods of wonder in tragedy.

In Book 3 of the *Rhetoric* Aristotle catalogues other stylistic techniques designed to make language lively, foreign, and surprising, techniques that appear with increasing frequency in the poetry of the late sixteenth century. These other forms of liveliness or *asteia* include "epigrammatic remarks (*apophthegmatōn*)," "well-constructed riddles (*eu ēinigmena*)," puns, similes, "proverbs (*paroimiai*)," and concise antitheses (3.11). Aristotle leaves hyperbole off this initial list, but classifies it as a kind of metaphor and discusses it immediately after his section on *asteia*. In explaining these techniques Aristotle implies that they share the metaphor's ability to spark the audience's inferences, that their impressiveness and value derive from their ability to jump-start the mind of the listener.

When analyzing these techniques, Aristotle puts less weight on maintaining a mean between clarity and distinctiveness than he had in discussing metaphor, and in elaborating on the sources of their power he provides later rhetoricians with the ingredients for a more thorough defense of obscurity.[11] Of antitheses, for example, he notes that "the more briefly and antithetically such sayings can be expressed, the more taking they are, for antithesis impresses the new idea more firmly and brevity more quickly" (1412b22–23). In his treatment of riddles, Aristotle hedges, criticizing overly obscure riddles and metaphors but admitting that their effectiveness in provoking inferences is proportional to their obscurity. Although insisting on some recognizable connection between the terms of a metaphor, he argues that these terms should not be filed too closely together in the mind's system of categories. On the one hand, "just as in philosophy also an acute mind will perceive resemblances even in things far apart" (1412a11); surprising metaphors show mother wit. On the other, metaphors will fail and "their inappropriateness will be conspicuous" if the signifier does not "fairly correspond to the thing signified" (3.2; 1405a10–12). Yet Aristotle also states that "Good riddles (*eu ēinigmenōn*) do, in general, provide us with satisfactory metaphors; for metaphors imply riddles, and therefore a good riddle can furnish a good metaphor" (1405b4–5). Riddles and hyperbole move speech farther from clarity than metaphor proper does, but in making it especially distinctive they too serve as means for later lyric poets to achieve wonder.

---

[11] See Kathy Eden, "Hermeneutics and the Ancient Rhetorical Tradition," *Rhetorica* 5 (1987): 59–86.

The Italian Critics

In disseminating the *Poetics*, literary critics of the Italian Renaissance conflate it with the *Rhetoric* and other authoritative critical texts, especially Horace's *Ars Poetica*, and produce versions of wonder that have their own distinguishing features. They contribute to the discourse of wonder primarily by expanding wonder into the sine qua non of poetry and by teasing out Aristotle's hints about the metaphor as a tragic fiction in miniature, as a wondrous strange equivalent of strange and admirable tales. J. W. Van Hook notes that Guido Morpurgo Tagliabue and Franco Croce have condemned baroque poetry for having "with mere cleverness transferred the Aristotelian *peripeteia*, or unexpected reversal, from the plot of tragedy to the individual images of lyric poetry" ("'Concupiscence of Witt,'"25). Cleverness would probably not have struck baroque poets in Italy or England as a crime, but if they were looking to defend themselves they would probably have pointed to the direct and indirect license that critics in the sixteenth century gave to their adoption of wonder as a goal. Or they might have plead ignorance. Theorists in the Renaissance, as in antiquity, laid down the law on tragedy and epic, but not on lyric forms; Giangiorgio Trissino, discussing lyric only briefly in the early sixteenth century, gave himself credit for having been only the second critic since Dante to touch it (Hathaway, *Marvels and Commonplaces*, 11). Lacking authoritative guides to the purpose of their genre, lyric poets might well have been expected to adapt Aristotle's treatment of the longer genres to their own.

Although wonder became less recognized as a goal of tragedy in the Middle Ages, Cunningham notes that "explicit recognition" that the "marvelous event, and so the marvelous story, provokes wonder . . . is common throughout the literature" of the period.[12] Both Albert the Great and Aquinas testified to the connection of poetry and wonder soon after the *Poetics* was recovered, and with the spread of the *Poetics* through printed editions and commentaries in the sixteenth century, wonder is frequently specified as an effect of both epic and tragedy. Trissino, Giraldi Cinthio, Antonio Minturno, Lodovico Castelvetro, Jacopo Mazzoni, Torquato Tasso, and Julius Caesar Scaliger all follow Aristotle in making this connection; Sidney, perhaps under the influence of Min-

[12] Cunningham offers the opening of the *Nibelungenlied* as an example (*Collected Essays*, 69); see also the first fitt of *Sir Gawain and the Green Knight*. Unquestionably the most significant developments in the Western concept of wonder between Aristotle and the sixteenth century grew out of Christian attempts to define, describe, catalog, and explain the miraculous: see Le Goff, *Medieval Imagination*.

turno especially, identifies "admiration and commiseration" as the tragic emotions.[13] When demanding wonder from other genres, significantly, Italian critics treated its production as a requirement that outweighed other generic expectations or rules.

Especially interesting is the case of comedy, a genre that like satire and epigram, the preferred forms at the turn of the seventeenth century, has traditionally been expected to adopt a plain style. In his *Oratione contra gli Terentiani* (1566), Benedetto Grasso joins Vincenzo Maggi, Giovanni Battista Pigna, and Giason Denores in demanding that comic poets astound. Terence, a Roman master of the plain style, fails Grasso's test.[14] As Bernard Weinberg explains, Grasso "concedes that Terence's diction is familiar and in the low style proper to comedy" yet criticizes him for "failing to arouse wonder through eloquence" (Weinberg, *History*, 1:179). Wonder is essential, plainness is not. Eloquence, Grasso says, "must use more choice and more beautiful words so that, by delighting with the diction, it will hold with wonder the minds of the listeners; and this thing simple and plebeian speech, because it is lacking in ornament and grace, cannot do." Grasso explicitly requires comedy to produce wonder through style, even though he knows this demand contradicts the traditional decorum of styles that would insist on plainness in comedy.

Insisting on wonderful eloquence, Grasso echoes the distinction a character in Pontano's dialogue *Actius* (c. 1500) makes between the poet and the orator. Within the dialogue, various characters elaborate on the definition of the poet's task as "to speak well and appropriately in order to arouse wonder." It is "at times the orator's business to speak sublimely and supremely well," Paulus Prassicius says, but it is "the poet's own peculiar business, on the other hand, to speak so always, even

---

[13] Sir Philip Sidney, *A Defence of Poesy*, ed. J. A. Van Dorsten (1971), 45. On wonder in the treatises of Sidney and the Italian critics see *Elizabethan Critical Essays*, ed. G. G. Smith (1904), 1:392; Allan H. Gilbert's appendix to the *Apology* in *Literary Criticism: Plato to Dryden* (1962), 459–61; the entries under "astonishing," "astonishment," and "marvelous" in Gilbert's index; the entries under "admiration" in the index to Bernard Weinberg, *A History of Literary Criticism* (1961); Marvin T. Herrick, "Some Neglected Sources of *Admiratio*," *Modern Language Notes* 62 (1947): 222–26; Cunningham, *Collected Essays*, 14–16, 53, 74–76; Mirollo, *Poet of the Marvelous*, 165–74; Hathaway, *Marvels and Commonplaces*; Greenblatt, *Marvelous Possessions*, 79–80; and Platt, " 'Not before either known or dreamt of.' "

[14] The key to comic wonder in Maggi's *De ridiculis* (1550) and Pigna's *I romanzi* (1554) is novelty; in Denores's *Discorso intorno . . .* (1586) it is the comic reversal (Weinberg, *History*, 1:417, 451, 622–28). Richard Janko reconstructs an Aristotelian theory of comedy that illuminates why it would be seen as capable of producing a tragic effect: see *Aristotle on Comedy* (1984). See also Marvin T. Herrick, *Comic Theory*, (1964), 36–86.

when he treats very small and humble matters, since indeed it is necessary that even in writing of very small and humble matters his excellence should appear."[15] This argument that arousing wonder is always in
order and outweighs other considerations may derive ultimately from
Aristotle's allowance for poetic "impossibilities," which he considers
faults that are justifiable "if they serve the end of poetry itself—if . . .
they make the effect of either that very portion of the work or some
other portion more astounding (*ekplēktikōteron*)" (*Poetics* 1460b23–26).
Although Aristotle is referring to errors of imitation, not to violations of
principles of style (much less to violation of the decorum of styles for
particular literary genres, established long after he wrote), Renaissance
critics seem to have latched onto his specification of wonder as the telos
of poetry. Grasso and Pontano's character view wonder this way, and see
style as a primary method of reaching this end.

By the middle of the sixteenth century the universal requirement of
wonder had become a tired commonplace. In Girolamo Fracastoro's
Naugerius, sive De Poetica Dialogus (1555), the character Bardulone re-
members "hearing Sannazaro, who was much younger than Pontano,
ask that good old man the customary question regarding the function of
the poet." "Pontano," Bardulone recalls, "said a good deal and then
made the customary reply that the function of the poet is to speak so as
to arouse admiration."[16] In the *Discourses on the Heroic Poem* (1594),
Tasso even felt compelled to defend the epic's special claim on wonder:
"While I do not blame Pontano for holding that the function of every
poet is to move wonder (*il qual volle che l'officio di ciascuno poeta
fosse muover meraviglia*), I still think it much less appropriate to all the
others than to the heroic poet."[17] By the 1590s, though, this claim had
already been jumped. Perhaps the best proof is Minturno's and Scaliger's
addition of provoking *admiratio* to the trio of duties transferred from
rhetoric to poetry: teaching, moving, and delighting. Minturno even explicitly sanctions wonder in lyric poetry, insisting that "all good poetry,
even lyric poetry, should arouse admiration in the reader and listener."[18]
Italian critics, therefore, encouraged and even required lyric poets to
pursue wonder as the goal of their activity. Baroque poets may, then,
have "with mere cleverness transferred the Aristotelian *peripeteia*, or

[15] In Girolamo Fracastoro, *Naugerius, sive De Poetica Dialogus*, trans. Ruth Kelso,
University of Illinois Studies in Language and Literature 9 (1924): 81–82.
[16] In Fracastoro, *Naugerius*, 58.
[17] Torquato Tasso, *Scritti Sull'Arte Poetica*, ed. Ettore Mazzali (1977), 2:347; the
English translation is from Torquato Tasso, *Discourses on the Heroic Poem*, trans.
Mariella Cavalchini and Irene Samuel (1973), 173.
[18] See Herrick, "Some Neglected Sources of *Admiratio*," 223–24.

unexpected reversal, from the plot of tragedy to the individual images of lyric poetry," but they did so with cause.

Renaissance critics, however, had not merely made the provocation of wonder a universal goal of poetry: they had gone far toward developing Aristotle's unstated comparison of the metaphor with the tragic plot. As James V. Mirollo and Bernard Weinberg explain, critics at the end of the sixteenth century, particularly Tasso and Camillo Pellegrino, equated metaphors, conceits, or *concetti* with what Aristotle called the "life and soul of a tragedy": plot (*Poetics* 6; 1450a38). Tasso in particular, Mirollo notes, treated the *concetto* "as the equivalent in a lyric poem of plot in longer works."[19] Pellegrino, similarly, and with reference to Tasso, says that *concetti* "are the soul and the form of a composition" (Weinberg, *History*, 1:243).

The *concetto* itself is not precisely equivalent to metaphor, but includes metaphor among its means of expression. A *concetto* might in the sixteenth century be not a particular verbal figure but the underlying approach, idea, or "fore-conceit" developed within a literary work; Mirollo explains that Pellegrino recognized this ambiguity, and that the characters in his dialogue *Del concetto poetico* (1598) tried to distinguish *concetti* as devices of style from *concetti* as methods of handling a subject.[20] For Pellegrino the relationship between the poetic *concetto* and the argument of the lyric poem, as Weinberg notes, is like that between the surprising turns in narrative and dramatic genres and the plot as a whole: "just as in tragedy, comedy, and the epic the digressions must bear a necessary and probable relationship to the plot, so in the lyric (which is its preferred genre) the "concetto" must have its roots in the main argument of the poem." The poetic *concetto*, then, both stands in the place of plot in a lyric poem, and imitates the plot's form and logical structure. Although metaphors and other figures are, strictly speaking, embodiments of a *concetto* rather than *concetti* themselves, in practice Pellegrino's characters designate individual devices of style as *concetti*. Like metaphor according to Aristotle, the poetic *concetto* is a natural product of invention. Pellegrino also allows the *concetto* greater latitude for distinctiveness and obscurity in verse than in prose, just as Aristotle had done in treating unfamiliar diction in general: "Prose in expressing conceits uses pure forms of expression, proper

---

[19] See Mirollo, *Poet of the Marvelous*, 170–74; and Weinberg, *History*, 1:184, 235–36, and 242–49. Mirollo and Weinberg both also treat Giulio Cortese as important in establishing the *concetto* as equivalent in importance to the plot, but make clear that for Cortese the *concetto* is less a verbal device than an approach to the subject of the poem.

[20] Mirollo, *Poet of the Marvelous*, 170–73.

words, and when it uses metaphors and figurative language it uses them rarely and with moderation; whereas verse, with greater liberty and sometimes with excessive boldness expresses its conceits with figures and metaphors distant from literal meanings" (Weinberg, *History*, 1:243–44).[21] Although the metaphor is not identical with the conceit, then, it is the principal method by which a poet expresses a conceit, which is to a lyric poem what plot is to tragedy, epic, or comedy.

The metaphor and other kinds of figurative language therefore bear the prime responsibility in a lyric poem for enabling the poet to fulfill the requirement of provoking wonder. In Pontano's *Actius*, for example, the character Paulus states that "comparisons . . . are not more suitable for teaching and illustrating than for arousing wonder." Poets, he says, wonderfully coin words and expressions through figurative language; "nay, even a digression or a hyperbole they frequently add, departing wholly from nature" (in Fracastoro, *Naugerius*, 84–85).[22] In the *Discourses* Tasso points to Homer's astounding adaptation of archaic and foreign diction, noting that "he transfers words not only from related terms but also from remote ones, just so that he may please the hearer, fill him with stupefaction, and enchant him with wonder (*purché addolcisca l'auditore e, riempiendolo di stupore, l'incanti con la meraviglia*)."[23] Even more indicative of how Italian critics creatively applied Aristotelian principles is the analysis of metaphor by Giason Denores in his 1553 commentary on Horace's *Ars Poetica*. To show the power of metaphor, Denores remarkably combines the various comments Aristotle makes on wonder, imitation, and the metaphor:

> I should hold that metaphors produce in all men greater admiration and pleasure (*admirationem, & voluptatem*) than do proper terms for the same reason for which we judge that poetry delights more than history, that is because poetry imitates. . . . it is certain that metaphors are most pleasurable, not only because they generate knowledge in us via resemblance and imitation, but also because they produce pleasure in us out of that knowledge. (in Weinberg, *History*, 1:427)

[21] Weinberg presents additional examples of how Pellegrino treats style as a source of *admiratio* (2:994), and notes a similar tendency in other critics, particularly Francesco Robortello (1:67), Francesco Patrizi (2:774), and Tommaso Campanella (2:795).

[22] On the uses of the comparison or *exemplum*, see Weinberg, *History*, 1:270; Rosemond Tuve, *Elizabethan and Metaphysical Imagery* (1961), 307, 347–50; Wesley Trimpi, *Muses of One Mind*, (1983), 371–81; and Eden, *Poetic and Legal Fiction*, 85–87, 166–72.

[23] Tasso, *Scritti*, 2:366; trans. in Tasso, *Discourses*, 191.

Denores here conflates the passage on metaphor and learning in Book 3 of the *Rhetoric* with the passages on delight and imitation in Book 1 of the *Rhetoric* and chapter 4 of the *Poetics*. The metaphor kills three birds with one stone, teaching, delighting and evoking wonder. If we consider arousing wonder comparable to moving the audience, the metaphor, performing all poetic functions, becomes the quintessence of poetic activity.[24]

Metaphors teach, delight, and astound by presenting a resemblance between two objects that the reader would not have considered susceptible to comparison. Like the plot of a tragedy, it convinces through what is contrary to the audience's expectation, yet upon reflection seems logical. That lyric poets of the late sixteenth and early seventeenth centuries in England and elsewhere should seize upon metaphor as the means for fulfilling the requirement of producing wonder and as an approximate equivalent to the *peripeteia* of tragedy, then, seems more than "mere cleverness." These poets' often-criticized adoption of metaphors that compare remote objects seems motivated by the desire to follow Aristotle's injunction to create wonder, an injunction repeated and expanded upon by influential Italian critics of the sixteenth century. The more remote the objects compared, the more contrary to expectation, paradoxical, astounding the comparison.

The Rise of Epigram

These elaborations on the Aristotelian analysis of poetic wonder, however, help to illuminate more than the increased use of obscure metaphor noticeable at the end of the sixteenth century. They also provide another way of understanding why English poets began to abandon the sonnet for the epigram, since the epigram is the lyric form that traditionally depends most on sudden reversal, its small shudder imitating tragedy's grand swoon. Richard Helgerson argues in *Self-Crowned Laureates* that the shift from the sonnet and pastoral of Sidney and Spenser to the epigram and satire of Donne and Jonson can be explained without reference to "the actual abuses that in the Elizabethan *fin de régime* deserved castigation and the high rate of unemployment among university and inns-of-court men that prompted them to do the castigating."

[24] On the relationship of *admiratio* to the function of moving the audience, see *Literary Criticism: Plato to Dryden*, ed. Gilbert, 459–61; *Elizabethan Critical Essays*, ed. G. G. Smith, 1:392; Minturno in Weinberg, *History*, 2:743; and Fracastoro, *Naugerius*, 18. On the metaphor and the three functions see Eden, *Poetic and Legal Fiction*, 71.

Instead Helgerson accentuates the "historical dynamic that opposes generation to generation and the literary system that sets genre against genre" (123). His argument is that young poets needed to work new fields, out of the shadow of the golden poets: their poems in the old modes, however distinguished, could not be sufficiently impressive.

For Helgerson the rejection of love poetry by Jonson's generation in favor of the more ostensibly prudential concerns of satire was a particularly appropriate reaction to the previous generation, which had itself adopted satire as a means of renouncing its errant, prodigal infatuation with verse: "what had hitherto been one way of marking the final stage of an amateur literary career became the principal differentiating mark of the newest age group" (*Self-Crowned Laureates*, 125). Novelty is a recognized source of wonder too, and I find Helgerson's explanation extremely helpful, but I would argue both that the increased pressure to distinguish oneself because of the overabundance of qualified courtiers contributes more heavily to this shift than he suggests, and that epigram and satire serve especially well the purposes of lyric poets hoping to provoke wonder.

Rather than stressing the generational factor, I would stress an alternative explanation, one that Helgerson's own analysis suggests: that the shift to epigram and satire, and the accompanying shift toward compressed and oblique style, was an updated version of the career paradigm typical of the earlier generation, the pattern of embracing, then rejecting, poetry.[25] Helgerson's theory answers the question it sets out to answer—why Ben Jonson enacts his laureate ambitions in such traditionally minor genres—but works less well, understandably, as an explanation of the behavior of deliberately amateur poets with courtly aspirations, poets writing under the lingering shadow of the stigma of print. For such poets pastures new were unquestionably desirable, but in choosing these pastures they headed for or happened upon those in which stylistic wonder could thrive.

Epigrams work because of the logic of their operation. In his treatise on the epigram (1569), Tommaso Correa describes how it "affects and almost seizes upon the inmost feelings of the soul." The form "requires great art, wit, sharpness of talent, becoming brevity, and a certain dexterity and discernment"; when written expertly "it arouses admiration

---

[25] Like all generational theories, Helgerson's also faces the problem of those who span these generations, especially Ralegh and Greville, in whose later work the satiric tone is especially evident; Sidney's schoolmate Greville exploits the syntactical ambiguity characteristic of the later generation in such poems as "Down in the depth of mine iniquity," "Wrapt up, O Lord, in mans degeneration," and "In Night when colours all to blacke are cast."

and produces an extraordinary pleasure." Correa's focus on the sharpness of the epigram and the mind that produces it echoes Aristotle's assertion that only sharp minds can produce metaphors and lively sayings. In unepigrammatic fashion Correa repeats himself for emphasis: "the brevity delights us, the sharpness arouses us, the harmony seizes us, the thought remains with us, the humor pervades our mind with an incredible pleasure." These are strong words to describe what Weinberg calls "one of the minor genres," but though the epigram lacks the scope of tragedy and epic, it does have, traditionally, the vehemence, efficacy, *energeia* that startle or astound an audience (Weinberg, *History*, 1:185–86). The epigram is a genre where the reversal or *peripeteia* belongs; in his *Conversations with . . . Drummond*, Ben Jonson complains that "A Great many Epigrams were ill, because they expressed in the end, what should have been understood, by what was said" (*Ben Jonson*, 11:143).[26] Failing to introduce something contrary to expectation in the final lines of an epigram means failing to complete its structure, and Jonson claims that the short poems of Sir John Davies, John Owens, and Sir John Harington do not even deserve the name epigram.

Like the metaphor, and especially like the bold metaphor that compares two items from different mental categories, epigrams operate contrary to expectation. That English poets of the 1590s devoted special attention to the epigram at the same time that they began to indulge in more ambitious metaphors or conceits was no coincidence: these developments reflect the growing seriousness with which they viewed their responsibility to create wonder. Our tendency to associate the epigram with plainness of style obscures this connection, but in *The Art of Poetry* (1674), Boileau looks back on the European vogue for conceits and epigrams, and sees them as partners in crime: "The epigram . . . is often just a witty remark ornamented with two rhyming words. Formerly unknown to our writers, conceits came into our verse from Italy. The crowd, dazzled by their false charms, ran avidly after this new attraction. Encouraged in their impudence by public favor, conceits in torrents inundated Parnassus" (262). After documenting how the dazzling conceit raided most literary genres as well as legal and religious discourse, Boileau describes its eventual capture, and confinement to the epigram:

> Outraged reason at last awoke and drove them out of serious discourse for good; but though declaring them disreputable in all such writing, out of mercy allowed them to appear in the epigram—so long as the

[26] See Wesley Trimpi, *Ben Jonson's Poems* (1962), 170–71.

wit, brilliant in relevance, turned on the thought and not on the words. And so on all sides the disorders came to an end. Yet some sorry comedians remained at court, insipid wags, pitiful buffoons, superannuated adherents of vulgar wordplay. (263)

Banished to its "birthplace," which is notably both the epigram and the court, the conceit returns to its earlier meaning, as figure of thought rather than play on words. Because, again, of the tendency to view the epigram as a humble genre befitting the plain style, we have overlooked its association with flash, wonder, and power.

In an unusual and overlooked discussion of letters—one more genre traditionally associated with plainness—Samuel Johnson in *Rambler* no. 152 divides letter writers into those who model them on epigrams and those who model them on sonnets. Johnson's division points to the boldness once associated with epigrammatic style:

> In letters of this kind [i.e., designed to entertain rather than to convey news] some conceive art graceful, and others think negligence amiable; some model them by the sonnet, and will allow them no means of delighting but the soft lapse of calm mellifluence; others adjust them by the epigram, and expect pointed sentences and forcible periods. The one party considers exemption from faults as the height of excellence, the other looks upon neglect of excellence as the most disgusting fault; one avoids censure, the other aspires to praise; one is always in danger of insipidity, the other continually on the brink of affectation.[27]

Put Johnson's set of distinctions here up against the usual, Roman measuring stick for sonnets and epigrams—that the sonnet is the province of the *genus medium* or *floridum* and the epigram that of the *genus tenue* or, especially, *humilis*—and the stick breaks. Despite his later attack on the rough, obscure, epigrammatic verse of the "metaphysical poets," what Johnson associates here with the height of style is precisely that. The key to unraveling the mystery of why he should do so may be contained in the single word "forcible," one of the many meanings of the protean Greek adjective *deinos*, especially as defined by Demetrius in *On Style*. Why should Correa, Boileau, and Johnson all associate the puny epigram with stylistic power? Why on the other hand should Boileau, who translated *On the Sublime*, and Johnson, who preferred Shakespeare's rough magic to Addison's smooth precision, attack lyric style for aiming at wonder? These questions may seem narrowly,

---

[27] Samuel Johnson, *Works of Samuel Johnson* (1958–), 5:47.

even claustrophobically formal, but they lead us where we need to go: back to Greek rhetoric, then out to the symbolic action performed by wit in the late Renaissance, especially in the genres of epigram and satire.

Unfamiliar and Unexpected: Wonderful Style in Greek Rhetoric

Crucial to any attempt at reconstructing lyric poets' motives for adopting roughness and obscurity in the late sixteenth century is recognition of the sometimes shadowy influence of the Greek rhetorical tradition. Rhetorical treatises taught poets how to choose and arrange words, and the Greek treatises of Demetrius, Dionysius of Halicarnassus, "Longinus," and Hermogenes both champion wonder (*deinotēs*) as a general effect of style and give detailed instructions in producing it. Late Greek rhetoric stresses the emotional power of obscurity, brevity, and the various figures Aristotle associates with distinctiveness (*semnotēs*) and liveliness (*asteia*); moving away from Aristotle's idea of a mean between clarity and distinctiveness, this tradition posits obscurity as a goal in itself.[28] In pioneering studies of Greek rhetoric's impact on Renaissance poetry and prose, Debora Kuller Shuger, John Monfasani, and Annabel Patterson have argued that this premium on forcefulness undermines Morris Croll's argument that the roughness and obscure brevity popular in the early seventeenth century were characteristics of an Attic plain style.[29] Croll saw these features as motivated by the desire to emphasize *res* over *verba*, teaching over delighting and moving. For Demetrius, Dionysius of Halicarnassus, "Longinus," and Hermogenes, however, these are features not of a plain or low style, but of the most powerful, most threatening style.

The key term in Greek examinations of wonderful style, *deinotēs*, is dazzlingly multivalent; its meanings register the ambivalence toward the Sophists' legacy that began almost as soon as they started teaching,

[28] Dionysius of Halicarnassus, however, retains Aristotle's idea of a mean, locating in the speeches of Demosthenes the proper balance between the obscurity of Thucydides and the plainness of Lysias ("Demosthenes," 8, 10). See Trimpi, *Muses*, 137n8. All citations of Dionysius, unless specified, are to the texts and translations in Dionysius of Halicarnassus, *Critical Essays*, trans. Stephen Usher (1974–85).

[29] See Debora K. Shuger, *Sacred Rhetoric* (1988); Annabel Patterson, *Hermogenes and the Renaissance*, (1970); and John Monfasani, "The Byzantine Rhetorical Tradition and the Renaissance," in *Renaissance Eloquence: Studies in the Theory and Practice of Renaissance Rhetoric*, ed. James J. Murphy (1983), 174–87. "Longinus" has of course long been the subject of scholarly attention, but Shuger especially has demonstrated how he influenced continental rhetorics well before Boileau's translation made his work more commonly available.

and that reemerged in the Renaissance. These meanings also register and produce confusion, wrecking all neat assumptions about levels of style and the literary genres that incorporate them. However annoying this confusion may be when trying to trace the itinerary of *deinotēs* in antiquity and through the Renaisssance, it was instrumental in the rise and fall of wit. Lyric poets found what they needed in the *deinotēs* cluster, given the various forces pressing them to produce wonder, and left the rest. Neoclassical critics, harmonizing *On the Sublime* with Quintilian and Horace, and operating within a different system of literary production and consumption, tended to read *deinotēs* differently, and to judge Renaissance efforts at lyric wonder to be sophistic rather than sublime.[30]

The Awful Power of Style

Two qualities predominate in Greek treatments of wonderful style: unusual diction and roughness. By definition, strange words and irregular rhythm are not what the audience expects: bold metaphors reformat the mind's sectors, and compressed rhythm and syntax mock the ear's desire for tock after tick. According to ancient critics, when speakers use obscure diction and condensed constructions they almost literally capture their audiences, seizing them by and through surprise. Persuasive *logos* carries one away in the kind of rapture that Gorgias claims in the "Encomium on Helen" is as impossible to resist as "Fate and the will of the gods."[31] Supplied with powerful speech, an orator can achieve the primary function of rhetoric, psychagogia, without bothering with evidence or discursive reasoning.

Aristotle's pupil Theophrastus thus wholly isolates force from logic, hypostasizing Aristotle's extremes of clarity and distinctiveness into two discrete kinds of language. Philosophers talk clearly, says the philosopher, but poets and orators "choose the more stately (*semnotera*) words, and not those which are common or vulgar," and combine them in such a way that "the listener shall be charmed and astonished and, with respect to intellectual persuasion, overmastered (*hēsai te ton akroatēn kai ekplēxai kai pros tēn peitho cheirōthenta echein*)."[32] Im-

---

[30] See William Edinger, *Samuel Johnson and Poetic Style* (1977), and chapter 5 below.

[31] Gorgias, "Encomium of Helen," 6.

[32] Quoted in G. L. Hendrickson, "The Origin and Meaning of the Ancient Characters of Style," *American Journal of Philology* 26 (1905), 255; I have adopted Cunningham's more precise reading of *ekplēxai* as "astonished," in place of Hen-

pressive style seizes the audience with the kind of rapture that Bottom claims to have experienced in the forest outside Athens. Later Greek authors continue to associate *semnotēs* or distinctiveness with wonder, but, unlike Theophrastus, usually see roughness and forceful brevity, not polish and sweetness, as its sources.

Roman rhetoric divides style into three kinds, but the binary tension sunk deep in Greek linguistic and cognitive procedures manifests itself in a tendency to set two models of speech against each other in a local agon. In *On Style*, Demetrius posits four characters of style, bouncing the grand off the plain and the forceful (*deinos*) off the elegant or charming. Not that all Greek writers reject the idea of three levels of style—coordinate to some degree with the forensic, epideictic, and deliberative kinds of speech that Aristotle had distinguished—but they seem drawn to one-on-one comparisons: for "Longinus," Demosthenes versus Cicero or Hyperides; for Dionsysius, Lysias versus Thucydides or Isaeus. When discussing the highest level of style, as Shuger explains in her overview of grand styles in antiquity, Greek writers seem especially eager to sepa- · rate one that is polished, lofty, and proper for epideixis from another that is rough, forceful, passionate, and practical.[33] Hermogenes, for example, separates the more forensic qualities of asperity and vehemence from the more epideictic solemnity and splendor in his Idea of Grandeur.[34] Cicero recognizes two kinds of grand style too, one "rough, severe, harsh . . . without regular construction or rounded periods," the other featuring "a smooth, ordered sentence-structure with a periodic cadence" (*Orator*, 20), but tends, like Quintilian and the author of the

---

drickson's "moved" (Cunningham, *Collected Essays*, 64). Plutarch similarly argues that philosophy adopted "perspicuitie of style" because it "was apt to teach and instruct, rather than that which by tropes and figures amused and amased mens braines" (*The Philosophie, commonlie called, The Morals*, trans. Philemon Holland [1603], 1199).

[33] On the place of these two elevated styles in ancient hierarchies see Shuger, *Sacred Rhetoric*, 14–41; Franz Quadlbauer, "Die genera dicendi bis auf Plinius d.J.," *Wiener Studien* 71 (1958): 55–111; Trimpi, *Muses*, 131–63, and his two articles on the rhetorical background of Horace's *ut pictura poesis*: "The Meaning of Horace's Ut Pictura Poesis" [hereafter, "MHP"], *Journal of the Warburg and Courtauld Institutes* 36 (1973): 1–34, and "Horace's 'Ut Pictura Poesis': The Argument for Stylistic Decorum" [hereafter, "HASD"], *Traditio* 34 (1978): 29–73; Manfred Fuhrmann, "Obscuritas (Das Problem der Dunkelheit in der rhetorischen und literarästhetischen Theorie der Antike)," in *Immanente Ästhetik: Ästhetische Reflexion*, ed. Wolfgang Iser (1966), 63–72; Dirk Marie Schenkeveld, *Studies in Demetrius on Style* (1964), 63–70; and Ludwig Voit, *Deinotēs* (1934).

[34] See Shuger, *Sacred Rhetoric*, 39; Patterson instead links these qualities with the two encomiastic categories of praise and blame (*Hermogenes*, 53).

Rhetorica ad Herennium, to collapse them.[35] Greek authors not only kept the rough and the polished forms of elevation distinct, but generally preferred the rough because of its agonistic power.

This Greek preference for rough style increased over time, but dates back at least to the fifth century B.C., when Alkidamas argued for a sketchy, improvised style in the teeth of Isocrates' insistence on smoothness, precision, and artistic embellishment.[36] When Aristotle classified the kinds of rhetoric as deliberative, epideictic, and forensic, he associated the first kind with issues of the greatest and widest importance and with an agonistic oral style that would be effective in moving a crowd, a style rougher than that appropriate in written, epideictic oratory (*Rhetoric,* 3.12).[37] Later this agonistic style became associated with Demosthenes, whose reputation as the quintessential orator helped equate forcefulness with the height of eloquence. Both Greek and Roman rhetoricians testify that force persuades, often by comparing Demosthenes' style to the body of a soldier and Isocrates' style to that of an athlete. The athlete flexes muscles; the soldier fights to the death: "the Isocratic style resembles a game, a display of rhetorical virtuosity that flourishes only in the shady halls of declamation or the schoolroom's shelter, while the oratorical grand style involves risk and commitment to the urgent issues pressing upon the state."[38] Although Iso-

[35] The importance Cicero attaches to periodic sentences in his treatises and his speeches indicates his preference for the latter kind. Quintilian, who identifies force (*vis*) as the prime requirement of the grand style (*Institutio,* 12.10.59), nevertheless rates Cicero slightly higher than Demosthenes overall, and in stirring emotion in particular, though the latter "is more concentrated" and uses shorter periods (10.1.106–112). Quintilian's ideal, like Cicero's, is an orator who uses each of the three kinds of style as appropriate, and he regards Cicero as more nearly ideal than Demosthenes not because he is the prime exemplar of force, but because he has "succeeded in reproducing the force of Demosthenes, the copious flow of Plato, and the charm of Isocrates" (10.1.108).

[36] For the increasing value attached to roughness and force in both Greek and Roman rhetorical theory, see Shuger, *Sacred Rhetoric,* 28–29; and Quadlbauer, "Die genera dicendi," 110–11.

[37] On Aristotle's distinction between deliberative and epideictic styles, and its influence on later rhetorical and literary theory, see Trimpi, "MHP" and "HASD."

[38] Shuger, *Sacred Rhetoric,* 22. Shuger cites examples of this analogy in Cicero, Tacitus, Quintilian, Seneca the Elder, Dionysius of Halicarnassus, and Saint Augustine, offering Cicero's treatment of Demetrius of Phaleron as representative (*Brutus,* 36–37): "his training was less for the field than for the parade-ground (*palaestra*). He entertained rather than stirred his countrymen; for he came forth into the heat and dust (*sol et pulvis*) of action, not from a soldier's tent, but from the shady retreat (*umbraculum*) of the great philosopher Theophrastus." The theory and practice of Theophrastus and Isocrates, Shuger further explains, combined with poetic criticism such as the debate between Aeschylus and Euripides in Aristophanes' *The Frogs* to

crates' style, with its smoothness and carefully balanced antitheses and patterns of sound, served as the primary model of excellence in epideixis, rhetoricians in Greece especially considered it no match for the rough style of Demosthenes in the arena of practical debate.

Whereas Cicero considered epideictic oratory the province of wonder, implying that wonder is a pleasant product of the *genus medium* (*Partitione Oratoria*, 21–22, 32), Greek critics usually associated wonder with dread, using *deinos* as an adjective that, like *phoberos*, describes "the fearful or terrifying."[39] Despite acknowledging that audiences found the styles of Gorgias and Isocrates in epideixis wonderful, Demetrius, "Longinus," Dionysius of Halicarnassus, and Hermogenes all attribute to powerful speech the dread and transport we feel at the most excellent and therefore least knowable objects or presences.[40] Expected to handle remote objects, strong emotions, or issues of the greatest public importance, grand speech overwhelms the way incomprehensible and uncontrollable forces in nature do. Its roughness intimates a power the

---

form a countertradition tempering the Greek emphasis on force (*Sacred Rhetoric*, 21–28).

[39] Aristotle, for example, uses *deinos* as equivalent to *phoberos* at *Rhetoric* 2.8;1386 (see Voit, *Deinotēs*, 3). The divergence between Greek and Roman views of the sources and provinces of wonder can be exaggerated. For Shuger Cicero's treatment of wonder as an effect of the middle style reflects a general Roman interest only in "the forensic emotions of anger and pity" (*Sacred Rhetoric*, 36–37). Roman rhetoricians might not have accepted the absolute disjunction she posits between wonder and the harsher forensic emotions of anger, fear, and indignation. Defining "charm (*suavis*)," Cicero treats wonder as compatible with a range of emotions: "And a statement has the quality of charm when it comprises causes for surprise and suspense and unexpected issues (*admirationes, exspectationes, exitus inopinatos*), with an admixture of human emotions, dialogues between people, and exhibitions of grief, rage, fear, joy, and desire" (*Partitione Oratoria*, 32). Roman authors did not associate admiration exclusively with the middle style; as Io. Christ. Theoph. Ernesti notes in *Lexicon Technologiae Latinorum Rhetoricae* (1797; 1962), 12, Cicero describes the wonder grand style provokes (*Orator*, 28), which apparently leads Quintilian to refer to the grand style as the "admirabile dicendi genus" (*Institutio*, 1.1.92). Contrariwise, Greek rhetoricians grant that there is a kind of bloodless wonder in polished style, but separate the aesthetic effect of display oratory from the emotional effect of political oratory. This qualified praise often takes the form of saying a speaker is no Demosthenes. See Dionysius of Halicarnassus, "Isocrates," 3; and "Longinus," *On the Sublime*, 8.3.

[40] As I discuss in chapter 4, Wesley Trimpi has identified an "ancient dilemma of knowledge and representation" (*Muses*, 97–98). He notes that we may evaluate our knowledge of an object according to how well we know it or according to how important we think the object itself is. The dilemma is that "the more excellent the object, the less apprehensible" it is; "on the other hand, the more accurately the object may be known and represented, the less removed and hence the less exceptional it is apt to be" (98).

speaker struggles to control, and its suggestive obscurity intimates that the subjects it handles are only partially intelligible.

Distinctive language packs chills and thrills, as Demetrius conveys by comparing the obscurity found in both the grand and forceful styles to the Mystery rites:

> Any darkly-hinting expression is more terror-striking, and its import is variously conjectured by different hearers. On the other hand, things that are clear and plain are apt to be despised, just like men when stripped of their garments.
>
> Hence the Mysteries are revealed in an allegorical form in order to inspire such shuddering and awe (*ekplēxin kai phrikēn*) as are associated with darkness and night. Allegory also is not unlike darkness and night. (Demetrius, *On Style*, 100–101)[41]

Like the rites, obscurity is aligned with both the terror of the night and the suggestiveness of the veiled body. Dionysius of Halicarnassus also testifies to the ecstatic power of speech, though with less emphasis on obscurity, when noting that Isocrates' oratory leaves him cold, but by Demosthenes he is rapt, "transported" like the enthused Corybantes ("Demosthenes," 22). Nowhere in ancient rhetoric is this connection of persuasion and astonishment, moving and wonder, more firm than in the sublime of "Longinus," where language transports not primarily because of its artistic refinement but because of the power of the forces it imitates: the sublime satisfies an "unconquerable passion," bestowed by Nature, "for whatever is great and more divine than ourselves" (*On the Sublime*, 35.2; cf. 35.3, 36.1).

"Longinus," like Demetrius, follows Aristotle in noting that "it is always the unusual which wins our wonder" (*thaumaston d'homōs aei to paradoxon*) (*On the Sublime*, 35.5). Despite their strangeness and even their flaws, ambitious works create an effect denied to the meticulously correct works created by the party Johnson says "considers exemption from faults as the height of excellence": "Correctness escapes censure: greatness earns admiration as well (*to mega de kai thaumazetai*)" (36.1).[42] As his examples of impressively destructive natural wonders show, this admiration is akin to fear of surpassing power. Little fires we control and streams that stay in their banks may be "clear and useful," but we

---

[41] Cf. 77 and 254, and Hermogenes, *Hermogenes' On Types of Style*, trans. Cecil W. Wooten (1987), 21; on the overlap between Demetrius' characters of grandeur and force see Shuger, *Sacred Rhetoric*, 39; and Schenkeveld, *Studies in Demetrius*, 58–60. As Eden remarks ("Hermeneutics," 83), Demetrius sanctions obscurity on the basis of its forcefulness, Aristotle on the basis of its usefulness as an instrument of learning.

[42] See Trimpi, *Muses*, 130–63.

reserve wonder for raging rivers and the sea, for "the fires of Heaven, which are often darkened," and for volcanoes in eruption (35.4). When comparing masters of the elevated style, therefore, "Longinus" prefers Demosthenes' concentrated force to Cicero's diffuse abundance. He compares them in order to explicate his statement that "Sublimity lies in elevation, amplification (*auxēsis*) rather in amount; and so you often find sublimity in a single idea, whereas amplification always goes with quantity and a certain degree of redundance" (12.2). For other authors amplification itself includes both methods of emphasis—through the single, qualitatively significant example, or through the heaping up of examples, *copia*—but "Longinus" collapses *auxēsis* into amplification through quantity alone.[43]

Demosthenes, whose style "Longinus" compares to "a flash of lightning or a thunder-bolt," exhibits "rugged sublimity" and "terrific power (*rōmēs deinotētos*)"; Cicero exhibits copious "diffusion" (12.4). Although acknowledging that Ciceronian *copia* marvelously suits "the treatment of a commonplace, a peroration, a digression, and all descriptive and 'show' passages (*epideiktikois*), history, too, and natural philosophy as well as various other kinds of literature," "Longinus" clearly prefers the agonistic strength of Demosthenes. Cicero's shine can't touch Demosthenes' burn.[44] Through his ability "utterly to dumbfounder (*ekplēxai*) the audience" (12.5), Demosthenes produces the transport beyond logical demonstration that Theophrastus associates with poetic and rhetorical style: "For the effect of genius is not to persuade the audience but rather to transport them out of themselves. Invariably what inspires wonder (*to thaumasion*) casts a spell upon us (*ekplēxei*) and is always superior to what is merely convincing and pleasing. For our convictions are usually under our own control, while such passages exercise an irresistible power of mastery and get the upper hand with every member of the audience" (*On the Sublime*, 1.4). That late Greek rhetoricians prefer the rougher form of elevation—speech that leaves the audience rapt—is clear; by praising the impressive artistry, diction, and balanced clauses and sounds found in Isocrates, however, they also provide a precedent for Cicero's connection of wonder with the middle style. Parallel to this space between milder and rougher kinds of wonder is the space between very different meanings of *deinos*, the dazzlingly multivalent Greek term for wonderful style, speech, or speakers.

[43] On amplification as qualitative elevation or quantitative dilation, see E. R. Curtius, *European Literature and the Latin Middle Ages*, trans. Willard R. Trask (1973), 490–92; Voit, *Deinotēs*, 7–11, 48–53; George L. Kustas, *Studies in Byzantine Rhetoric* (1973), 148; and Tuve, *Elizabethan and Metaphysical Imagery*, 89–90.

[44] Cf. Quintilian, *Institutio*, 10.1.106–7, and Hoskyns, *Life, Letters*, 136–38.

Deinotēs and the Styles of Wonder

Greek rhetoricians use the adjective *deinos* and its cognates in confusing if not contradictory senses. This confusion, however, is part of the story, since it allows Italian critics in the sixteenth century—and Joshua Reynolds in the eighteenth—to describe *deinos* Michelangelo as the Homer of painting, even though Joseph Addison and Samuel Johnson treat *deinos* John Donne as the Cellini or Salviati of poetry.[45] In part these judgments reveal the resilience of the hierachy of genres; Michelangelo's use of grand historical subjects renders his work comparable to epic, but Donne's use of brevity and boldness in short lyrics led critics to view his wit as forced. "Longinus" exalts wonder, and his emphasis on short, sharp wonder offers a potential defense of epigrammatic style, but he also prefers ambitious works, works on a grand scale foreign to seventeenth-century lyrics.

For *deinos*, Liddell and Scott list three main classes of meaning, in chronological order:

I. "fearful, terrible, dread, dire"
II. 1. "with a notion of Force or Power, *mighty, powerful*"
   2. "wondrous, marvelous, strange"
III. "able, clever, skilful."[46]

These meanings, of course, float and mix. When Demetrius, "Longinus," Dionysius of Halicarnassus, and Hermogenes describe style as *deinos*, they tend to hint at all three, but with some sense of disjunction between senses I. (terrible) and III. (clever): they emphasize one quality or the other, depending on whether they are referring to a forcible grand style or to the Sophists' style in epideixis.[47] Both styles are treated as "wondrous, marvelous, strange," but one promotes dread, and the other features the skill and cleverness involved in speaking impressively. These clusters of meaning for *deinos* resemble the two meanings Liddell and Scott give for the noun *deinotēs*: I. "terribleness . . . harshness, sternness, severity" and II. "natural ability, cleverness, shrewdness." As *deinos* and *deinotēs* shift, the verb form *deinoō*, "to make terrible: to exaggerate" remains relatively stable; Voit argues that as the founder of

---

[45] See David Summers, *Michelangelo and the Language of Art* (1981), 234–41, and chapter 5 below.
[46] Henry George Liddell and Robert Scott, *A Greek-English Lexicon*, rev. Sir Henry Stuart Jones, supplement ed. E. A. Barber (1968), 176–77.
[47] Ludwig Voit, arguing that true *deinotēs* is the agonistic, passionate style of Demosthenes, sees descriptions of sophistic style as *deinos* as anomalous (*Deinotēs*, 3); see also G. M. A. Grube, *A Greek Critic* (1961), 136–37.

this lexical family it bequeaths an overtone of dread to all the other parts of speech (Voit, *Deinotēs*, 4–5). From this verb comes another noun, *deinōsis*, "exaggeration," which names the kind of amplication that "Longinus" calls sublime: the concise but brilliantly effective choice of example. Homer uses the adjective *deinos* in its two earlier senses, and according to Liddell and Scott, the third sense—"natural ability"—develops out of sense II.1, "*mighty, powerful.*"[48] Through this third sense the quality of being *deinos* became especially connected to those able to speak well, in particular the Sophists of the fifth and fourth centuries B.C., whose educational program equated skill in speaking with skill, and therefore power, in all social and political realms.

Those who were *deinoi legein*, "skillful in speaking and interpretation," assumed political superiority over the untrained *idiōtai*, "laymen," whose reaction to the Sophists Voit describes as "das unheimliche Staunen des Laien vor dem Fachmann, vor dem Unbegriffen, nicht Erreichbaren": "the uncanny wonder of laymen at the expert, uncomprehended and out of reach."[49] To be *deinoi legein*, that is, meant to be *deinoi* in general, flat out wonderful. Dionysius of Halicarnassus reports that Gorgias "astounded (*katēplexato*) the Assembly," and lumps him with those who "confused the ordinary members of their audiences (*ton idiōten*) by using recondite and exotic words, and by resorting to unfamiliar figures of speech and other novel modes of expression" ("Lysias," 3).[50] Plato satirizes Sophistic claims to *deinotēs* in the opening of the *Apology*, where Socrates, the ironic layman, resists his accusers' insinuation that he is *deinou ontos legein*, "a skillful speaker"—"unless, of course by a skillful speaker they mean one who speaks the truth" (17B).[51] *Deinotēs* is thus equated with *panourgia*, deception, a charge that echoes in Renaissance critiques of style as sophistic. These charges, from Plato on down, are only in a minor sense aesthetic: they register anxiety about the political power the eloquent can wield. Those pursuing and defending admirable style in the late sixteenth century may have resurrected sophistic epistemology, which embraced contingency, but the power accruing to those capable of evoking wonder was at least as great an attraction, and was certainly the focus of most attacks.

Slippage in the meaning of *deinos* and *deinotēs*, though, makes identi-

[48] See Heinrich Ebeling, *Lexicon Homericum* (1885; 1963), 1:283; Richard John Cunliffe, *A Lexicon of the Homeric Dialect* (1963), 86.

[49] Voit, *Deinotēs*, 11; my translation.

[50] Cf. Aristotle, *Rhetoric*, 3.1.9;1404a29–33. on the popularity of Gorgias' style among "the majority of the uneducated (*hoi polloi tōn apaideutōn*)."

[51] For Socrates' often oblique attacks on the value of being *deinos* in interpretation (*Protagoras*, 341A-B; *Phaedrus*, 260C; *Cratylus*, 407A-B; *Ion*, 531A-C), see Eden, "Hermeneutics," 65–66.

fication of a uniform admirable style in the Renaissance impossible: we need to speak of admirable styles, at least, and to recognize that for practicing poets the line between rough boldness and sophistic style was blurry, despite the extraordinary training in rhetorical figures that early modern grammar schools provided. The outlines are clear enough: like the distinction between the two grand styles, the key distinction between forceful *deinotēs* and sophistic *deinotēs* is that the latter is more regular, smooth, and polished. Rough wonder persuades, even in a sense commands; smooth wonder delights.[52] Rough *deinotēs*, coordinate with the style of deliberative oratory and designed to move the audience, provokes the wonder akin to fear; sophistic *deinotēs*, coordinate with the epideictic style designed to please, elicits the more purely pleasant wonder we feel at dazzling verbal cleverness, sleight of mouth. As epitomized in Gorgias' "Encomium on Helen" and parodied in Agathon's definition of love in the *Symposium* (195a), sophistic rhetoric flaunts its artifice on its gaudy sleeve. It employs the delightful but noticeable repetition of initial and final sounds that Lyly's *Euphues* made popular again briefly in the sixteenth century.

Disentangling these styles may illuminate the motives for wonder in seventeenth-century lyric poetry, but it also distorts them by making them seem more distinct. The protean quality of *deinotēs* in Greek rhetoric shadows the protean quality of later wonder: conflation produces synergy. When the different strands of what Greek rhetoric recognized as *deinotēs* met, they merged with other strands of wonder to form a cultural text of enormous if transitory tensile strength. Their point of intersection, their blurry center, was concise wit. And when neoclassical critics began to unravel the text of wonder, they started by sorting the warp of rough *deinotēs* from the woof of the sophistic variety.

Rough Wonder

In *On Style*, Demetrius makes the most diligent effort in Greek rhetoric to define *deinotēs*; force is the primary quality of his *charaktēr dei-*

---

[52] Different styles produce different kinds of wonder because they serve different rhetorical functions. When Aristotle juxtaposes deliberative style to epideictic style in *Rhetoric*, 3.12, he compares them to two kinds of painting: one sketched with stark contrasts, the other elaborately detailed and colored. Like the deliberative style, Demetrius' *charaktēr deinos* is unpolished, even jarring. Epideixis demands precision because it will be examined more carefully than public speeches before a crowd. Political oratory, dealing with the present and the immediate future, is urgent; epideixis generally deals with the past, and is both composed and enjoyed in leisure. See Trimpi, *Muses*, 138.

nos, which he tries, not quite successfully, to dissassociate completely
from sophistic style. Even if Italian critics had not developed Aristotle's
hints about the marvelousness of metaphor and epigrammatic remarks,
Renaissance poets would have found in Demetrius' text an already thorough explanation, building on Aristotelian principles and examples, of
how brevity, roughness, and obscurity evoked wonder by defying expectations. In aligning roughness and obscurity as sources of *deinotēs,* then,
Demetrius offers us a way of bridging the perceived gap between strong
lines and metaphysical conceits, a gap that Samuel Johnson did not recognize in the *Life of Cowley* when he named Jonson and Donne
cofounders of the poetry of admiration. Because Demetrius connects
wonder both to specific methods of making style obscure—especially to
the figure known as *emphasis*—and to the general quality of *energeia*
that amplification supplies, *On Style* is a crucial source of later conceptions of wonderful style.

Analyzing Demades' quip that "Alexander is not dead . . . or the
whole world would have scented the corpse," Demetrius highlights the
force of the *charaktēr deinos,* its capacity to frighten. Demades' words,
Demetrius says, "convey a thrilling effect (*ekplēktikon*). . . . And every
such sensation is forcible, since it inspires fear (*pasa de ekplēxis deinon,
epeidē phoberon*)" (283). Once a brief saying has been elaborated upon,
howver, "it suggests the expositor rather than the intimidator (*ekpho-
bounti*)" (8). Yet by exemplifying *deinotēs* through this and other witticisms (259–262, 282–291), Demetrius also associates it with the
cleverness that produces startling expressions. Since he also includes
witticisms in the opposite category of style—the *charaktēr glaphuros,*
or elegant style—Demetrius perhaps implicitly acknowledges the ability of a smooth yet distinctive style to amaze. But the style he equates
with wonder is anything but smooth.

In syntax, rhythm, and grammar, the *charaktēr deinos* defies convention: it features brevity, asymmetrical form, climactic structure with
many brief periods, hiatus, sheer cacophony, and such solecisms as end-
ing sentences with conjunctions. Demetrius points to the dynamic ag-
gression condensed style wields: "As a wild beast gathers itself together
for the attack, so should discourse gather itself together as in a coil in
order to increase its force" (8). Forcible style aims "to be sharp and short
like the exchange of blows" (274), so it jabs with paratactic sentence
structure and rough composition. He especially praises Hipponax, who
"shattered his verse" when attacking his enemies, making "the measure
suitable for energetic invective, since correct and melodious rhythm
would be fitter for eulogy than satire" (301). Like the epigram, satire is
often associated with plainness, especially as handled by Horace, but

Demetrius reminds us that satire was alternately conceived as aggressively powerful, as the genre for rhyming an enemy to death.[53] This point was not lost on John Cleveland, or whoever wrote the satire attributed to him "On the Pouder Plot":

> Satyres run best when Classhing tearms do meet,
> And Indignation makes them knock their feet.
> To bee methodicall in Verse, & rhime
> In such invectives is the highest crime.
> Who Ever saw a firy passion breake
> But in abruptnes?[54]

In part through its roughness, its denial of the audience's expectations concerning rhythm, satire can astound. Like Quintilian (*Institutio*, 9.3.102) and others, Demetrius also prefers passion served raw: "The fact is that words which are actually unpremeditated, and are as it were a spontaneous growth, will give an impression of vigour, especially when we are manifesting our anger or our sense of injustice. Whereas anxious attention to niceties of smoothness and harmony does not betoken anger so much as elegant trifling and a desire to exhibit one's powers" (300). Forcible style raises strong passions—strikes—by denying the audience what it expects: completely expressed meaning, sentence structure that makes logical connections explicit and unambiguous, and rhythm that satisfies the ear's desire for harmony, euphony, and regularity. This is precisely the kind of "negligence" Samuel Johnson associates with the bold epigram.

Brevity induces cognitive as well as aural wonder. Especially forceful are "brief utterances (*brachylogiais*)" that leave the audience "to infer (*hyponoēsai*) the chief of the meaning from a short statement, as though it were a sort of riddle" (243). Because of its obscurity, "a sudden lapse into silence is often yet more forcible" (253). As exhibited especially in the wit of Demades, *deinotēs* consists of "allegory, hyperbole, and innuendo (*emphasis*)" (286), all of which Demetrius, significantly, associates with poetry. His treatment of these covert figures, and of analogy in general, borrows heavily from Aristotle's analysis of *asteia* or liveliness in the *Rhetoric* (3.10–11). But, as Kathy Eden notes, although Demetrius

---

[53] On the grand style in satire see Robert C. Elliott, *Power of Satire* (1960); Inez Gertrude Scott, *Grand Style* (1927); Trimpi, *Ben Jonson's Poems*, 112; and Raman Selden, *English Verse Satire 1590–1765* (1978).

[54] *Poems of John Cleveland*, ed. Brian Morris and Eleanor Withington (1967), 72. The editors include Robert Wilde's warning to the reader to "pray that the Satyrist be in that minde / that thou art below his laughing at"; if not, "his strong lines have not yet so thinne a twist / but thou maist finde them whipcord if he list" (lv).

draws even his examples of concise speech from Aristotle, he departs by attaching a nearly unqualified value to obscurity: "And (strange though it may seem) even obscurity often produces force, since what is distantly hinted is more forcible, while what is plainly stated is held cheap" (254).[55] This suggestive brevity "suits apophthegms and maxims; and it is a mark of superior skill to compress much thought in a little space, just as seeds contain potentially entire trees" (9). These claims about how obscurity affects the audience, about its rhetorical force in the widest sense, point to the aura—social, political, and religious—that later accompanies concise style.[56] By displaying concise wit, as I will argue, poets could demonstrate their "superior skill" and "avoid being held cheap": in late Elizabethan England, these were the prerequisites for survival at court.

In rhetorical terms, *deinotēs* amplifies. As practiced by Demades, the *charaktēr deinos* fulfills Quintilian's definition of amplification: "the gift of signifying more than we say, that is *emphasis*, together with exaggeration and overstatement of the truth" (9.2.3; cf. 9.1.45). Quintilian explains that *emphasis* is close to *brachylogia*, a figure that when successful "expresses a great deal in a very few words," and when unsuccessful results "merely in obscurity" (8.3.82). *Emphasis*, however, "is on a grander scale," and "succeeds in revealing a deeper meaning than is actually expressed by the words." Implying that emphasis is a kind of amplification that depends on the power of inference, Quintilian provides a glimpse into the psychological mechanism of wonderful obscurity (8.4.26).[57]

As "Longinus" claims when praising Demosthenes, the single suggestive example sets the audience on fire. Not by being detailed and therefore visualizable, but by being obscure yet illustrative: it provokes the audience to supply what is missing. In Greek terms, it provides *energeia* or force, but not—or at least not immediately—*enargeia* or vividness. Demetrius, admittedly, associates *emphasis* with *enargeia* (51, 212, 216), but does little to indicate that the style presents powerful visual images; the force in his forcible style seems closer to *energeia*, or what Renaissance critics called "energy," "life," or "spirit." *Energeia* and *enargeia* are wound together inextricably thanks to Aristotle, "according

[55] Eden, "Hermeneutics," 83.

[56] Bacon applies the Aristotelian metaphor of the powerful yet compact seed to sententious style in the *Advancement of Learning* (*Works*, 3:413), and Nicholas of Cusa and Erasmus invoke it to explain why a hidden God is most divine (see Edgar Wind, *Pagan Mysteries in the Renaissance* [1968], 221–22).

[57] Cf. 8.3.83 and the description of *significatio* in the anonymous *Ad C. Herennium: de ratione dicendi (Rhetorica ad Herennium)*, trans. Harry Caplan (1954), 4.67.

to whom metaphor achieves its vivid effect by describing things 'in active state' (*energounta*)."[58] In the *Metaphysics*, Aristotle uses *energeia* to describe whatever is actual, or what results when the potential (*dynamis*) of a thing has been fully converted into being (9.6); in *de Anima*, *energeia* is his term for the activation of the intellect, which requires a sensible image. This image is projected to the eye and the mind by a sensible object: "And clearly the sensible object makes the sense-faculty actually operative (*energeiai*) from being only potential (*ek dynamei*)" (3.7).[59] Because the mind requires images in order to think, writing that is vivid—that has *enargeia*—will make the minds of the audience active, or stimulate *energeia*. Such writing persuades by placing the scene described before the eyes (*pro ommmatōn*) of the audience, making them virtual witnesses.[60]

The *charaktēr deinos* is not vivid directly, but indirectly. Its emphasis on stimulation of the intellect (*energeia*) rather than on vivid description (*enargeia*) parallels the distinction that literary historians routinely make between the lyric poetry of the seventeenth and sixteenth centuries. Like writing that has *enargeia*, though, a suggestive style aims at making the members of the audience witnesses. In defining persuasiveness (222), Demetrius presents the view of Theophrastus that "not all points should be punctiliously and tediously elaborated, but some should be left to the comprehension and inference (*logizesthai*) of the hearer." The hearer, allowed to draw such inferences, "becomes not only your hearer but your witness, and a very friendly witness too. For he thinks himself intelligent because you have afforded him the means of showing his intelligence." The audience has the pleasure of thinking through the case—pleasurable to the peripatetic Theophrastus because it involves wondering and learning—and, since this inferential process requires the phantasms that energize the mind, they emerge as friendly witnesses. Wonderful speech does not contain vivid images of its own, but provokes them in the minds of the audience through suggestion.

Quintilian later solidifies this connection between *deinotēs* and *energeia* when he lists the various kinds of force, *vis*. Indeed, Ernesti asserts that *vis*, crucial to eloquence for Quintilian and other Roman rhetoricians, is simply the Latin term for *deinotēs*.[61] Among the methods of

---

[58] Kustas, *Byzantine Rhetoric*, 174; see also Eden, *Poetic and Legal Fiction*, 71–74; Tuve, 29; and Patterson, *Hermogenes*, 131–34.

[59] Aristotle, *On the Soul*, trans. W. S. Hett (1964).

[60] See Eden, *Poetic and Legal Fiction*, 15–17 and 71–111, and William J. Jordan, "Aristotle's Concept of Metaphor in Rhetoric," in *Aristotle: The Classical Heritage of Rhetoric*, ed. Keith V. Erickson (1974), 235–50.

[61] Io. Christ. Theoph. Ernesti, *Lexicon Technologiae Graecorum Rhetoricae* (1795;

insuring that speech has it, Quintilian includes both *deinōsis* or exaggeration and *"energeia,* or vigour, a near relative of all these qualities [the various kinds of force], which derives its name from action and finds its peculiar function in securing that nothing that we say is tame" (8.3.88–89). Demetrius' description of the *charaktēr deinos* serves as a handbook for avoiding tameness, and for ensuring *vis* or *energeia.*

Quintilian's term for "exaggeration"—*deinōsis*—is the final member of the lexical family, and deserves mention because it both helps explain the relationships between various styles of wonder and indicates one of the ways in which Greek ideas of wonder were available in the Renaissance independently of the texts of Demetrius and other Greek rhetoricians. Voit observes that the sophist Thrasymachus of Chalcedon, believed to be the first author to investigate rhetorical pathos, divided the techniques for raising strong emotions such as anger, indignation, and fear from those that raise pity, compassion, or mercy. The art of evoking indignation, of amplifying the harsher emotions, is *deinōsis,* and that of evoking milder emotions such as pity (*eleos*) or compassion (*oiktos*) is *eleeinolgia.*[62] The first is generally the art of the prosecutor, the second of the defense. Quintilian thus defines *deinōsis* as "a certain sublimity (*altitudo*) in the exaggerated denunciation of unworthy conduct" (*Institutio,* 8.3.88). By both identifying *deinōsis* as the power to move harsh feelings and attributing to it "a certain sublimity," Quintilian perhaps here transmits some of the Greek preference for rough forms of elevation. He also perhaps allows later poets to determine that sublimity is compatible with the "exaggerated denunciation of unworthy conduct" that is an essential feature of satire and a usual feature of the epigram, the genres of choice for the English poets of the 1590s who began the fashion for rough, difficult, and obscure poetry.

These genres also frequently feature compression and gnomic statements or *sententiae.* When discussing maxims (*gnōmai*) in the *Rhetoric,* Aristotle alludes to *deinōsis,* implying a connection between brevity and this kind of intensification.[63] "To declare a thing to be universally true when it is not," he advises, "is most appropriate when working up

---

1962), 420. Support for this assertion is found in Gerardus Vossius' translation of Hermogenes' seventh idea of style, *deinotēs,* as *dicendi vis,* see Shuger, *Sacred Rhetoric,* 260.

[62] See Voit, 122–26, and the excellent note on *deinōsis* and amplification in Caplan's edition of the *Rhetorica ad Herennium,* 146n(b).

[63] As Voit observes (4–6 and 94–97), Plato aligns brevity with *deinōsis* in the *Phaedrus* (267A and 272A) and in the *Republic* (336B–337A), where Socrates describes the aggressive verbal style of Thrasymachus in language very similar to that in Demetrius, *On Style,* 8.

feelings of horror and indignation (*en schetliasmōi kai deinōsei*) in our hearers; especially by way of preface, or after the facts have been proved" (2.21; 1395a8–10). Aristotle lumps *deinōsis* with fallacious topics and arguments, designed to lead the audience to make unjustified inferences: "Another commonplace is the use of indignant language (*to deinōsei*), whether to support your own case or to overthrow your opponent's. We do this when we paint a highly-coloured picture of the situation (*auxēsēi to pragma*) without having proved the facts of it. . . . Here there is no genuine enthymeme: the hearer infers (*paralogizetai*) guilt or innocence, but no proof is given, and the inference is fallacious accordingly" (2.24; 1401b3–9).[64] Here *deinōsis* is characterized as independent of the proof of a case, or even contrary to it (cf. Quintilian, *Institutio*, 6.4–5). By treating *deinōsis* as amplification unconnected to logical demonstration, Aristotle perhaps triggers the dichotomy Theophrastus later posits between a poetic or rhetorical style designed to astound the audience and a philosophical style designed to establish facts through logic. The effect of *deinōsis* for Aristotle, of the style that astounds for Theophrastus, and of the sublime for "Longinus," is that the audience is "with respect to intellectual persuasion, overmastered." The success of this exaggeration depends, like that of the obscure brevity in Demetrius' *charaktēr deinos*, on the speaker's ability to manipulate the inferences of the audience.[65]

Greek critics other than Demetrius devote less sustained attention to *deinotēs*, but follow him in coordinating roughness and metaphorical boldness as sources of wonder. With the exception of Dionysius of Halicarnassus, they also try, not quite successfully, to keep the forcible style and the sophistic style distinct.[66] Dionysius praises the wonderfully forceful styles of Isaeus and Thucydides, which he juxtaposes to the plain, Attic style of Lysias. Lysias, he says, aims at "charm," Isaeus

---

[64] By translating *auxēsēi to pragma* as "paint a highly-coloured picture of the situation," Roberts demonstrates how easy amplification is to confuse with vividness, *energeia* with *enargeia*. J. H. Freese offers the more literal "exaggerates the supposed fact" in Aristotle, *The "Art" of Rhetoric*, trans. J. H. Freese (1926).

[65] In the *Saturnalia Convivia* (c. 400 A.D.), Macrobius also links gnomic style with passion; he advises speakers to heighten indignation, *deinōsis*, by opening abruptly and designing an oration "rich with brief sentences and a variety of figures" (quoted in Voit, *Deinotēs*, 150). For examples of "the brilliant abrupt openings for which metaphysical poetry is famous," see the introduction to *The Metaphysical Poets*, ed. Helen Gardner (1966), 22.

[66] Dionysius of Halicarnassus and Hermogenes diverge from Demetrius by frequently using *deinotēs* for what Roman rhetoricians call decorum: not a particular style or set of stylistic qualities but the masterly mixing of them according to the dictates of *kairos*. See Patterson, *Hermogenes*, 8; Shuger, *Sacred Rhetoric*, 260; Voit, *Deinotēs*, 30–47; and Ernesti, *Lexicon Technologiae Graecorum Rhetoricae*, 68–69.

at "forcefulness (*tou deinos*)" ("Isaeus," 18), produced by a style "which is condensed and bold in the brevity, succinctness and unorthodoxy of its composition and which is not universally or readily understood" (13). The style of Lysias, especially by contrast, is clear but flat: "It certainly does not excite us or move us to wonder, nor does it portray pungency, intensity or fear" ("Lysias," 13). Before Thucydides, Dionysius claims, historians wrote like Lysias: they were "pure, clear and concise," but void of force ("Thucydides," 23).[67] Thucydides filled this void:

> In his choice of words he preferred those which were metaphorical, obscure, archaic and outlandish. . . . In the construction of both shorter and longer clauses he chose the arrangements which were dignified, severe, compact and firm-footed, and those which jarred the ear by the clashing of inconsonant letters rather than those which were melodious, smooth, polished and free from any conflict of sound. To figures of speech, in which he was especially eager to outstrip his predecessors, he devoted particular attention. ("Thucydides," 24; cf. "Demosthenes," 10; "Second Letter to Ammaeus," 3–14)

In short, Thucydides tried "to express as much as possible in the fewest possible words, and to combine many ideas into one, and to leave the listener still expecting to hear something more." These goals "help to make his brevity obscure." Yet Dionysius confuses the issue—or offers evidence of the indeterminacy of *deinotēs*—by seeming to align Thucydides' occasional "parallelisms in length and sound, word-play and antithesis, which were excessively used by Gorgias" with force; for Demetrius these qualities simply destroy it.[68] In *On Literary Composition*, however, Dionysius describes Thucydides as a master of austere composition, in which parallelism and regularity are as out of place as in the *charaktēr deinos* of Demetrius (22; cf. "Demosthenes," 39). It is worth noting that Dionysius chooses Pindar, the lyric poet famed for a nearly tragic style, as his other prime model of austerity. Despite his inconsistent treatment of composition, Dionysius joins Demetrius in coordinating strange diction, roughness, and obscurity as sources of wonder.

When "Longinus" and Hermogenes use *deinos* and *deinotēs*, the equation of metaphoric boldness with roughness is less pronounced, because the critique of sophistic style and its over-the-top metaphors is sharper.

---

[67] Their writing lacks "sublimity, eloquence, dignity, and grandeur." "Nor," he finds, "is there any intensity, any gravity, or any emotion to arouse the mind, nor any robust, combative spirit, all of which are essential to what we call genius (*deinotēs*)" (cf. "Lysias," 3, 4, 12, 16; "Demosthenes," 2; and Demetrius, *On Style*, 258).

[68] Dionysius of Halicarnassus, "Thucydides," 24; Demetrius, *On Style*, 27–29. Dionysius also aligns force with artifice in "Isaeus," 3, 7, 16.

"Longinus," again, parallels *deinotēs* with fearfulness. "No one," he claims, "is ever panic-stricken while reading Hyperides," a master of epideixis; Demosthenes, however, immediately "shows the merits of great genius in their most consummate form, sublime intensity, living emotion, redundance, readiness, speed . . . and his own unapproachable vehemence (*deinotēta*) and power" (34.4).[69] Hermogenes similarly points to Demosthenes' wonderful power, but is nothing if not inconsistent in his use of *deinotēs*. As W. R. Roberts notes, Hermogenes actually discusses three kinds of *deinotēs*: "one which seems it and is it, a second which is it without seeming it, a third which seems it without being it" (*On Style*, 268). Hermogenes' first kind most parallels Demetrius' *charaktēr deinos*: terrible and vehement speech, exemplified by the public orations of Demosthenes against Philip of Macedon. The second kind, exemplified by Lysias and by Demosthenes' private speeches, succeeds by hiding its art. The third, the sophistic style of those who are *deinoi legein*, ignores decorum, especially by using exalted language for trivial subjects, displaying the ingenious mastery of epideixis that leads Cicero to treat wonder as an effect of the middle style.[70]

Hermogenes analyzes Force (*deinotēs*), like all of his seven ideas of style, into three elements: "thought or content (*ennoia*); approach (*methodos*), which he eventually identifies with figures of thought; and style (*lexis*), which includes diction, figures of speech, clauses, word order, cadences, and rhythm" (*On Types of Style*, xi). The thoughts in the kind of Force that both is and seems forceful are "paradoxical, profound, compelling, or, in general, . . . cleverly contrived" (104); its approaches are likewise "ingenious and profound" (105). Finally, "Solemn words and words that are harsh and vehement and, generally speaking, words that are used figuratively are forceful, because it is appropriate to use them whenever you want to describe something vividly." He considers "especially suitable" the "figure that involves concentrating many thoughts concisely into one sentence"—again, suggestive brevity, *emphasis*, is a hallmark of *deinotēs*.

Hermogenes' third kind—that which seems to be *deinos* but is not—

[69] Roberts renders *deinotēta* here as "*terror*" (his italics) (Demetrius, *On Style*, 267). "Longinus" also juxtaposes Archilochus to Eratosthenes and Pindar to Bacchylides as examples of lyric excellence, and Sophocles to Ion of Chios as tragedians (33.5); in each case he judges the latter poet impeccably smooth, yet lesser. Smoothness is thus the antithesis of the sublime for "Longinus," the austere style for Dionysius, and the *charaktēr deinos* for Demetrius.

[70] Significantly, given the intimate connection between *sprezzatura* and wonder for Castiglione, Dionysius of Halicarnassus had also referred to Lysias' art of concealing art as *deinos*: "it is in the very illusion of not having been composed with masterly skill (*en autoi toi me dokein deinōs*) that the mastery (*to deinon*) lies" ("Lysias," 8).

is the "style of the sophists, that is, of Polus and Gorgias and Meno and
their followers, and of quite a few in our own times [late second century
A.D.]." The pseudo-forceful style "is created primarily by diction, when
a speaker uses rough and vehement or even solemn words to express
thoughts that are shallow and commonplace" (106).[71] He admits, citing
Isocrates, that "it is one of the duties of an orator to be able to treat
insignificant matters in a grand way and significant matters slight-
ingly," but feels that deliberate indecorum requires a heightened sense
of discretion (107).[72] He resists, that is, the argument Grasso makes
when criticizing Terence for his plainness in comedy: that wonder has
universal value and is always required, much less appropriate. Hermogenes considers pseudo-forceful the kinds of speeches Isocrates himself attacks in his encomium on Helen: "eristic disputations" and paradoxical encomia.[73] Those who choose "an absurd and self-contradictory
subject" (hypothesin atopon kai paradoxon)" (Isocrates, Helen, 1) set
themselves less of a challenge: "No one who has chosen to praise bum-
ble-bees and salt and kindred topics has ever been at a loss for words. . . .
and while on famous subjects one rarely finds thoughts which no one
has previously uttered, yet on trifling and insignificant topics whatever
the speaker may chance to say is entirely original" (Helen, 12–14; cf.
Panathenaicus, 36). He claims that the Sophists who specialize in these
speeches and in arguing abstruse philosophical questions maintain their
hold on students because the young "are and always have been inclined
toward what is extraordinary and astounding (tas perittotētas kai tas
thaumatopoiias)" (Helen, 7). For Hermogenes, the cleverness or deinotēs of the Sophists is not truly deinos—it is not forceful speech on
important subjects.

   Hermogenes' critique of the Sophists' discordant metaphors, although
appearing in his section on Solemnity (semnotēs) rather than Force (deinotēs), is also apposite. Labeling excessively bold metaphors "frigid images," he notes that Demosthenes has no use for them but "In the

---

[71] Cf. Dryden on the difference between Cleveland's satires and Donne's: "the one
gives us deep thoughts in common language, though rough cadence; the other gives
us common thoughts in abstruse words" (An Essay of Dramatic Poesy, in Essays of
John Dryden, ed. W. P. Ker [1900], 1:52). Hermogenes also criticizes inappropriately
grand "thoughts" and "approaches."
[72] Isocrates, Panegyricus, 8, in Isocrates.
[73] Isocrates, Helen, 1–15. On Isocrates' objections to the speeches of other sophists
as insufficiently pragmatic, see Trimpi, Muses, 11–17. Isocrates especially criticizes
their failure to prepare students for public service and to recognize that "likely conjecture about useful things is far preferable to exact knowledge of the useless" (Helen,
5).

works of the pretentious sophists you would find very many indeed" (23). His example is Gorgias' description of vultures as "living tombs." Such language may be acceptable in tragedies and, significantly, in poets "like Pindar, who use a tragic style," but Hermogenes finds "no excuse for those who use such crudities in practical oratory." "Longinus," too, holds his nose at Gorgias' vulture image, criticizing "pseudotragic" images that "make for confusion rather than intensity (*dedeinōtai*)" and that under close examination decline "from the terrible to the ridiculous" (*On the Sublime*, 3.1–2; cf. 9.5). Hermogenes and "Longinus" refuse to admit that sophistic style, with its bold metaphors heisted from tragic diction, is truly *deinos*, and neoclassical critics echo their complaints when attacking "metaphysical" style.

If Greek descriptions of *deinotēs* held the seeds of these later attacks, however, they also held the seeds that allowed admirable style to grow. Most important for the later itinerary of wonder is Demetrius' coordination of roughness, metaphorical obscurity, and suggestive brevity, and the frequent conection of these qualities with poetry. Through its association with both tragic fear and deliberative force, the rougher kind of *deinotēs* provides a model for the "manly" style that Renaissance lyric poets used to imitate the marvelous effect of tragic plots. But the delightful wonder of sophistic style, with its unabashed antitheses and ingenious paradoxical encomia, was never completely separated out of later views of astounding style, in part because of the confusion I have tried to chart.[74] Together they help shape the practice of wit in the late Elizabethan period, wit that can amuse as well as amaze.

Greek rhetoric in general and Greek views on *deinotēs* and *deinōsis* in particular became increasingly accessible in the late Renaissance through new editions, translations into Latin, commentaries, and continental treatises such as those by Sturm and Vossius.[75] As Bernard Weinberg explains, *On Style* was first printed in 1508, as part of Aldus

---

[74] George Williamson argues persuasively that the antithetical prose popular in the late sixteenth century was often associated with the sophistic style pioneered by Gorgias and later considered Asiatic; see *The Senecan Amble* (1966), esp. 20–53, 75–88.

[75] See the studies cited by Shuger, *Sacred Rhetoric*, 56n3; and Summers, *Michelangelo*, 236. "During the Renaissance," P. O. Kristeller states flatly, "the entire body of Greek rhetorical literature became accessible to the West, both through the original texts and through Latin and vernacular translations" ("Rhetoric in Medieval and Renaissance Culture," in Murphy, ed., *Renaissance Eloquence*, 4). On continental rhetorics in English libraries and private collections see Shuger, *Sacred Rhetoric*, 110–17. For allusions to Hermogenes and Demetrius by Gabriel Harvey and John Milton, see Patterson, *Hermogenes*, 24–26.

Manutius' edition of the Greek rhetors, and first printed separately (anonymously) in 1542.[76] The text was translated into Latin in whole or in part several times over the course of the sixteenth century, and was the subject of at least four commentaries. The section on letter writing (223–35) took on a life of its own, especially after Justus Lipsius appended a Latin translation of the section to his *Institutio Epistolica* (1591). Demetrius' description of the *charaktēr deinos* does not seem to have enjoyed independent transmission of this kind—with the exception of Tasso's summary in Book 6 of *Discourses on the Heroic Poem* (1594). But traces of *deinotēs*, of the strange and admirable, appear in other texts encouraging authors to produce wonder through style. In particular, the qualities of style that produce wonder receive emphasis in treatments of amplification and wit within manuals of poetry, rhetoric, and conduct. As Daniel Javitch, Frank Whigham, Heinrich Plett, Richard Helgerson, and others have shown, of course, the boundaries separating these kinds of texts dissolve when courtiers read them and put their tenets into practice: courtiers' amateur poetry was always at least in part rhetorical performance. The most influential English handbooks seldom explicitly connect with wonder the techniques of style that Aristotle offers in his discussion of *asteia* or that Demetrius includes in the *charaktēr deinos*. But they do insist, like Aristotle as elaborated by Demetrius, on style that is strange and admirable.

Amplification and Wonder

Balancing their demand for clarity, Thomas Wilson's *The Arte of Rhetorique* (1553), Henry Peacham's *The Garden of Eloquence* (1577), and George Puttenham's *The Arte of English Poesie* (1589) also demand that language be forceful. The more explicit emphasis in the Greek rhetorics on making style wonderful becomes in the English rhetorics an emphasis on amplification, on giving style life, spirit, and *energeia*. To amplify speech is to make it lively and strange, evoking wonder. Amplification is particularly crucial in the conclusion of speeches, where Wilson says a prosecutor, "stirryng the hearers by large utteraunce," can "set the Judges on fire, and heate them earnestly against the wicked offender" (137). Indignation or *deinōsis* is not the only kind of wonder amplification can produce: "In praisyng, or dispraisyng" generally, Wilson claims, "wee muste exaggerate those places towardes the ende, which make menne wonder at the straungenesse of any thyng" (138).

[76] See Bernard Weinberg, "Demetrius Phalereus," in *Catalogous Translationum et Commentariorum*, vol. 2, ed. P. O. Kristeller (1971), 27–41.

For all three authors, figurative language is the primary means of exaggerating and strangifying, and in setting out the motives for metaphor Wilson starts with those most resonant of Demetrius. Writers deliberately avoid the most apt words in favor of figures or "places" either because they "counte it a poynte of witte to passe over such woordes as are at hande, and to use suche as are farre fetcht and translated" or "because the hearer is led by cogitacion upon rehearsall of a Metaphore, and thinketh more by remembraunce of a word translated, then is there expreslye spoken" (193).[77] Peacham waxes more alliteratively eloquent in praise of "places," referring to "that great and forcible floud of Eloquence" that is "most plentifully and pleasantly poured forth by the great might of Figures" (*Garden*, Aiii.r). For Puttenham too, exornation provides the strangeness that makes language distinctive; it "resteth in the fashioning of our makers language and stile, to such purpose as it may delight and allure as well the mynde as the eare of the hearers with a certaine noveltie and strange maner of conveyance, disguising it no little from the ordinary and accustomed" (*Arte*, 137; cf. 240). To be convincing, speech must be strange.

In his manuscript *Directions for Speech and Style* (c. 1599), John Hoskyns links amplification to admiration even more explicitly than the published critics do: "To *Amplifye* and *Illustrate*, are two the chiefest ornaments of eloquence; & gaine of mens myndes two the chiefest advantages admyracon & beliefe, for how can yow commend a thing more acceptably to our attencion, then by tellinge us it is extraordynary, and by shewing us that it is evident" (131).[78] Moving "admyracon and beliefe" involves highlighting a subject's strangeness and presenting it with *evidentia*, the Latin term for *enargeia*. Hoskyns seems to align amplification with "admyracon" and illustration with "belief," but fails to keep the categories entirely distinct: his inconsistencies reflect again

---

[77] Wilson also notes that metaphors open a new perspective on a subject, serving as a means of discovery, and that they provide *enargeia* (193; cf. 196, 201, and Peacham, *Garden*, Aiii.r; Bii.r.; Niiii.r). On Puttenham's treatment of vividness, see Linda Galyon, "Puttenham's *Enargeia* and *Energeia*: New Twists for Old Terms," *Philological Quarterly* 60 (1981): 29–40.

[78] Circulating only in manuscript until partially incorporated first in Jonson's *Discoveries* and later in Thomas Blount's *Academie of Eloquence* (1654) and John Smith's *The Mysterie of Rhetorique unvail'd* (1657), Hoskyns's text is most safely handled not as an influence on contemporary poets but as a record of the views of a representative "scholar, lawyer, parliamentarian, occasional poet, wit, stylist, and critic" (John Hoskyns, *Life, Letters*, 1). Editor Louise Brown Osborn points out, however, that Hoskyns "was wont to bring . . . his own weight of erudition into circles of some of London's bravest wits." See also Annabel Patterson, "All Donne," in *Soliciting Interpretation*, ed. Elizabeth D. Harvey and Katharine Eisaman Maus (1990), 37–67.

the tendency to conflate *energeia, efficacia,* or force with *enargeia, evidentia,* and "cleereness."[79] Hoskyns, like the published critics, includes among the methods of amplifying speech, or provoking wonder, the devices that made up the *charaktēr deinos* of Demetrius: metaphor, emphasis, allegory or enigma, hyperbole, ambiguity, aposiopesis, and others.

Without grouping these devices together in a single character of style, authors of English rhetorics and poetry manuals find valuable distinctiveness in metaphor, in witticisms, and in the figures allegory, enigma, and emphasis.[80] Obscurity acquires its prestige at least as much from Renaissance esoteric traditions, but these manuals hint at how and why poets thought they could use signs to be taken as wonders. Puttenham, like practicing poets such as Hoskyns later and George Gascoigne before, follows Wilson in recognizing the value of obscure comparisons, as in his treatment of *"Parabola* or Resemblance misticall,"* to be practiced "whensoever by your similitude ye will seeme to teach any moralitie or good lesson by speeches misticall and darke, or farre fette, under a sence metaphoricall applying one naturall thing to another, or one case to another" (*Arte,* 245). He does not say that similitudes are more excellent as they are more obscure, but brings prestige to his most obscure category of similitudes by citing as examples Aesop's fables, "other apologies invented for doctrine sake by wise and grave men," and even "all the preachings of Christ in the Gospell" (245).

In his *Certayne Notes of Instruction . . .* (1575), Gascoigne more definitively insists that poets pass over topics and comparisons at hand in search of inventive approaches to poetic matter, of *aliquid salis.* Instead of praising a woman for qualities that are *"trita et obvia,"* he says, he

---

[79] See Tuve, *Elizabethan and Metaphysical Imagery,* 27–40 and 67–68. Hoskyns makes *evidentia* parallel to "cleerenes" in the sense derived from the Latin *claritas:* "brightness, vividness." Slippage between clearness and force also emerges in his discussion of *progressio:* "This is a most easie cleere and usuall kinde of amplificacion, for it gives more light & force out of everie circumstance" (142). Cf. George Chapman's struggle to distinguish vividness from clarity: "That, *Enargia,* or cleerenes of representation, requird in absolute poems is not the perspicuous delivery of a lowe invention; but high, and harty invention exprest in most significant, and unaffected phrase" (in *Literary Criticism,* ed. Tayler, 35).

[80] Wilson observes that "An Oration is wonderfullye enriched, when apte Metaphores are gotte and applied to the matter" (*Arte,* 195). He also refers to those expert at "Whittie jestyng" as "wonderfull to beholde" (204). Peacham authorizes schemes that "cause something to want"—leaving some of the sense to the reader to figure out—because this want "is yet pleasaunte, for that it doth marvelously serve to brevity" (*Garden,* Eiii.v). Puttenham's figure *"Paradoxon,* or the Wondrer" is simply the English equivalent of the Latin idioms *mirabile dictu* and *mirabile visu:* "a wonder to speak of" or "to behold."

would either "find some supernaturall cause whereby my penne might walke in the superlative degree" or paradoxically turn "any imperfection that she hath" into a point in her favor. (Just as "superlative degree" here is a Latinism for "hyperbolically," "supernaturall" may be a Latinism for "metaphysical.") Avoiding the trite and obvious means embracing hyperbole, paradox, and obscurity: "Like wise, if I should disclose my pretence in love, I would eyther make a strange discourse of some intollerable passion . . . or discover my disquiet in shadowes *per Allegoriam*, or use the covertest meane that I could to avoyde the uncomely customes of common writers."[81] By treating a plain declaration of love as "common," Gascoigne blurs the line between aesthetic and social judgment, or rather his equation reveals that the distinction is anachronistic: for the amateur poets he addresses, to be common is to be uncomely. Taking the high road means joining the crowd, never the goal of the poet-courtier, especially not in the later decades of the century; Gascoigne's own poetry, to be sure, treats plainness as its highest virtue, but his declaration might later be read as sanctioning pursuit of the bizarre.

Poets can be inventive without being obscure, and the most famous poem following Gascoigne's advice to write against convention is Shakespeare's hardly metaphysical sonnet 130, "My mistress' eyes are nothing like the sun." But whereas Shakespeare departs from the norm sparingly, and retains the sonnet form, Donne and his contemporaries continually pursued paradox and hyperbole, and in different forms. Sonnet 130 stands out, but in Donne's early love lyrics paradox is the norm, its absence the exception.

Love-wits especially ring changes on three paradoxes: inconstancy is superior to constancy, older women to younger, and "ugly" women (by conventional standards) to beautiful.[82] Donne produces his famous range of perspectives on love in part by taking multiple stances on inconstancy: praising it to some degree in, for example, "Womans Constancy," "Change," "Confined Love," "The Indifferent," and "Loves Deitie" (cf. Thomas Stanley, "The Repulse"); indicting it in "Song: 'Goe, and catche a falling starre,'" "Tutelage," "The Good Morrow," "A Jeat Ring Sent," "The Apparition," "The Message," and "The Legacie" (cf. Abraham

---

[81] In *English Literary Criticism*, ed. O. B. Hardison, Jr. (1963), 75–76.

[82] Donne's friend Edward, Lord Herbert of Cherbury, follows Shakespeare (sonnets 127 and 130–32) in frequently questioning the Northern European judgment of fair hair, eyes, and complexion as most beautiful: "The Brown Beauty" most explicitly relates aesthetic judgment to ethnic prejudice. Cf. John Cleveland, "A Faire Nimph scorning a Black Boy Courting her," and the editors' note listing other poems on the racial theme, in *Poems of John Cleveland*, 22, 101.

Cowley, "The Change"); and anatomizing it in "The Broken Heart," "Loves Growth," "Loves Infiniteness," and "A Lecture upon the Shadow" (cf. Edward Herbert, Lord Herbert of Cherbury, "An Ode Upon a Question Moved, whether Love Should Continue for Ever").[83] For ugliness, Donne similarly offers praise (in "The Anagram," the imitation of Tasso that Gardner describes as the elegy appearing most frequently in miscellanies) and over-the-top critique (in the elegy "The Comparison," odious and odorous).[84]

The same principle Gascoigne announces in regard to invention applies to metaphor. Hoskyns defends the rhetorical effect of obscurity when he calls comparison of "things equall indeed" less "forcible an Amplification" than comparisons in which "things seeming unequall are compared" (*Life, Letters*, 132). Writers "shall most of all profitt by inventing matter of agreement in things most unlike, as London, and a Tenis Court, for in both all the gaine goes to the hazard" (132). This comparison obviously satisfies Samuel Johnson's definition of a metaphysical conceit, yoking heterogeneous ideas together by violence. *Discordia concors* provides forcible amplification, which in turn provokes wonder, "admyracon." Like Wilson, Puttenham, and Gascoigne, Hoskyns applies the touchstone of obscurity; poems that amaze through invention and style pass the test.

If to this point the motives and strategies for provoking wonder have seemed all too clear, the ways in which English amateur poets of the 1590s put them into action move us into stranger land. As symbolic action, even ritual, the use of wit to provoke wonder leaves logic behind, or obeys a looking-glass logic. The insistence in Greek rhetoric on frustrating the audience's expectations, like Hoskyns' desperate metaphor of London and the tennis court, points us to the entrance of a dif-

---

[83] Misogyny is probably the only constant in these three approaches to inconstancy. He accepts presumed female inconstancy in "Womans Constancy" and "Change" simply to license his own (as in "Communitie"), and attacks it in the second group of poems while contrasting it to his own implicit faithfulness. Both strategies enable him to seem especially "manly." The third group is distinct: the poems take the transitory nature of love as their subject in a more serious way, but this position leads to the rejection of earthly love found so frequently in the sonneteers (Wyatt, Sidney, Greville), and expressed so fiercely as rejection of womankind in "Loves Alchymie" and "Twicknam Garden."

[84] For poems praising "ugliness" or "deformity," see Sir Benjamin Rudyerd, "On Deformity in Man" and his verses "Written by one that was a suitor to a gentlewoman more virtuous than fair, to a friend of his that disliked her . . ." (possibly a companion poem to Donne's "The Comparison"), in *Sir Benjamin Rudyerd, Knt., Containing His Speeches and Poems*, ed. James Alexander Manning (1841); and the editors' note on John Cleveland, "A young man to an old Woman Courting him," in *Poems of John Cleveland*, 98.

ferent world. Here not only does the ability to compare seemingly dissimilar objects produce wonder and uncommon distinction, but the best
way to emerge as a capable member of the aristocracy is to appear desperately subversive.

In his study of symbolic images, E. H. Gombrich presents the analysis
by Girolame Ruscelli of an *impresa* that "shows the sun behind clouds
... with the motto *hinc clarior* ('hence brighter')": its sudden emergence
makes it more wonderful than it could possibly have seemed if always
visible.[85] Gombrich, like Steven Mullaney more recently, adduces Hal's
famous soliloquy in *Henry IV, Part I*, as a comparable emblem of the
wonder generated by unexpected brightness:

> I know you all, and will awhile uphold
> The unyoked humour of your idleness.
> Yet herein will I imitate the sun,
> Who doth permit the base contagious clouds
> To smother up his beauty from the world,
> That, when he please again to be himself,
> Being wanted he may be more wonder'd at
> By breaking through the foul and ugly mists
> Of vapours that did seem to strangle him.
> If all the year were playing holidays,
> To sport would be as tedious as to work;
> But when they seldom come, they wish'd for come,
> And nothing pleaseth but rare accidents.
> So, when this loose behaviour I throw off,
> And pay the debt I never promised,
> By how much better than my word I am,
> By so much shall I falsify men's hopes. (1.2.190)

Hal, Mullaney notes, takes on as a matter of policy the behavior and
language of Eastcheap: he is "a Prince who plays at prodigality, and
means to translate his rather full performance into the profession of
power."[86] He deceives the courtly audience's expectations, falsifies their
hopes.[87] What Hal does in Eastcheap is comparable to what wits such as

[85] E. H. Gombrich, *Symbolic Images* (1972), 163.
[86] Steven Mullaney, "Strange Things," 83–84. The playing out of Hal's deliberate
transformation needs to be distinguished from presentations of the rebel's absorption
into social conformity as inevitable, a theme handled most frankly in The Clash's
"Death or Glory," on *London Calling* (1979).
[87] The audience in the theater will not be deceived, because he has revealed his
strategy to us. As insiders, however, we are invited to share the pleasure as well as

Donne do, or tried to do, through quick wit. In both cases wonder is the intended, even necessary, result. Hal's burden of wonder is greater, since Renaissance political theory requires majestic wonder to be nearly divine, and as heir to an usurper he must play his role especially well to heal the rupture in royal ideology. But the crowd of qualified courtiers seeking a place at court made the burden on any individual courtier heavy too, and as the odds against succeeding at court rose, so did their willingness to take the risk involved in playing the quick wit.

The stylistic authorities considered so far have seemed largely to be forces encouraging, even if unwittingly, witty obscurity, but playing the wit had its downside. Traditional injunctions against being overly witty, against living in perpetual holiday, exerted a counterpressure, as did the more sinister implications of being quick-witted, especially the association of verbal wittiness with melancholy, Machiavellian policy, Jesuit equivocation, and tyrannical doubleness. When viewed as action, as a strategy taken by courtier-poets rather than simply a style or a set of genres chosen by poets on aesthetic grounds, witty style in the satires and epigrams of the 1590s emerges as a practice conditioned by its need to manuever between various sets of cultural values. To describe the action of producing wonder through wit thickly, we need to recognize that clarity and obscurity both had value in Renaissance poetics and rhetoric, that jesting could be both encouraged and proscribed. The negotiation that courtier-poets accomplished was in no sense the mechanical charting of a course between these extremes: the danger involved in being a quick wit was itself part of the attraction, and playing it safe seemed to be becoming increasingly risky itself, given the abundance of educated young men. They calculated the risk according to a complex calculus that required recognition of how witty wonder played into these different systems of value.

By using a tennis court as an analogy for London—meaning the court and its environs, the place where an ambitious courtier would make or break his fortune—Hoskyns points to the kind of stakes involved, and to the sense young men had that Dame Fortune was alive and well and living there. It also points to his own ambivalence toward wit and its social function. When presenting this desparate comparison, Hoskyns notes that writers "shall most of all profitt by inventing matter of agreement" between things unlike; he may simply be using a dead metaphor, but the literal sense of "profitt" as economic and social gain shows signs

---

pain involved in his transformation from Hal, companion of Falstaff, to Henry V, King of England. On the tradition of the Renaissance confidence man and Henry's place within it, see Rebhorn, *Foxes and Lions*, 1–44, esp. 15–16 and 33–35.

of life in this context. When read with Hoskyns' other discussions of wit and patronage, skipping over the literal sense of "profitt" becomes especially questionable, as blind as ignoring the cluster of terms for economic exchange that Hal uses when calculating the ultimate value of his reformation.

Hal catapults to a place of wonder on the battlefield at Shrewsbury, calling in the glory his "factor" Hotspur has amassed, but this traditional method of gaining status had become nearly obsolete by the end of the sixteenth century, as Lawrence Stone has demonstrated.[88] Hoskyns' generation took up the sword of wit as earlier generations had taken up the more obvious weapon of awe, advancement, and competition, as John Aubrey confirms when noting in his biography that Hoskyns's "excellent Witt gave him letters of Commendacion to all ingeniose persons."[89] Not that Hoskyns (or Donne) matched Hal's success, but when the actor playing Hal looked into the audience at the end of his first scene, the Inns of Court men who haunted the theaters must have felt a shock of recognition or a flame of inspiration. No strategy is foolproof in a game where all the gain goes to the hazard, but even when writing from the Tower in 1614 Hoskyns was unrepentant about his weapon of choice: "I cannot be persuaded that any man that hath witt of his own is afrayd of anothers witt, as no good soldier that hath a sword feares another mans sword.[sic] and for my part I had rather dy with witt then live without it." (*Life, Letters,* 71). If Hoskyns bristles here at being accused of being overly witty, it was a charge he himself had leveled in the *Directions* at those addicted to catachresis (125):

> *Catachresis* (in English *Abuse*) is nowe growne in fashion (as most abuses are,) It is somewhat more desperate then a *Metaphore*, it is the expressing of one matter by the name of another, which is incompatible with it, & sometimes cleane contrary. . . . this is a usuall figure with the fine conversants of our tyme, when they strayne for an extraordinary phraze, as I am not guilty of those phrases, I am in danger of preferment.

As his examples make clear, Hoskyns is here largely attacking *ironia,* or what we might call simple sarcasm.[90] Hoskyns's protest that his failure

---

[88] *Crisis of the Aristocracy* (1965), 265–67, 401–3, and 454–58. On the Inns of Court as "the career open to talents, the ladder on which able young men could climb to power and riches," see Wilfred R. Prest, *Inns of Court* (1972), 21–22.

[89] *Aubrey's Brief Lives,* ed. Oliver Lawson Dick (1950), 169.

[90] One of his examples is "I gave order to some servaunts of myne, (whome I thought as apt for such charities as my selfe) to lead him out into the forrest & there to kill him."

to indulge in all forms of wit threatens his chances for advancement demonstrates that courtier-poets sought to provoke wonder through style, but his critique also registers deep ambivalence. And if he was later content to die by wit, he was not sure he wanted his son to rise or fall the same way, as his poem in the witty vein of Ralegh's "Three things there be" shows:

> My little Ben, whil'st thou art young,
> And know'st not how to rule thy Tongue,
> Make it thy Slave whil'st thou art free,
> Least it as mine imprison thee.[91]

However paradoxical a witty epigram about constraining wit may seem (and however hypocritical, given his pledge of allegiance), Hoskyns was not alone in feeling tugged in at least two directions by wit, or in ultimately risking being quartered.

[91] In Aubrey, *Aubrey's Brief Lives*, 69.

2 The Most Dangerous Game: Wonder, Melancholy, and Satire

> This is the paradox of charisma: that though it is rooted in the sense of being near to the heart of things, of being caught up in the realm of the serious, a sentiment that is felt most characteristically and continually by those who in fact dominate social affairs, who ride in the progresses and grant the audiences, its most flamboyant expressions tend to appear among people at some distance from the center, indeed often enough at a rather enormous distance, who want very much to be closer. Heresy is as much of a child of orthodoxy in politics as it is in religion.
> —Clifford Geertz, "Centers, Kings, and Charisma: Reflections on the Symbolics of Power"

When Athens' cool-headed Duke Theseus dismisses the lovers' story of their adventures in the green world of *A Midsummer Night's Dream*, he charges them with guilt by association. With their fellow travelers in the sin of indulging imagination, lovers in general form the trio of "the lunatic, the lover, and the poet" (5.1.7). Although identified as the usual suspects in gloss after gloss on the Platonic, Neoplatonic, and pseudo-Aristotelian origins of the idea of melancholic genius, this trio should strike us as strange and admirable, something, like the lovers' story itself, to wonder at. Theseus's list is strange not for what it contains, but for what it omits, and what it omits is the politician or governor, whom most authorities had included in the ranks of those touched by melancholic genius. By failing to recognize the public function of imagination, the hard-witted Theseus indicts himself, becoming the butt of a joke he tells but cannot get.

That Shakespeare and at least part of his audience were in on this joke seems likely from the frequency with which Renaissance accounts of melancholy, wit, and genius echo the idea, wrongly but repeatedly credited to Aristotle, that "all those who have become eminent in philosophy or politics or poetry or the arts are clearly melancholics" (*Problems*, 30.1). The upstart crow need have looked no further than Robert Greene's *Planetomachia* (1585), which defends the Saturnine disposition both on the authority of Plato and Aristotle and through the example of such supposedly melancholic statesmen as Pericles, Scipio, Julius Caesar, and even pious Aeneas.[1] In *The Arte of English Poesie*, George Puttenham champions those "of rare invention" even more strongly; bristling at the scorn expressed by those who call poets "phantasticall," Puttenham anxiously distinguishes *phantastici* from *euphantastiote*, or those afflicted with melancholy from those blessed with genius, and highlights the pragmatic benefits of imagination: "of this sort of phantasie are all good Poets, notable Captaines stratagematique, all cunning artificers and enginers, all Legislators, Polititiens, & Counsellours of estate, in whose exercises the inventive part is most employed, and is to the sound & true judgement of man most needful" (18–20). By dismissing imagination, Theseus ironically presents himself as lacking in this necessary component of public excellence.

But Theseus, after all, is only a character; for us the consequences of sharing his omission are more serious: miss the association between political skill and imagination, and we may misread the cultural function of a variety of poetic practices in the Renaissance, especially witty satire. Nod instead of winking at Theseus' view of poetic invention and the wonder it produces, and we may find ourselves listening only to the soberly negative assessment of wit that Roger Ascham and the Tudor elders present, and ignoring other powerful voices. Theseus's omission points to the difficulty of reading the status of satire in the 1590s, and the status of the wit and wonder with which it was associated. I want to argue not that Theseus's judgment of the imagination is unique, because it is not, but that it coexists with Hippolyta's praise of the strange and admirable—that the two judgments both register significant forces within English culture late in Elizabeth's reign. The opposition in act five of *A Midsummer Night's Dream* echoes a set of oppositions that runs all along the fault line connecting imagination to melancholy, melancholy to wit, wit to wonder, wonder to policy, and policy to satire. By recognizing the forces creating this chasm, we will better understand why young courtier-poets walked its edge.

[1] In *The Life and Complete Works in Prose and Verse of Robert Greene, M.A.*, ed. Alexander B. Grosart (1883), 5:46.

All down the line, young men like John Hoskyns or John Donne who sought a way to power could not help hearing both voices, the warnings to stay back and the sirens' call to fare forward. Witty satire inspires such radically different kinds of evaluation as a practice because both wit and satire are capable of performing radically different functions: the display of wit may mark one as frivolous, impractical, and fantastic, or as a member of an intellectual elite capable of maintaining the state; satire may express personal, political, and religious discontent, challenging authority through its oblique complaints about those in power and the satirist's lack of advancement, or it may reinforce conventional social, moral, and political norms by mocking deviations from them.

As scholarship on the melancholy malcontent has shown, the forces, attitudes, and activities with which satire was associated in the 1590s were considered far more sinister than those listed by Theseus.[2] In other circumstances, poets might have listened only to the alarms, but in the desperate competition for preferment in the 1590s, they took the risk of appearing witty, melancholy, curious, malcontented, Italianate, Machiavellian, even traitorous. In a paradox as witty as those devised by the Monarch of Wit, witty satire offers young aspirants a medium in which to make the transition from student to courtier not in spite of its dangerous associations, but precisely because of them. Playing a most dangerous game, they wrote witty satire.

In ritual terms, such satire serves as a liminal activity, a practice in which one transgresses the norm only to join the elite that maintains it. This game is one that only those who have not yet invested significant symbolic capital in social norms can play: as Pierre Bourdieu notes, the "great" in a society "can least afford to take liberties with the official norms."[3] Yet the ante is high, since it involves the risk of all potential for gaining symbolic capital, all opportunity for social advancement.

If the status of wit were not complicated enough by itself, the status of the melancholy with which it was associated would provide sufficient challenge. Renaissance views of melancholy, as the debate between Theseus and Hippolyta indicates, were notoriously ambivalent, and with good reason: the cluster of symptoms it included make up what is now diagnosed as the bipolar condition of manic depression. Melancholics were almost always viewed with deep suspicion, but melancholy was also often recognized as the prerequisite for poetic genius,

---

[2] On representations of the melancholic in Elizabethan literature see Bridget Gellert Lyons, *Voices of Melancholy* (1975); Lawrence Babb, *The Elizabethan Malady* (1951); and Zera S. Fink, "Jaques and the Malcontent Traveler," *Philological Quarterly* 14 (1935): 237–52.

[3] *Outline of a Theory of Practice*, trans. Richard Nice (1977), 193; see also 124–39.

furor poeticus, and, though a target of satire, melancholy is also a source of satire. Curiouser and curiouser: the more one chases wit in the cultural matrix of England in the 1590s, the stranger it becomes.

When Marsilio Ficino missed the irony in Plato's treatment of poetic inspiration in the *Ion* and in *Phaedrus* 245a, and combined it with the pseudo-Aristotelian explanation for "fits of exaltation and ecstasy (*nosemasin . . . manikois e enthousiastikois*)," thus "creating the modern notion of genius," he was countering but not effacing the tradition in Galenic humour theory that Saturnian melancholy, if not tempered, produced madness, paranoia, and depression.[4] In *The Optick Glasse of Humours* (1607, rpt. 1631), Thomas Walkington tries to contain these explosive counterpressures within the field of melancholy by splitting those born under Saturn into two groups, identifying them as "*aut Deus aut Dæmon*, either angel of heaven or a fiend of hell," in whom "the soule is either wrapt up into an *Elysium* and paradise of blesse by a heavenly contemplation, or into a direfull hellish purgatory by a cynicall meditation" (125).

Like the varying functions of wit and satire, the varying evaluations of melancholy complicate any thick description of satire in the 1590s. Those responding to the fashion for melancholy seem to have played both angel and devil, combining claims to *furor poeticus*—manifested in mastery of verbal wit—with the cynical stance of the satirist. The melancholic's solitary, bitter character made him privy mocker par excellence, in turn making the role of satiric poet especially fashionable. The logic that encourages the adoption of a mode with such dangerous associations is the same logic that encourages comparisons of ostensibly dissimilar objects. So is the goal: just as the ability to yoke heterogeneous ideas provokes wonder, so does the ability to land at the top after plunging downward. Again the parallel with Hal is worth considering, since even if he considers his truancy a holiday, his father makes explicit the fear that it signifies potential treason (*1HIV*, 3.2.121–8).

By posing as melancholic and even Machiavellian wits, prospective courtiers could also provoke wonder along the way to their eventual reformation. Because of Castiglione's association of jests with wonder and natural ability, and Ficino's revival of the association of melancholy

[4] See Raymond Klibansky, Erwin Panofsky, and Fritz Saxl, *Saturn and Melancholy* (1964), 24, 250; on familiarity with the notion of poetic frenzy in the Middle Ages, however, see Curtius, *European Literature*, 474. For the influence of Ficino's *De vita triplici* on English travelers, see Babb, *Elizabethan Malady*, 60–67. Renaissance texts on melancholy that present themselves as strictly medical nevertheless vacillate among medical, moral, religious, and political perspectives; see Carol Thomas Neely, "Did Madness Have a Renaissance?" *Renaissance Quarterly* 20 (1991): 766–88; and Debora Kuller Shuger, *Habits of Thought* (1990), 50 and 78–90.

with genius in poetry and politics, courtiers playing the melancholic wit automatically hedge their bets. Such endorsements of wit limit the risk involved in practicing an obscure, admirable style tainted by its similarity to the equivocation practiced by Jesuits and the doubleness of tyrants such as Tiberius. Such endorsements also, of course, mitigate the still-thriving prejudices against quick wits as lightheaded, poets as phantastical, and melancholics as dangerously diseased. Even as witty satirists act out mock-rebellion and holiday, then, they keep one foot in the door of advancement, the world of everyday.

Hard Wits, Quick Wits, and Daedalus Wings

As Richard Helgerson has shown, the critiques of "quick wits" by Roger Ascham and others encouraged courtier-poets in the sixteenth century to downplay and eventually renounce their poetry as prodigal play, unsuited to one holding public responsibility. Ascham accuses quick-witted students of addiction to novelty, merriment, and change, calling them "overquick, hasty, rash, heady, and brainsick" (*The School-master*, 22). These overly quick wits engage too often in satirical flyting: they are "ready scoffers, privy mockers, and ever overlight and merry." Hard wits, Ascham continues, though slow early, eventually overtake the hare-brained, who "decay and vanish, men know not which way." When advising their sons, Sir Henry Sidney and Lord Burghley echo Ascham's warning against gaining a reputation as a jester.[5] This parental anxiety extends through the middle of the next century, when Francis Osborne cautions his son to "spend no time in reading, much less writing strong lines."[6] Although often cited as evidence of the shift in taste away from the bold wit of Donne to the proper wit of Dryden and Swift, Osborne's advice emerges in context as a politic caution, a social rather than strictly aesthetic objection to admirable style. These warnings signify that wit carries both a stigma and an allure: if there had been no temptation, there would have been no warnings (and the warnings themselves, of course, no doubt heightened the allure).

Like Hoskyns when writing to his son from the Tower, these fathers are concerned about their sons' advancement: they are not humorless, but pragmatic, fearful that the reputation as quick wit will mar their

[5] See Richard Helgerson, *Self-Crowned Laureates*, 27. Sidney's warning is reprinted in James M. Osborn, *Young Philip Sidney*, 1572–1577 (1972), 12–13, Burghley's in *Advice To a Son: Precepts of Lord Burghley, Sir Walter Raleigh, and Francis Osborne*, ed. Louis B. Wright (1962), 13.

[6] *Advice to a Son* (1656), in *Advice to a Son*, ed. Wright, 45.

sons' chances for preferment. (Here again the parallel with Hal is worth considering, since in 3.2 Henry IV delivers to Hal a long lecture on how ill-advised his behavior is, how unlikely it is to gain him the kind of wonder majesty requires. Throughout this speech the audience is aware, as Henry IV is not, that Hal knows the importance of wonder. He has, however, out-politicked his father by adopting a new strategy to create wonder, just as the young satirists of the post-Sidney generation did.) Questions about the ability of quick wits to perform public service last into the seventeenth century, surfacing in *The New-found Politicke* (1626), translated anonymously from Traiano Boccalini's *Ragguagli di Parnasso* (1612). The Ministers of Boccalini's Parnassus habitually chose officials who fit the profile of Ascham's "hard wits" (164):

> It is worth the observation, that in so great a number of concurrents for places, they had elected persons of a slow Genius, of cold constitutions, and in their actions perplext, irresolute, and addicted to drowsinesse, even almost to disability: and on the contrary, that they had excluded those which for the quicknesse and vivacity of their wits, appeared to be far fitter, and more worthy of employment than others.

The Ministers "doe firmely beleeve, that those wits which are over lively, nimble, & fiery, prove very unapt to rule others, having great need themselues of a curbing-bit, and a head-straine to save them from falling downe headlong into ditches" (165). Like such famous stumblers as Horace's mad poet (*Art of Poetry*, 457–59) or Plato's star-gazing Thales (*Theaetetus* 174a), quick wits are seen as impractical by temperament.[7] Busily seeking continual change, they tend to stir up rather than pacify the state: "The world, which requires good government, turnes quickly seditious and imbroyled with the phantasticall *chymaeraes* of certain hotspurres, which in all their affaires by seeking to become over-wise in their owne conceit, they doe in stead of quenching and appeasing troubles and combustions, kindle them the more by unseasonable remedies" (164). Quick wits, then, are more than incompetent in the political sphere: they are dangerous, practicing a wild brand of homeopathic medicine.

But as Boccalini's indictment of slow wits for "drowsiness" suggests, the quick wit associated with a saturnine dispostion is not so easily

---

[7] Socrates presents the "leaders of philosophy" as wholly ignorant of civic affairs: "From their youth up they have never known the way to market place or law court or Council Chamber or any other place of public assembly; they never hear a decree read out loud or look at the text of a law" (*Theaetetus*, 173d). Cf. Sidney, *A Defence of Poetry*, 28–29.

dismissed, especially because it enables one to dissemble and to recognize the dissimulation of others, skills crucial for acquiring and maintaining power: in Puttenham's favorite adage, "Qui nescit dissimulare, nescit regnare (Whoever does not know how to dissemble, does not know how to rule)" (*Arte*, 186).[8] Above all, wit is the faculty by which the courtier can fulfill Castiglione's injunction to make "all men wonder at him, and hee at no man" (*Courtier*, 129). When Castiglione's Federico Fregoso catalogues the varieties of verbal dissimulation in Book Two, he presents figures that had also been specified in the ancient rhetorical tradition as capable of provoking an audience's wonder. Drawing on the *De Oratore* (2.54.217–2.71.290) as well as Quintilian's analysis of wit (6.3), what Castiglione presents is a miniature manual of wonderful wit.[9] Like Cicero's treatment of *facetiae* in the *De Oratore*, Castiglione's treatment of *arguzie* broadly overlaps with Demetrius' treatments of wit in relation to the graceful style (*charaktēr charis*) and the wonderful (*charaktēr deinos*).[10]

Castiglione follows Cicero and Demetrius in including among short, sharp witticisms those based on ambiguity (148–149), antithesis (154), metaphor and other forms of comparison (154–58), hyperbole (158), irony ("to answere contrarie to that he woulde with whom he talketh, but drily and (as it were) with a certaine doubting and heedfull consideration," 167), and a form of dissimulation that, like *emphasis* for Demetrius, signifies something more or other than what it says, but not the exact opposite (159). Both Cicero and Castiglione make explicit the relationship of wit to wonder, especially when describing the effect of ambiguity:

---

[8] My translation; see Javitch, *Poetry and Courtliness*, 36–119; and Rosemary Kegl, *The Rhetoric of Concealment* (1994), 11–42.

[9] Caesar identifies seven categories of verbal wit: the ambiguous or equivocal; the unexpected; play on words or names that involves changing spelling or pronunciation slightly (*paranomasia*); apt quotation of proverbs or familiar verses; taking another's words literally yet contrary to their intention; using allegory, figurative senses, and irony; and, finally, using antithetical expressions (*De Oratore*, 2.61.248). Quintilian tightens the connection between wonderful style and wit by emphasizing brevity (6.3.45); he covers Caesar's categories, and interestingly mentions in succession hyperbole, irony, metaphor, allegory, and emphasis—all elements of Demetrius' *charaktēr deinos*—as sources of jests (67–70). On witticisms in the sixteenth century see Joanna Brizdle Lipking, "Traditions of the *Facetiae* and Their Influence in Tudor England" (Ph.D. diss., Columbia University, 1970); and Anne Lake Prescott, "Humanism in the Tudor Jestbook," *Moreana* 24 (1987): 5–16.

[10] Richard Janko argues from the similarity of the discussions of laughter in Demetrius, Cicero, Quintilian, and the anonymous *Tractatus Coislianus* that the *Tractatus* preserves much of the lost second section of Aristotle's *Poetics*, on comedy (*Aristotle on Comedy*, 161–208).

Of those readie jeastes [*arguzie*] therefore that consist in a short saying, such are most lively that arise of doubtfulnesse, though always
they provoke not laughing: for they bee rather praysed for wittie, than
for matters of laughter. . . . But because those doubtfull wordes have a
pretie sharpenesse of wit in them, being taken in a contrarie signification to that all other men take them, it appeareth . . . that they rather
provoke a man to wonder than to laugh. (148–49; cf. *De Oratore*
2.61.253–54)[11]

If only by virtue of the extensive treatment Castiglione gives to wit, *The
Book of the Courtier* would have served to balance the Tudor elders'
weighty doom. By intimately associating wit with the evocation of
wonder—the double duty of the courtier-poet (as courtier and as poet)—
Book Two does more.

Castiglione's analysis picks up the most visible thread running through
the tangled tradition of wonder, the value placed on the ability to surprise, to write or speak what is contrary to expectation. In both verbal
witticisms and humorous stories, Castiglione concludes, "the chief mattere is to deceive opinion, and to answere otherwise than the hearer
looketh for" (168).[12] Like the tragic plot and the metaphor, the witticism
achieves its effect by manipulating and frustrating the audience's expectations. Defining *sprezzatura* in Book One, Count Ludovico further explains why style that appears to mean more than it says is admirable:
like the ideal courtier's other kinds of performance, wit makes the difficult appear easy, natural. The effect of such "readiness" in "rare matters" where "every man knoweth the hardnesse of them" is "great
wonder" (46).

Witty style is particularly admirable because it is likely to be perceived as natural and not duplicable by art: its magic remains mysterious. Introducing the discussion of wit in Book Two, "Sir Fredericke"
(Federico Fregoso) admits that "jestes and merrie conceites are rather a
gift, and a grace of nature, than of arte" (134; cf. Puttenham, *Arte*, 302–
07). He is echoing Cicero's *De Oratore*, where the characters Caesar and

---

[11] "Caesar" describes ambiguity as "particularly clever (*acuta*)," and notes that
Greek authorities considered other varieties of witticisms, including "*admirationes*"
or "astonishments" (2.71.288). In the *Partitiones Oratoriae*, Cicero further cements
the relationship between unexpected turns of speech and the marvelous, twice connecting wonder at what is surprising with delight (6.22; 9.32).

[12] See also 153 and 157. Just as Gorgias identifies the just tragedian and the wise
audience as those who will deceive and be deceived (Eden, *Poetic and Legal Fiction*,
25–28, esp. 26n2), Castiglione implies that a sharp audience—those who get the
joke—will laugh at having been deceived. Wit, like *deinotēs*, shades into *panourgia*,
crafty deception.

Antonius insist that *facetiae* "are assuredly the endowment of nature and in no need of art" (2.54.217; cf. 2.56.227); they, in turn, are adapting Aristotle's identification of metaphor as a sign of natural genius, "the one thing that cannot be learnt from others" (*Poetics*, 22; 1459a6; cf. *Rhetoric*, 3.2; 1405a7–9). Wit, artless because beyond the reach of art, is therefore an inalienable mark of natural distinction, like nobility by birth. This apparent causelessness makes the wielder of wit all the more imposing. Those who display "readiness" in wit, tossing off jests "without paine," arouse our wonder.

Frank Whigham's discussion of *sprezzatura* is particularly helpful here. Whigham emphasizes that aristocracy maintains its exclusivity by creating a group of qualifications that are both unachievable by effort and difficult to define: the emphasis is not on possession of a skill so much as on the manner in which the skill is performed.[13] I would argue that verbal wit, because treated as natural, exemplifies this "governing principle of the display of *effortlessness* . . . designed to imply the natural or given character of one's social identity, and to deny any earnedness, any labor or arrival from a social elsewhere" ("Interpretation at Court," 626). The emphasis on success through wit rather than study, nature rather than art, underlies the aristocratic stigma against appearing in print, which prompted George Pettie's bourgeois complaint: "Those which mislike that a Gentleman should publish the fruites of his learning, are some curious Gentlemen, who thynke it most commendable in a Gentleman, to cloak his arte and skill in every thyng, and to seeme to do all thynges of his owne mother witte as it were: not considering how we deserve no prayse for that, which God or Nature hath bestowed upon us, but only for that, which we purchace by our owne industry."[14] Pettie's complaint supports Whigham's hypothesis concerning mystification of the courtier's arts, arts which may be openly displayed in conversation at court and in coterie poetry, but must remain unprinted so as not to seem to involve labor. His withering repetition of "Gentleman" seems designed to throw the word's stability into doubt, pointing to the debate over the true site of nobility frequently rehearsed in the sixteenth century. Even if those with humble origins

---

[13] Whigham, "Interpretation at Court," 623–39. Sidney's reference to the awkwardness of "professors of learning" in comparison to "smally learned courtiers" may be the most famous English example (Sidney, *Defence of Poesy*, 72); see J. W. Saunders, "The Stigma of Print: A Note on the Social Bases of Tudor Poetry," *Essays in Criticism* 1 (1951): 139–64.

[14] In the preface to Pettie's translation of Stephen Guazzo, *The Civile Conversation of M. Steeven Guazzo*, ed. Edward Sullivan (1925), 1:8. See Daniel Javitch, "Rival Arts of Conduct in Elizabethan England: Guazzo's *Civile Conversation* and Castiglione's *Courtier*," *Yearbook of Italian Studies* 1 (1971): 196.

who sought to rise into positions at court had sympathy with Pettie's position, however, they were more immediately concerned with becoming "Gentlemen" than with debating the merits of nobility by birth versus nobility by effort. They were more interested, that is, in learning how to cloak.

Pettie focuses on natural wit in the general sense of powers of understanding—"mother witte"—but other English authors follow Aristotle, Cicero, and Castiglione in pointing to the innateness of verbal wit in particular, wit as the ability to make surprising verbal combinations. For Thomas Walkington wits are those "excelling in active nature, acute, having a quicke insight into a thing, a lively conceit of a thing: that can invent with ease such witty policies, quirks and stratagems, as he that is not of so sharpe a wit, would eve[r] admire, never can compass" (*Optick Glasse*, 82). Quick verbal wit, according to Richard Flecknoe in "Of Wit" (1666), is "a soaring quality, that just as *Daedalus* wings, elevates those who have it above other men; and is the same in the *brain*, as *Nobility* is in the *blood*." Like Abraham Cowley, Flecknoe finds wit "easier to admire, then tell you what it is: not acquir'd by *art* and *Study*, but *Nature* and *Conversation*."[15] Wit appears natural and admirable, making claims to be a certain sign or even a cause of a hierarchy of power as well as intellect. The claim on wit is a claim on power.

Also crucial to an elite's self-description is indeterminacy. Drawing upon Sartre's analysis of the mechanism of exclusion in *Anti-Semite and Jew*, Whigham says that "the aristocrat has 'that certain something' which cannot be achieved . . . because it is never fully defined or specified; because of this indeterminacy," he further argues, "the role of audience ratification grows. While logical criteria can claim to transcend group ratification, with magical criteria the group reasserts its power."[16] Wit, of course, fulfills this condition perfectly: only one who has it can recognize it. In a court such as that of Castiglione's Duke Guidobaldo, or of Elizabeth in the 1590s, you have to know one to be one, and must always act and speak—and interpret others' actions and speech—so as to remain an insider. There is no margin for social awk-

[15] Richard Flecknoe, *A Farrago of Several Pieces* (1666), 59. Robert Johnson argues similarly in his essay "Of Wit": "Men of slowe capacitie are more apte to serve, then to rule" because "their conceite is so tough" that nothing can improve it (*Essaies, or, Rather Imperfect Offers* (1607), ed. Robert Hood Bowers (1955), no page).

[16] "Interpretation at Court," 628; although he does not address the special case of wit, Whigham notes that Castiglione's injunction to courtiers to pursue wonder employs "a crucial critical term [maravigliasse] for the desired effect worked by literature, used throughout theoretical discussions in the sixteenth century" (628n10).

wardness or lack of perception; as Robert Burton puts it, "if the king laugh, all laugh."[17]

Those who hope to be close to the emperor admire his new suit even more than those already there. Operating not just as a marker distinguishing the elite from other classes, covert style and satire offered aspiring courtiers a means of setting themselves off from their companions in the universities, Inns of Court, and other satellites of the court, where, according to Nicholas Breton, days were filled with "Riddles, Questions and Answers" as well as "Poems, Histories, and strange Inventions of Witt, to startle the Braine of a good understanding."[18] A court where none can afford the exclusion that results from failing to get the joke provides the ideal atmosphere for obscure wit, and for poetry that demands that the reader validate its wittiness, and his or her own.

But to play the wit often meant to play the melancholic, since wit and melancholy, read as the source or sign of genius, were so closely associated. Even the conservative medical investigators of melancholy testify to this link. Laurentius, for example, notes that melancholics "are accomted as most fit to undertake matters of weightie charge and high attempt" and credits Aristotle with the idea "that the melancholike are most wittie and ingenious."[19] He finds that "their conceit is very deepe," and that "when this humour groweth hot . . . it causeth as it were, a kinde of divine ravishment, commenly called *Enthousiasma*, which stirreth men up to plaie the Philosophers, Poets, and also to prophesie: in such maner, as that it may seeme to contain in it some divine parts."[20] Although Thomas Walkington challenges the connec-

---

[17] *The Anatomy of Melancholy*, ed. Holbrook Jackson (1977), 1:66. Cf. *The Courtier:* "If a prince be inclined to one that is most ignorant, that can neither do nor say any thing, his manners and behaviors, (be they never so fonde and foolish) are many times commended with acclamation and wonder of all men, and it seemeth that all the Court beholdeth and observeth him, and every man laugheth at his boording and certaine carterly jestes, that shoulde rather move a man to vomit than to laugh" (123). In "Mine own John Poins," Sir Thomas Wyatt prides himself on being unable to "Grynne when he laugheth that bereth all the swaye" (line 53). In Ben Jonson's *Every Man Out of his Humour*, Cordatus describes Orange as "one that can laugh at a jest for company with a most plausible, and extemporall grace; and some houre after, in private, aske you what it was" (3.1.25–28).

[18] Nicholas Breton, *The Court and the Country* (1618), no page. Although not printed until 1618, Breton's work was probably written decades earlier; see W. G. Crane, *Wit and Rhetoric in the Renaissance* (1937), 124.

[19] M. Andreas Laurentius, *A Discourse of the Preservation of the Sight: of Melancolike Diseases; of Rheumes, and of Old Age*, trans. Richard Surphlet (1599; 1938), 85; cf. Timothy Bright, *A Treatise of Melancholie* (1586; 1940), 140; and Sir Thomas Elyot, *The Castel of Helth* (1541; rpt. no date), fol. 73r.

[20] Laurentius, *Discourse*, 86. Robert Burton quotes this statement almost verbatim

tion of melancholy with genius by arguing that the sanguine temperament "is the paragon of all," he rehearses the commonplaces, admitting
that melancholy has been considered "the pretious balme of witte and
policy: the enthusiasticall breath of poetry, the foyson of our phan-
tasies" (131). Ironically, he demonstrates that satiric jesting and admirable style were popularly associated with melancholy by protesting so
much that the sanguine disposition, not the melancholic, is best "for a
nimble, dextericall, smirke, pregnant, extemporary invention, for a sud-
daine *angchinoia*, a pleasant conceit, a comicall jeast, a witty bourd, for
a smug neat stile" and all that makes up "an astounding Rhetoricall
veine" (129-30). In challenging the standard view, Walkington reveals
how powerful the connections among melancholy, admirable wit, and
satirical jesting were for his audience. Despite the warnings of the
Tudor elders, a young aspirant hearing the siren song of wit had reason
to steer for it.

Satire, with its rude roots and sometime association with an Horatian
plain style, may seem far from these heights of enthusiasm. But Elizabethan satire, as Alvin Kernan, Robert C. Elliot, Raman Selden, Annabel
Patterson, and Richard Helgerson (among others) have shown, often
aligned itself with the Juvenalian mode and with the rough, bold, and
elliptical style of wonder discussed in the previous chapter.[21] Which is
why both the author of *The Return from Parnassus* (Part Two) and Jonson's Cordatus in *Every Man Out of his Humour* ("After the second
Sounding" 147–50), mock contemporary satirists' claims to *furor poeticus*.[22] In the preface to the 1635 edition of his translation of Persius,
Barten Holyday remained unwilling to relinquish this claim: "When a
Satyrist . . . is set on fire to see the desperate securitie of prophanenesse:
the furie of his passion doth so transport him, that there is no time left
for the placing or displacing, choosing or rejecting of some particular
word; but as most commonly their passions are uneven, rough and fu-
rious: so is that also which they write being in this poeticall perturba-
tion."[23] English satirists around the turn of the century almost certainly

---

in *The Anatomy of Melancholy*; like Laurentius (and Theseus) he notably omits politics from the realms where melancholics excel (1:401). Cf. Plutarch on the inspiration
that Apollo gives to Pythia: "As for him, he representeth unto her, fancies onely and
imaginations, kindling a light in the soule to declare things to come: and such an
illumination as this, is that which they call *Enthusiasmos*" ("Why the Prophetesse
Pythia giveth no answers now from the oracle in verse or meter," in *Morals*, 1189).
    [21] See Alvin Kernan, *The Cankered Muse* (1959), 94–108; Elliott, *Power of Satire*,
102–18; Selden, *English Verse Satire*, 29–72; Patterson, *Hermogenes*, 97–121; Helgerson, *Self-Crowned Laureates*, 118–44; and Trimpi, *Ben Jonson's Poems*, 111–13.
    [22] See *The Three Parnassus Plays* (1598–1601), ed. J. B. Leishman (1949), 82–92.
    [23] Quoted in the introduction to *The Poems of John Cleveland*, lx.

bought the false genealogy (contained, for example, in Puttenham) relating satire, through "satyr," to tragedy. Milton, using Bishop Hall's shady past as a satiric wit against him in *An Apology . . . against Smectymnus* (1642), could still score points using it: "For a Satyr as it was borne out of a *Tragedy*, so ought to resemble his parentage, to strike high, and adventure dangerously at the most eminent vices among the greatest persons, and not to creepe into every blinde Taphouse that fears a Constable more then a Satyr" (*Works*, 3.1.329). Hall had led Milton to the target himself by opening the "Post-script to the Reader" of his *Virgidemiarum* with a defense of the lofty satiric vein: "It is not for every one to rellish a true and naturall Satyre, being of it selfe besides the native and in-bred bitternes and tartnes of particulers, both hard of conceipt, and harsh of stile, and therefore cannot but be unpleasing both to the unskilfull, and over Musicall eare, the one being affected with onely a shallow and easie matter, the other with a smooth and currant disposition."[24] Like Johnson's and Boileau's comments on the epigram, Hall's claims for satire and Milton's boomerang signal that although the rough genres could be pegged as lowly, they were also often expected to aim high.

The equation of satire with the "satyr" could admittedly work against its association with boldness of style, because of the satyr's humble, unlearned status. John Marston, the probable butt of the *furor poeticus* lampoons, registers concern in the *Scourge of Villainie* that his "sacred rage" may be indecorously lofty:

> O how on tiptoes proudly mounts my Muse,
> Stalking a loftier gate then Satyres use.
> Me thinkes some sacred rage warmes all my vaines,
> Making my spright mount up to higher straines
> Then wel beseemes a rough-tongu'd Satyres part.[25]

Marston's apology reveals a measure of anxiety about violating generic expectations, but it is clear that he would rather lay claim to enthusi-

[24] *The Collected Poems of Joseph Hall*, ed. Arnold Davenport (1949), 97; cf. satires 4.1 and 6.1.
[25] In *Poems of John Marston*, ed. Arnold Davenport (1961) 158; see Helgerson, *Self-Crowned Laureates*, 118. In his preface, Marston claims to "hate to affect too much obscuritie, & harshnes" (*Poems*, 100), a claim Selden undermines (*English Verse Satire*, 55). Although abjuring obscurity himself, Marston notes that some readers judge satires to be "bastard" unless they are "palpable darke" and "rough writ." He laments that "there are some, (too many) that think nothing good, that is so curteous, as to come within their reach," and that his obscure first satire will earn praise in "new-minted Epithets, (as *Reall, Intrinsecate, Delphicke*)" (*Poems*, 100).

asm than play by the supposed rules. The scholar who exploded the false etymology of "satire," Isaac Casaubon, makes a similar exchange in the *Prolegomena* to his 1605 edition of Persius: what he takes from satiric roughness, he gives to satiric obscurity. Responding to Scaliger's charge that Persius is overly obscure, Casaubon adduces numerous ancient defenses of obscurity, including the allowance for Plato's "untempered and harsh metaphors" by "Longinus" (*On the Sublime*, 32.7) and the praise of Thucydides' obscure and forceful style by Dionysius of Halicarnassus. In concluding this section, Casaubon mentions again that "Longinus" sanctions bold, figurative expressions in general and in his defense of Plato specifically. Equating height of style with genius, he aligns criticism of Plato's metaphors with the criticism of Demosthenes by Aeschines, "when he said that 'monstrosities (*thaumata* [*miracula*])' of such a high-flown nature are not 'words.'" (The translation of *thaumata* as "monstrosities" fits with Aeschines' tone, but "wonders" would be as accurate.) Finally Casaubon, reverses direction, arguing that Persius deserves praise, not defense: "Indeed if we are to believe Dionysius Halicarnassus—that 'in many cases force contains obscurity' (*tēn asapheian pollachou deinotēta einai* [*obscuritati vim & acrimoniam non raro inesse*])—Persius ought not to be excused by us but rather celebrated in 'musical' commendation."[26] Even if the degree of Casaubon's influence in England is unclear, the nature of his defense is significant: he implicitly connects genius and boldness with satire, and explicitly connects obscurity with *deinotēs* and wonder.

Melancholy and Quick Wit as Mock Rebellion

Against the background of Castiglione's encouragement to produce wonder, the widespread identification of *maraviglia* as the goal of all poetry, and the recovery of discussions of wonderful style in Greek rhetorical manuals—as well as the imported fashion for melancholy—the adoption of satire and epigram in the 1590s stands out as an updated, more desparate version of the earlier Elizabethans' choice to play the quick wit before taking up the burden of public service. Satire could offer a vent for the frustration many young men felt at their lack of advancement, but might also serve as a form of mock-rebellion prior to

[26] Peter E. Medine, "Isaac Casaubon's *Prolegomena* to the *Satires* of Persius: An Introduction, Text, and Translation," *ELR* 6 (1976): 296 (text, 285), 297 (text, 286). Medine notes that Casaubon paraphrases Dionysius on Thucydides, and that he can find no passage that matches the second phrase, on obscurity and force. Casaubon, like Vossius, translates *deinotēs* as *vis* (and *acrimonia*).

their entry into public service. Unlike Wyatt, Gascoigne, and Ralegh, whose satires on the court, however conventional and gnomic they might have been, carried the weight of the authors' experiences, young poets like Donne proleptically put the disillusionment before the bitter experience. Satirists figuring forth the misprision of the court are comparable to Petrarchan sonneteers figuring forth their sweet torment in love. Both wounds are largely self-inflicted (though attributed to the cruelty or blindness of another who fails to recognize one's worth), and both say at least as much about the psyche of the seeker as about any verifiable external situation.[27] Young satirists might pretend to have been slighted simply to draw attention to themselves, and attack behavior they knew only too well from their own indulgence in it.[28]

Satires by political hopefuls are self-consuming artifacts to the degree that once the amateur poet has obtained a position of power, the rationale for such poetry ceases to exist. This claim may seem to indicate too narrow a focus on the pursuit of power, but it was made first (and more rudely) by John Marston, in the fourth satire in *The Scourge of Villanie* (59–66; *Poems*, 120):

> There is a crew which I too plaine could name . . .
> That lick the tayle of greatnes with their lips:
> Laboring with third-hand jests, and Apish skips,
> Retayling others wit, long barrelled
> To glib some great mans eares, till panch be fed,
> Glad if themselves, as sporting fooles be made,
> To get the shelter of some high-growne shade.
> *To morrow* yet these base tricks thei'le cast off,
> And cease for lucar be a jering scoffe.

Such jesters, Marston makes clear, aspire not to prestige as satirists, but to prestige; as he puts it in the following satire, on cunning or "sleight"

---

[27] As Helen Gardner notes in the introduction to *The Elegies and the Songs and Sonnets*, Donne "never speaks in the tone of a man overwhelmed by what he feels to be wholly undeserved good fortune" or expresses "the sense of unworthiness in face of the overwhelming worth of the beloved" (xvii).

[28] On having to be one to satirize one see Fink, "Jaques," 245; Lyons, *Voices of Melancholy*, 21; and Arthur Marotti, "John Donne and the Rewards of Patronage," in *Patronage in the Renaissance*, ed. Guy Fitch Little and Stephen Orgel (1981), 212; and his *John Donne: Coterie Poet* (1986), 25–36. Cunningham treats the implied situation of Donne's satire as representative of that facing "a scholarly young man of good family, interested in poetry" around 1590: "He will write some toys in verse, partly to display his wit, and partly in the hope he will be noticed by someone in power, some official of the state who might further his ambitions—Lord Essex, let us say, or Sir Thomas Egerton" (*Collected Essays*, 312).

as "the onely gally-ladder unto might": "A nimble quick-pate mounts to dignitie."[29] By making fools of themselves in order to rise, the jesters in the fourth satire display their understanding of what the times demand, as Marston acknowledges in the fifth (98–102; *Poems*, 133):

> Faire Age!
> When tis a high, and hard thing t'have repute
> Of a compleat villaine, perfect, absolute,
> And roguing vertue brings a man defame.
> A packstaffe Epethite, and scorned name. . . .

Among Marston's examples of villains who thrive is Flavus (48–55):

> I heard old *Albius* sweare, *Flavus* should have
> His eldest gurle, for *Flavus* was a knave.
> A damn'd deep-reaching villaine, & would mount
> (He durst well warrant him) to great account.
> What though he laid forth all his stock & store
> Upon some office, yet he'le gaine much more,
> Though purchast deere. Tut, he will trebble it
> In some few termes, by his extorting wit.[30]

Flavus is less explicitly adopting villainy as a strategy than other characters in the satire, but is especially notable for his wit and his willingness to gamble. Another of Marston's examples is Tuscus, who has learned only in bankruptcy to practice proper treachery; now he "Cogs, sweares, and lies," and "since he hath the grace, thus [to] gracelesse be / His neighbors sweare, he'le swell with treasurie" (73–75). Marston's description of his strategy as a graceless grace plays off of Hoby's translation of Castiglione's term *sprezzatura* as a graceful "disgracing" (*Courtier*, 46). The move Marston sarcastically advocates—sinking one's own reputation in order to raise it—is again curiously reminiscent of Hal's strategic holiday in Eastcheap. Like young quick wits, Hal manipulates his reputation. In his interview with Henry IV in act three, scene two, Hal be-

---

[29] *Poems*, 132, 131; I have removed italics. Cf. lines 25–30 of Benjamin Rudyerd's poem "In Praise of a Painted Woman" (*Memoirs of Sir Benjamin Rudyerd*, xlii):
> Take me a face as full of fraud and lies
> As gipsies, or your running lotteries,
> That is more false, or more sophisticate
> Than are saints' reliques or a man of state;
> Yet such being glazed by the sleight of art
> Gains admiration,—

[30] I have inserted the parentheses in the fourth line quoted here.

comes increasingly indignant about being slighted—"And God forgive them that so much have sway'd / Your Majesty's good thoughts away from me!" (lines 130–31)—yet he is the ultimate author of these slights. They are crucial to his strategy of concealment and miraculous display, and enable him finally to mount, like Marston's Flavus, to "great account."

Hal concludes his holiday to the wonder of his various audiences, but the adoption of a style calculated to evoke wonder enabled desparate seekers of patronage in the Tudor court to pursue holiday and admiration simultaneously. No institution nourished either the development of admirable style or the enjoyment of the holiday atmosphere more than the Inns of Court.[31] Although many did manage to learn the law at the Inns (or at least to become lawyers after their residence there), students at the Inns by all accounts spent much of their time in theaters, taverns, and brothels, enjoying a prolonged holiday prior to the public careers they expected to pursue. The Inns provided the perfect setting for mock-rebellion, and for Donne's satires.

Wit, Misrule, and the Inns of Court

Located for the most part outside the City, the Inns of Court occupy a cultural space somewhat comparable to that of the theaters located in the "Liberties," as brilliantly analyzed by Steven Mullaney in *The Place of the Stage*. Even more than Oxford or Cambridge, which fed them, the societies of the "third university" were the scene of transitions into power and place. Scholars like the subject of Francis Lenton's *The Young Gallants Whirligig* (1629), whose "Tutor said hee had a ready wit," rightly recognized the Inns as conduits to power. Once there, however, they were not always in a rush to leave holiday for everyday:

> Instead of *perkins* pedlers French, he sayes
> He better loves Ben: Johnsons booke of Playes,
> But that therein of wit he findes such plenty,
> That he scarce understands a Jest of twenty.[32]

[31] See Philip J. Finkelpearl's invaluable portrait of the Inns in *John Marston of the Middle Temple* (1969), esp. 9–10; D. S. Bland, "Rhetoric and the Law in Sixteenth-Century England," *Studies in Philology* 54 (1957): 498–508; and Wilfred R. Prest, *The Inns of Court*.

[32] Quoted in Finkelpearl, *John Marston*, 13–14.

Jonson himself dedicated *Every Man Out of his Humour* (1599), with its mock-identification of satiric style as "right *Furor Poeticus*" and its satire of courtly sycophants, to the "Gentlemen" of the Inns, suggesting that they enjoy his play "when the gowne and cap, is off, and the Lord of liberty raignes" (*Ben Jonson*, 3:421). The gown and cap seem to have been off as often as on, but the Lord of liberty had special authority during the Christmas revels featuring a mock prince whose "reign was often characterized by disorderly conduct, abuse of authority, and a general atmosphere of 'solemn foolery.'"[33] As the rare records of such revels at Gray's Inn and at the Middle Temple show, these were barely controlled saturnalian events, but the young men who turned the world upside down were not the perennially powerless of popular festivals; instead, they were men on their way to positions of power, and their rites were rites of passage rather than rites of simple inversion.

The Middle Templars of the 1590s are worth an especially close look: they include Richard Martin, Benjamin Rudyerd, John Hoskyns, Henry Wotton, and John Davies. All but ringleader Martin were poets, and all were friends of John Donne.[34] These wits, as Philip Finkelpearl notes, "came from the same background, pursued the same course in life, shared the same tastes and preferences, and often tended to act in very similar ways" (46). Although all but Wotton were ultimately called to the Bar, they took both their misrule and their wit very seriously along the way: Davies and Martin were among a group who got into trouble in 1591 for "forcibly breaking open chambers in the night and levying money as the Lord of Misrule's rent"; Hoskyns, who had given a "bitterly satyricall" address at Oxford that led to his dismissal, later spent time in the Tower for a slur on Scots in Parliament; Wotton displeased James by wittily defining an "ambassador" as "an honest man, sent to lie abroad for the good of his country"; Davies, upset over his treatment during the Middle Temple revels of 1597–98, broke Martin's head with a bastinado.[35] Together, they brought Sir Henry Sidney's and Lord Burghley's nightmares about quick wit to life.

[33] Finkelpearl cautions that "it is not clear that Christmas revels always had such a tone or that it was ever purely a time for satiric or disorderly conduct," but at the very least we may say that students at the Inns were accustomed to holiday rituals and to assuming roles within an inverted hierarchy (37).

[34] Annabel Patterson examines Donne's continuing relationships to Hoskyns, Wotton, and Martin in "All Donne." On Donne's acquaintance at Oxford with all but Rudyerd, see R. C. Bald, *John Donne: A Life* (1970), 43; and on Donne's friendship with Rudyerd, see Sir Benjamin Rudyerd, *Memories of Sir Benjamin Rudyerd, Knt., Containing His Speeches and Poems*, ed. James Alexander Manning (1841), 22. Rudyerd's poems were posthumously printed by Donne's son.

[35] Their acquaintance Thomas Bastard, the epigrammatist, "was deprived of his fellowship at New College for writing a libel about the sexual activities of certain

Because Martin and his group, like John Donne and John Marston, were not especially wealthy, they were under special pressure to distinguish themselves. Although they may have been unique in their dedication to wit and their extension of the world of misrule into everyday, they were standard products of the Inns in their competitiveness. Wilfred Prest argues that the desire of young gentlemen to set themselves off from common lawyers led to "the competitive aping of court modes in dress and taste, the cult of wit, the incessant versifying (for private circulation, not mercenary publication), even perhaps the obsessive drinking, gaming, and womanising." Sharpening this cuthroat competition were their rhetorical exercises, especially the moot cases "involving one or more controversial questions of law" inherited from the Roman schools of declamation.[36] Like the Roman *controversiae* and *suasoriae* criticized by Quintilian, these often ex tempore debates rewarded displays of quick-wittedness, and put a premium on ingenuity of argument and expression.[37] Their training—to the degree that they attended to it—continually encouraged them to overgo their companions verbally.

Even in the readings performed by more advanced members of the profession but (at least in theory) attended by the younger students, ingenuity and obscurity seem to have become the rage in the late sixteenth century. Bacon and Coke might have been invoking a golden age that never was, but both found contemporary readings degenerate. When lecturing at Gray's Inn in 1600, Bacon claims that in the "former ancient form of reading" the intention was to instruct, not to "stir conceits and subtle doubts"; in the *Institutes* (1628), Coke similarly blasts readings for being "long, obscure and intricate, full of new conceits, like rather to riddles than lectures, which when they are opened they vanish into smoake."[38] Given such models for imitation, the nature of their

prominent members of the academic community" (Finkelpearl, *John Marston*, 46). On the group in general, see Finkelpearl, *John Marston*, 46–55; on Hoskyns, see *Life Letters*, 19 and 36–47; on Wotton, see *The "Conceited Newes" of Sir Thomas Overbury and His Friends*, ed. James E. Savage (1968), xlii–lvi.

[36] *Inns of Court*, 43 and 116.

[37] See Kenneth Charlton, "Liberal Education and the Inns of Court in the Sixteenth Century," *British Journal of Educational Studies* 9 (1960): 28. On the Roman schools see Trimpi, *Muses*, 306–27 and the studies he cites in 306n1. Although Arthur Marotti is loosely justified in describing the Inns' exercises as belonging to an "agonistic mode" ("John Donne," 211), the scholastic style and exercises of the schools of declamation were juxtaposed to the agonistic style of deliberative oratory throughout antiquity as well as in the Renaissance.

[38] Quoted in Charlton, "Liberal Education," 34 (Bacon) and Prest, *Inns of Court*, 127 (Coke). See also Marotti, *John Donne*, 70. For praise of obscure lecturing, see Prest, *Inns of Court*, 128.

exercises, and the increasingly shrinking paths to court patronage in the 1590s, how could the Inns avoid cultivating wit? As institutions geographically and culturally on the threshold of power, providing liberty for rehearsals of power and the establishment of credit, the inns were the perfect medium for growing wit.

Nothing better demonstrates this ascendancy of witty dissimulation, and the participants' acute awareness of the risks involved in mock-rebellion, than the records of the raucous "Prince D'Amour" revels ruled over by Richard Martin at the Middle Temple in 1597–98.[39] Transcribed as *Le Prince d'Amour, or the Prince of Love*, the record of Martin's reign was printed by William Leake in 1660 with *A Collection of Several Ingenious Poems and Songs by the Wits of the Age* (mostly anonymous poems, ranging from the 1580s through the 1640s). What the transcripts reveal are the students' painfully elaborate stabs at wit, primarily the smirking wit of an all-male society—thinly veiled double entendres and over-the-top declarations of true love—but also wit exercised at their own expense. In addition to speeches by poets Hoskyns and Davies, *Le Prince d'Amour* contains the fascinating text of "A briefe Chronicle of the Dark Reigne of the bright Prince of burning Love" by poet Benjamin Rudyerd, whose paradoxical and epigrammatic poems were edited in 1660 by John Donne the younger.[40] Hoskyns's speech, a "fustian" parody of euphuistic style, plays off the demand for ready wit and *sprezzatura*. Although the speech is obviously rehearsed, *Le Prince d'Amour* introduces it as an instant, reluctant performance: "The Princes Orator having made a ridiculous and sensless speech unto his Excellency, the Clerk of the Council [Hoskyns] was requested to make an Answer thereunto at *ex tempore*, which at the first he refused; but being importuned, he began. . . ." (37). The manuscript text of this speech identifies those doing the importuning as both "the prince"—Richard Martin—and "Sir Walter Rawlegh," Hoskyns' future wit-mate in the Tower (Hoskyns, *Life*, 100). Ralegh's presence and the progress of the Prince's court to the

[39] See also the description of the Gray's Inn revels of 1594–95, presided over by Henry Helmes. Here knights of the "Order of the Helmet" are "required to frequent the theater and the better sort of taverns 'whereby they may not only become accomplished with Civil Conversations, and able to govern a Table with Discourse; but also sufficient, if need be, to make Epigrams, Emblems, and other Devices appertaining to His Honour's learned Revels'" (Finkelpearl, *John Marston*, 30). The ironic reference to Guazzo's *Civile Conversation* shows how students at the Inns used the conduct books to sanction their recreation.

[40] James Alexander Manning prints a transcription of Rudyerd's autograph manuscript as well as texts of Rudyerd's poems in *Memoirs of Sir Benjamin Rudyerd*. For the attribution of speeches to Hoskyns and Davies, see Hoskyns, *Life, Letters*, 10–11; and *Directions for Speech and Style, by John Hoskins*, ed. Hoyt H. Hudson (1935), 108–13.

lord mayor's residence underscore the stakes involved in the festive performances, their blurry border with the world of everyday and real advancement.

Mock Prince Martin's askew rules for his knights include the demand
that "once in three dayes he speak with some spice of Wit, and to the
purpose twice every night if it be possible" (*Le Prince d'Amour*, 43).
Martin himself, although eventually embracing the role of mock king
ferociously enough, at first expressed anxiety over the risk involved in
flouting authority yet again. Like Hoskyns, Martin seems to have been
both proud of his wit and afraid of its consequences. Having been Prince
before, and having been censured and even temporarily expelled for ex-
torting rent from the citizenry of London in the name of the Lord of
Misrule in 1591 and 1592, Martin hesitated. That is, he ran away. As
soon as he heard himself being proclaimed chief knave he bolted, "es-
teeming it," in Rudyerd's words, "a solemn leading to some fatal execu-
tion" (79). Later, when verbally refusing, Martin faced the initial problem of overcoming his audience's suspicion that any refusal might
simply be pro forma, a falsely modest request to be asked twice like
Hoskyns:

> All that week was Seignior *Martino* continually importuned by his
> own friends, pressed by a mighty expectation, and overborn with the
> stream of Rumor overborne; all which he answered, more then for
> fashion sake, with these Reasons, That other men heretofore, if they
> denyed it, might hide theyr willingness under form of denial, for they
> for their years were unsettled; for their life not so well known as they
> would be; for their experience untravelled; and for their course unre-
> solved; for his part, he rather now desired to settle his name then to
> spread it, and thought it would be but a subject to spend his former
> credit upon (*Prince*, 79–80).

Before finally relenting for "love of that company," Martin calculated:
he knew that the venture was not worth the risk for him, although it
would have been for someone younger and more desperate for any kind
of attention, even notoriety.

In the conclusion of his chronicle, presumably written much later,
Rudyerd captures Martin's career in a sentence: "Fortune never taught
him to temper his own Wit or Manhood" (90). For Rudyerd, Martin's
inability to resist taking on the role speaks to his temperament, but it
also speaks to the climate at the Inns, where caution was judged cow-
ardice, effeminacy. (Henry Sidney's letter to young Philip had warned
that if he controlled his wit he would likely be "rebuked of light fellows

for maidenlike shamefastness."[41] Not that any of those importuning
Martin would have failed to understand his reasoning, but as a group
they would have rejected it as treason to their code of bluster. Nor
would his language of credit and capital venture have seemed at all foreign. When he commanded that libels of "Stradilax" (Sir John Davies) be
posted around London—the action that eventually earned Martin a
busted head—many revelers jumped ship. Some of these traitors to misrule, Rudyerd notes, were "not without excuse, for one said he would
willingly stay, but he must always have a care to the main chance" and
another begged off "because he had no money, and his Wit was not yet
come to his head, nor his land to his hands" (80–81). Even in midwinter,
everyday calls holiday's bluff.

An incident early in the revels further confirms Martin's friends as
politic. As soon as the Prince's dominion over the realm of love has
been proclaimed, a "strange Knight" challenges his claim on behalf of
his "dread Soveraign," by whom "the whole face of the earth is struck
with admiration" (9–11). This sovereign, "who though the Beams of her
Majesty infuse Awe and Reverence, yet tempers the dazeling raies
thereof with the gracious aspect of Bounty," is presumably Elizabeth,
but is never explicitly identified. When her champion and the Prince's
are on the verge of fighting for the crown, the Prince defers the battle,
asking his counsel "whether he should expose the tryal of his Title to
the hazard of a single combat" (16). When the Secretary of Martin's
counsel speaks, he specifies some of the "considerations infinite" that
made Shakespeare's Henry IV think twice about letting Hal join Hotspur in single combat for the English crown. The Secretary advises the
Prince always to take a course with a fall-back position:

This is not spoken to that end that I would have the noble Prince
d'Amours . . . either basely to turn his back, or cowardly to creep into
corners, no more then I would have the bright Beams of the Sun to be
obscured with a cloud, or with darksome night to be overshadowed.
But if, by some disastrous fortune of the field, his unmatchable Forces
should at some incounter, by devise or stratagem, happen to be overmatched; or if by slie intelligence, or secret Ambuscadoes any part of
them should be intrapped and intercepted; they might yet again and
again be reunited, and his Excellency shine brighter then before in the
midst of his Troopes, to the terror of the enemy, like the Sun when it
hath been newly eclipsed (18).

[41] In Osborn, *Young Philip Sidney*, 12–13.

It would be too much to say that Hal's speech of self-revelation is the source of this speech, exactly, since the emblem *hinc clarior* was widespread. But the Secretary's reasoning here and his examples of how *fortuna* may "falsify men's hopes" point to an ethos and a language shared with Hal. Even when "the valour of the one be never so assured, yet by the Agility, Slight, or Policy of the other it may be overmatched," or there may "happeneth some unexpected accident which utterly overthroweth our hope, and deludeth our expectation" (18–19). The Secretary trusts neither in valor nor in fortune, but in wit: success comes to those who wittily anticipate policy and devise witty counterstrategies. The episode ends anticlimactically, with the Prince accepting the Secretary's argument and simply ignoring the challenge, but the sword of wit has been championed here as firmly as in Hoskyns's declaration to die by it.

For the most part, Martin's party stayed within the bounds of their liberty, content to invert only the students' own giddy world. In the mock court of the "Prince d'Amour" all "male-contented, way-ward, false, jealous, leud, wanton, dissembling and disdainful persons" were charged with treason for "making Love, and [sic] outward shew and shadow, and a deceitful practice, which should be indeed inward compunction and passion of the heart" (48–49). Here the melancholic malcontent appears to be an apostate of true love. Yet the Prince further decreed that if any of his subjects "hath abused the Favor of his Mistris by the Act of dissimulation, or the Mystery of double dealing, he shall be punished by dismembring" (63). As Philip Finkelpearl asserts, the severity of this punishment and its inclusion in revels creating "a world where the right true end of love is the maximum number of female conquests," are clear signals of its ironic intent. The rule carries approximately the same force as the "commendation of woman's inconstancy"—possibly Donne's first paradox—"scheduled but not delivered" during the same revels: in the world of misrule, all proclamations must be read asquint.

Donne's *Satyre I*

Since the Middle Temple revels were largely "a series of short sallies of satiric wit directed at the manners and morals of the inhabitants of the Inns," their own habits of witty dissimulation, the revelers became both the archers and the targets.[42] Likewise Donne's *Satyre I*, which he seems to have written in 1593 at Lincoln's Inn, during his second year of

---

[42] Finkelpearl, *John Marston*, 56.

being one of those "Of study and play made strange Hermaphrodits" ("Epithalamion made at Lincolnes Inne"). Perhaps no satire of the 1590s is as firmly grounded in the practices at the Inns, and the speaker's self-involvement in the satirized behavior of the unnamed other in the poem has been the focus of most readings, beginning with Donne's own reflection in the *Sermons* (7.408): "We make *Satyrs*; and we look that the world shall call that *wit*; when God knowes, that that is in great part, self-guiltinesse, and we do but reprehend those things which we our selves have done, we cry out upon the illness of the times, and we make the times ill; so the calumniator whispers those things, which are true, no where, but in himselfe."[43] Like the proclamations of Richard Martin as Prince D'Amour, Donne's satire winks, both abjuring and claiming the role of moral arbiter that Horace voices in *Satire* 1.9, Donne's primary model. This double movement is apparent from the very first line, where Donne takes on the persona of satirist even while declaring "Away thou fondling motley humorist." The epithet "fondling motley humorist" fits perfectly with the details of the Other that the poem goes on to provide, but it also boomerangs, serving as an apt description of the satirical jester himself, Donne's own role. Further undercutting the dismissal is the irony that he wants to be left alone in the company of, among others, "Giddie fantastique Poëts." In writing the poem Donne implicitly joins this giddy company, but he insists that his friend repent his own "giddinesses" before they hit the street. Donne's own repentance, then—his own escape from giddiness—would be to relinquish the role of satirist altogether, a move he cannot make without abandoning the goal of displaying himself as wit. Like the Prince d'Amour and his cronies, Donne preempts the charge that might be brought against him—in his case, the charge that he is "fantastical"—by leveling it against himself. It is a brilliant hedge, since it allows him to proceed with the business of self-display.

Throughout the poem he sustains this pattern of alternately, or even simultaneously, separating himself from the friend and identifying himself with him. Comparison with Horace's street nightmare points up

---

[43] Recent readings of the satire as self-critique include Arthur Marotti, *John Donne*, 37–40; Stanley Fish, "Masculine Persuasive Force: Donne and Verbal Power," in *Soliciting Interpretation: Literary Theory and Seventeenth-Century English Poetry*, ed. Elizabeth D. Harvey and Katharine Eisaman Maus (1990), 235–41; and James S. Baumlin, *John Donne and the Rhetorics of Renaissance Discourse* (1991), 67–93. John Shawcross reads the poem as a dialogue between the speaker's body and soul (see *The Complete Poetry of John Donne*, ed. John T. Shawcross [1967], 397). I have used John Donne, *The Satires, Epigrams and Verse Letters*, ed. W. Milgate (1967) for the texts of Donne's satires.

this feature: the unknown barnacle latches onto Horace in the street and Horace finally scrapes him off and leaves him there, but Donne's journey begins and ends at home, where the intimate companion rejoins him at the poem's end. Horace is wandering aimlessly, but Donne's decision to leave home is deliberate. Initially reluctant, resisting his friend's importuning, he eventually accedes to his friend's desire to make the zany rounds: "Come, let's goe" (52). His decision is ultimately to "follow headlong, wild uncertain thee," with the comma after "headlong" in the 1633 text marking it as an adverb describing Donne's precipitous following rather than an adjective heaped on the "wild uncertain" friend (12). Donne asks the Other to "sweare by thy best love in earnest" not to abandon him, then wonders parenthetically whether "thou which lov'st all, canst love any best" (13–14); the sarcasm seems hypocritical coming from the poet who brags in "The Indifferent" that "I can love her, and her, and you and you, / I can love any, so she be not true" (8–9). Later, Donne confesses that he has "sinn'd against" (66) his conscience by going into the street, and requests pardon, but his confession appears after the Other has not only repented "like a contrite penitent, / Charitably warn'd of thy sinnes" but has also immediately reverted to his "giddy" behavior (lines 49–52). The other's failed repentance casts a shadow over the speaker's own, suggesting that he will make further forays into the active life of the street and into the giddy role of satirist. Still, the confession stands, marking Donne's speaker as witty but not phantastical, capable of recognizing folly for what it is.

Another contrast with Horace's poem illuminates the nature and goal of Donne's performance. Horace's pest eventually reveals that he wants an introduction to the patron Maecenas (43–60); like the Other in Donne's poem, he is a desperate seeker. Unlike Horace, though, Donne himself is no more secure than his friend. The access, position, and favor his friend seeks in the street itself are what Donne seeks through his description of the street, and of his "friend's" behavior there. Despite Donne's jibes at courtiers and captains, like the Prince d'Amour revels the satire lowers its boom most frequently on his own company, on young men in precisely his condition. Whoever the Other in Donne's poem is modeled on "is"—his chambermate Christopher Brooke, his own body as John Shawcross suggests, or an amalgam of the most ridiculous actions he and his friends at the Inns have performed—the Other is someone like young Jack Donne. No one who has seen Donne's melancholy pose with crossed arms, unlaced collarband, and cocked hat in the Lothian portrait—probably painted in 1595, after the poem was written—can avoid smirking when Donne asks "What fashion'd hats, or ruffes, or suits next yeare / Our subtile-witted antique youths will weare" (61–62).[44] Like the attacks on wayward lovers in Martin's revels, Donne's indictment of melancholy must be read asquint. Donne caps these doublings in the middle of the poem when the companion takes to the wall, like a shadow. Doing so gains him status, but at the expense of his "libertie": just as the speaker began the poem "in prison" in his small room at Lincoln's Inn, so his *semblable* is now "imprison'd, and hem'd in by mee" (69–70). Symmetry in Donne is no accident, and his "shadow" is more a reflection than an Other.

James S. Baumlin and Stanley Fish see Donne's self-consciousness about language and about the absence of a moral ground from which to deliver judgments on his companion as reflecting an awareness that the poem is a failure and the genre of satire is bankrupt. If the poet lacks "the capacity to curse and cure," and "if his words fail to reform," Baumlin argues, "then the classical model and the genre itself have equally failed."[45] Baumlin marshals classical and Renaissance theorists to demonstrate that the classical function of satire is indeed to curse and cure, and Fish implies that what Donne should be doing in the satire is "to distinguish himself from the variability and corruption" around him.[46] Their analysis is entirely accurate, but misdirected, holding the text up to a set of expectations other than those the poet seems to have embraced. Donne is implicated in giddiness not *despite* his role as satirist, but *because* of it: his "self-guiltiness" results from his adoption of the role of quick-witted satirist as much as from his unresisted urge to fare forward with his companion. Whatever the continuing force of the classical conception of satire, Donne is writing witty satire in the spirit of the revels, and with the goal of self-promotion that marks his early verse. He is not writing with the Horatian goal of establishing norms, nor the Juvenalian goal of scourging the vicious. The position of the solitary railer, singing "high and aloof" and damning the madness of the crowd, is simply untenable for one whose ambitions lie in public service and participation in the all-too-giddy life of the court.

Instead, he identifies himself both as fantastic and as seeing through the behavior of his fellow fantastics. He steps into the street parade, the world of holiday, but like Hal in Eastcheap is always partly removed from it, always immune to its allure, always headed back to everyday. He can play the quick-witted privy mocker—the melancholy satirist—

---

[44] Donne's *adynata* in lines 53–62 display both his concern with curiosities and wonder and the affinity between the satires and other early lyrics, such as "Song: 'Goe, and catche a falling starre.'"

[45] Baumlin, *John Donne*, 78.

[46] Fish, "Masculine Persuasive Force," 235.

yet in exercising his wit also show that he is not ignorant of the dangers
of being "overquick, hasty, rash, heady, and brainsick." It is a manuever
characteristic of the poet Arthur F. Marotti describes as "both jauntily,
if not self-destructively, *subversive of* as well as contritely *deferential
toward* the Establishment."[47] Aware of the stakes, Donne hedges, playing both sides of his culture's ambivalence toward satire and jesting.
While exploiting the form, writing the kind of witty poem that can at-
tract him notice, bring him credit, he also demonstrates that he knows
exactly where liberty and misrule end.[48] In making himself and his relatively powerless friends the primary target of his wit, Donne seems to
be rehearsing, as though he were trying to test the waters before committing to the even more dangerous game he plays in *Satyre IV*, where
the primary targets are much closer to the center of power, and the self-
accusations more damaging.

[47] *John Donne*, 182.
[48] Like Hal in Eastcheap, he hints at a reformation, although his strategy is perhaps
safer than Hal's, is Hal's turned inside out. Hal progresses through the medium of
time, and has a premonition when rehearsing the interview with his father that *occasio* or *kairos* is on the wing, that the fulcrum springing him from shame to wonder,
Hal to Henry, is shimmering into view. Donne's speaker in *Satyre I* is not yet ready
to move from Jack to John, but also unwilling to risk presenting himself now as more
Jack than John; John Donne speaks the poem, distancing Jack but unable to extin-
guish him.

3 Suspicious Boldness

When amateur poets in the 1590s adopted satire, epigram, and obscure style as their version of mock-rebellion before taking up the burden of public service, they played an even more dangerous game than the earlier Elizabethans had. The continuing influence of Castiglione's encouragement to produce wonder and the increasing identification of *maraviglia* as the goal of poetry sweetened the pot, but the association of wit with Machiavellian policy made gaining a reputation as the wrong kind of wit riskier. Earlier Tudor fathers feared their sons might lose reputations for *gravitas* through displays of wit; Ralegh, in the death's-head-jest of "Three Things There Be," warns his son not to lose his neck. Whereas the earlier Elizabethans chose such ostensibly apolitical genres as sonnet and pastoral (a genre of course especially political as handled by Spenser and Sidney), poets in the 1590s displayed their quick wits in the socially charged genres of satire and epigram, and in the equivocating style associated with Papist plotters, conscienceless tyrants, and the *prince de tenèbres*, Tacitus.

Anyone displaying wit makes a pitch for admission to the elite. Like all pitches, however, it has a spin. The attacks by Ascham and others on Italianate manners and wit were still in the wind, as were crosscurrents that made the trajectory of wit and witty satire anything but straight.[1] Thomas Walkington's description of the witty as having "lyvely con-

[1] See Fink, "Jaques," 239–51; Klibansky, Panofsy, and Saxl, *Saturn*, 241–74; Lyons, *Voices*, 17–44; and Babb, *Elizabethan Malady*, 73–101.

ceit" and "excelling in active nature" would seem to indicate that quick-wittedness made possible an ideal combination of *gnōsis* and *praxis*, but Walkington fears that excessive contemplation will lead the melancholic to become "a brocher of dangerous machiavellisme, an inventor of stratagems, quirks and pollicies" (*Optick Glasse*, 66v). Quick wits "invent with ease," according to Walkington, but what they invent are "witty policies, quirks and stratagems," making their effortlessness more dreadful than desirable.

Walkington's ambivalence registers the tension between moral and pragmatic approaches to political behavior, a tension also registered in the contradictory meanings of "prudence," which for Aristotle involves action in accordance with political or ethical virtue, but for Tacitus involves covering your back. Wit is a true anamorph: the qualities associated with it look from one view like lapses of virtue, but from another like indispensable elements of virtù. The very kinds of behavior and modes of thought that met such resistance from the dominant culture of late Elizabethan England were indispensable to those hoping to negotiate its cultural terrain: curiosity, equivocation, and suspicion. In this chapter I will explore various ways in which witty obscurity and brevity were judged, especially in political discourse, show how Roman as well as Greek rhetoric helps to illuminate the development of admirable style, and examine English references to the strong lines of Donne and others. I will conclude by examining Donne's *Satyre IV*, a poem in which Donne shows acute awareness of the risks he runs by adopting the satiric persona, and tries, as in "The Flea," to flip the weaknesses in his position to his advantage.

In the standard view, quick wits are likely to be melancholics; melancholics, addicted to innovation, plotting, and policy, are likely to be Machiavellian malcontents. In *Wits Miserie* (1596), Thomas Lodge satirizes the "right malcontent Devill" with "lookes suspitious and heavie": "well spoken he is, and hath some languages, and hath red over the conjuration of Machiavel: in beliefe he is an Atheist, or a counterfait Catholicke; hating his countrie wherein hee was bred, his gratious prince under whom he liveth" (17).[2] The touring gallant was suspected of having brought home Catholicism wrapped up in a melancholy demeanor and a Machiavellian pragmatism. Even the Catholic William Watson judges Jesuits guilty on all these counts, attacking them in *A sparing discoverie of our English Jesuits* (1601) as "haughtie-aspiring-touring-wits" and finding Robert Parsons more spiteful than "*Don Lucifer* the wittiest fiend in hell." For Watson the techniques of dissimula-

[2] In *Complete Works of Thomas Lodge* (1883; 1966), 4:17.

tion and ambiguity that Castiglione and Puttenham considered essential to the courtier's art, like the stratagems Saturnian wits produce with astounding ease, are morally equivalent to the Jesuits' equivocating "sleights of wit." The Jesuits, he says, playing "by Machivels rules," support their religion "by equivocation, detractions, dissimulation, ambition, contention for superioritie, stirring up strife, setting kingdomes against kingdomes, raising of rebellions, murthering of princes, and by we know not how many stratagems of Sathan."[3] Long before the Gunpowder Plot and before Donne portrayed Machiavelli and Ignatius Loyola fighting to hold the title of king equivocator and to be Satan's right-hand man in *Ignatius His Conclave* (1611), Watson and others saw the Jesuits as belonging to *"Nicke Machivels* crue." Tying a noose disguised as a logical chain, he elides any space between dissimulation, policy, quick-wittedness, and treason: "A right Politician is a very Machiavell, a very Machiavell is an upright Atheist, and an upright Atheist, is a downeright dastardly coward, void of all religion, reason, or honestie: so by consequent it may be said, that in politicall government or Machivilean pollicie none goeth beyond the Jesuits at this day."[4] Wittiness, invention, and cunning dissimulation—the qualities that distinguish melancholics, and that courtiers wishing to pose as melancholics cultivated—were also the signs by which Machiavels and Jesuits were identified.

The admirable wit is a very melancholic, the very melancholic is a plotting Machiavel, the plotting Machiavel is an equivocating Jesuit. Watson's equation of Jesuits with atheists may seem logically strained—even if typical of sixteenth-century polemics—but it points to a further link in this sinister chain: the plotting Machiavel and equivocating Jesuit is a disciple of Tacitus. Despite Machiavelli's slight use of Tacitus, the two were considered identical in their amoral method of studying history, and came in for the same kind of criticism.[5] This connection

[3] Quoted in Sydney Anglo, "More Machiavellian than Machiavel," in *John Donne: Essays in Celebration*, ed. A. J. Smith (1973), 371, 372. On equivocation and treason see also Steven Mullaney, "Lying Like Truth: Riddle, Representation and Treason in Renaissance England," *ELH* 47 (1980): 32–47; and Frank L. Huntley, "*Macbeth* and the Background of Jesuitical Equivocation," *PMLA* 79 (1964): 390–400. Stark division between practical and ethical perspectives on dissimulation also of course characterizes the debate of counsel between Morus and Hythladeus in Book I of the *Utopia* (see Stephen Greenblatt, *Renaissance Self-Fashioning* [1980], 34–36).

[4] *A Decacordon of Ten Quodlibeticall Questions* (1602), ed. D. M. Rogers (1974), 59, 64.

[5] On Machiavelli's use of Tacitus, see J. H. Whitfield, "Livy, Tacitus," in *Classical Influences on European Culture A.D. 1500–1700*, ed. R. R. Bolgar (1976), 285–91.

ultimately brings us back to the question of style, since Tacitus was one of the primary Latin models for admirable strong lines.

Equivocation, Curiosity, Suspicion, and Obscurity

To understand how the melancholic pose and admirable style intersect, we need to recognize how intellectual qualities attributed to masters of policy manifest themselves in style. Beneath the surface resemblance between those wearing melancholy's crest and those attacked as Tacitean, Machiavellian, or Papist plotters lurk deeper forms of likeness. The psychological profile of those afflicted with melancholy shares features with the Tacitean method of studying history, and with the personalities of the tyrants Tacitus and Sallust present. Like Tacitus, melancholics are curious, digging too deeply into the causes of things and into the *arcana imperii* for the comfort of those in power; like the imperial tyrants he and Sallust describe, melancholics are suspicious, and their suspicion leads them to speak or write obscurely. For the various intellectual qualities in this cluster there is a similar problem of interpretation—the problem of determining whether they are attributes of particular kinds of people in power or attributes of those claiming to be those kinds of people, representative qualities or qualities of self-representation.

There is also a problem of evaluation, of determining how beneficial curiosity, equivocation, and suspicion may be, and for whom. Curiosity was characterized both as a wholesome thirst for knowledge, and as dropsy. Through its association with genius, melancholy was recognized as the source of a beneficial curiosity, the kind of productive wonder described by Plato in the *Theaetetus* and Aristotle in the *Metaphysics* as what sets the philosopher apart. In *Examen De Ingenios: The Examination of Mens Wits* (trans. Richard Carew, 1594), Juan Huarte commends "wits full of invention" because they are likely to have a soul that "never resteth settled in any contemplation, but fareth forthwith unquiet, seeking to know and understand new matters" (67). But since the lack of apparent cause is the most profound source of wonder, such striving for knowledge threatens to diminish reverence for divine or monarchical power. As political theorists continually insisted, the opposite of reverent awe is contempt. Curiosity is thus branded a threat to the individual and to the state. As the Epilogue to *Doctor Faustus* warns, potential Icaruses should learn from Faustus's "hellish fall":

Only to wonder at unlawful things,
Whose deepness doth entice such forward wits,
To practise more than heavenly power permits.
(Epilogue, 23–27)[6]

As for the state, or more precisely the monarchy, James I's famous blast at Parliament for "searching out as it were the very bowels of Curiositie" when it took up the implications of Union registers concern at the demystification of his own power and its sources (*Political Works*, 291). Because viewing his own authority as mirrored in God's, in *Basilikon Doron* James cautions Prince Henry against overly curious interpretation of scripture: "The scripture is ever the best interpreter of it selfe; but preasse not curiously to seeke out farther then is contained therein; for that were over unmannerly a presumption, to strive to bee further upon Gods secrets, then he hath will ye be" (*Political Works*, 14).[7] This is the logic of the golden rule: if Henry would have his subjects wonder at him from below, he should wonder at God above. Like Marlowe's Chorus, James advises even the most powerful wit to "admire reverently such obscure places as ye understand not" (*Political Works*, 14). The inquiry wonder excites could hardly be dismissed so easily, but concern at how far forward wits will fare fuels late Renaissance resistance both to quick wits and to politic historians in the mold of Tacitus and Machiavelli.

As indicated in the previous chapter by Ascham's critique of quick wits for their addiction to novelty and Boccalini's Ministers' complaint that such wits are continually upsetting the settled order, the melancholic's curiosity was frequently not appreciated. John Leslie, Bishop of Ross, considered the "fyne witted clerkis of Machivellis scoole" addicted to change, eager to "employ thair braynes for altering of commoun wealthes and depriving and setting up of Princes at thair plesour."[8] In the medical treatises, the usual blurring of psychology and politics occurs. Walkington blames the melancholics' "contemplative facultie" and "assiduitie of sad and serious meditation" for their tendency to become Machiavels, and Timothy Bright and Thomas Wright warn

---

[6] Cf. Fulke Greville's *Caelica*, 88, "Man, dream no more of curious mysteries," in *Poems and Dramas of Fulke Greville, First Lord Brooke*, ed. Geoffrey Bullough (1945), 136. As J. B. Steane cautions, of course, "*Faustus* is not a simple Morality that can be summed up in the last words of the chorus" (Christopher Marlowe, *Complete Plays*, ed. J. B. Steane [1969], 23).

[7] See Jonathan Goldberg, *James I and the Politics of Literature* (1989), 65–85.

[8] Quoted in Anglo, "More Machiavelliavellan than Machiavel," 381; Anglo notes that "Throughout the sixteenth century *innovation* and *novelties* had carried religious connotations—and invariably bad ones" (352–53).

at length against the destructive curiosity to which melancholics are prone.[9]

Politic historians were seen as possibly even more insidious, with too much curiosity about the mechanics of government, the *arcana imperii*, and too little concern for the providence that set the machine in motion. For William Rankins, Baconian attempts to free scientific inquiry from questions of divine causation and historians' attempts to investigate human affairs without recourse to providential explanations were equally misguided, and proof that the authors were born under Saturn. In the section *"Contra Saturnistam"* of *Seven Satires* (1598), he attacks those "that reaching Polliticians will be nam'd" for "urging that nature all the world hath fram'd, / Affirming God in things is needlesse nam'd."[10] Tacitus in particular had the reputation of having discovered and exposed illicit secrets through illicit means: Famiano Strada warns students of history to "watch out for whoever reveals I-know-not-what hidden arts and secrets of ruling while putting together a history."[11] Whatever its explicit intentions, such history challenges authority simply by its attempt to find causes for political phenomena; diminish the mystery of apparent causelessness and you diminish the wonder.[12] By seeing through rulers' attempts at dissimulation, and especially by inquiring too intently into the origins of political institutions, the politic historians inspired by Tacitus threatened to demystify the workings of power.

In the translation of Boccalini's *Ragguagli Di Parnasso* (Venice, 1612) as *The New-found Politicke* (1626), the perceived ability of Tacitus to see into the hearts of his subjects even earns him the reputation of having created "Diabolicall spectacles." Whoever wears these X-ray specs

---

[9] See Walkington, *Optick glasse*, 129; Bright, *Treatise*, 199–200; and Wright, *The Passions of the Minde in Generall* (1604; 1971), 314–15.

[10] William Rankins, *Seven Satires* (1598), ed. A. Davenport (1948), 15.

[11] Quoted in Kenneth C. Schellhase, *Tacitus in Renaissance Political Thought* (1976), 150.

[12] Christopher Pye, analyzing Hobbes' treatment of the mysterious origin of the commonwealth, emphasizes how terrifying this lack of discernible cause can be: see "The Sovereign, the Theater, and the Kingdome of Darknesse: Hobbes and the Spectacle of Power," in *Representing the English Renaissance*, ed. Greenblatt, esp. 287–91. In the *Natural Questions*, Seneca is entirely aware that his mechanistic explanations are incompatible with myths created to instill religious awe for moral and political purposes, such as the attribution of the lightning bolt to Jupiter (2.42; *Workes*, trans. Lodge, 796): "These Wisemen pretending to bridle in the mindes of the ignorant, made them believe, that there was an inevitable feare, to the end wee should dread a divinity, that is above us. It was neccessary, in so great intemperance and corruption of manners, that there should be some power, against which no man should thinke himselfe able to prevaile."

sees "the pure essence and qualitie of the mindes and purposes of
Princes, what they are inwardly, and not what with their trickes and
artifices (necessary for to rule and raigne) they endevor to appeare out-
wardly."[13] Later Gabriel Naudé "speaks of Tacitus as a *deus ex machina*,
occupying a seat above the theatrical stage of history, 'from which, amid
stupor and amazement (*cum stupore et admiratione*), he resolves political difficulties'; for this, 'he is venerated silently, as befits a deity.'"[14] In
a world where all are wondering, Tacitus, the master both of curiosity
and of justified suspicion, is not. Able to see through others' guises and
uncover hidden causes with a single glance, he is the model and inspiration for courtiers, who as Donne writes in "To Sir Henry Wotton," need
"Suspicious boldness."

In *The New-found Politicke*, the connection between Tacitus and policy is emphasized both by Apollo and by "Lipsius," the editor and champion of Tacitus, who must defend himself against the charge of idola-
trously preferring Tacitus to Apollo. Lipsius praises Tacitus as "the true
Doctor of Princes, the *Pedagogue* of Courtiers" (17), but Apollo, temporarily rehearsing the position of the anti-Taciteans, describes him as "a
slye cunning Doctor of false simulation, the only subtile artificer of
treacherous tyrannies" (18). Apollo (dis)credits Tacitus with authorship
of the doctrine of equivocation, identifying him as "a sublime *pedagogue* to instruct others in that most villanous doctrine to smother and
suppresse the conceits and meanings of a true-meaning heart, and yet to
speake with a false-lying tongue; the ingenious Architect of fallacies
and deceits" (18). Boccalini apparently intended Apollo's over-the-top
speeches as parodies of the kind of criticism leveled at Tacitus.[15] When
Apollo has finished what he later reveals to be only a test of Lipsius'
loyalty to Tacitus—testing the constancy of the author of *de Con-
stantia*—he himself acknowledges Tacitus as "the father of humane
wisdom, and true inventor of modern *Policie*" (26). Although not trans-

[13] Quoted in Alan T. Bradford, "Stuart Absolutism and the 'Utility' of Tacitus,"
Huntington Library Quarterly 46 (1983): 137. Bradford also notes that Sir William
Cornwallis found Tacitus to have "so piercing an eye into the designes of Princes and
States" that he wishes his works were restricted to those already in power, and cites
parodies of those who lay claim to such sight, including the Overburian character of
"A Mere Fellow of an House," who "If he hath read Tacitus, Guicchardine, or Gallo-
Belgicus, he condemns the late Lord Treasurer, for all the state policy he had" (*A
Book of "Characters,"* ed. and trans. Richard Aldington [1924], 129) and Jonson's Epi-
gram 92, "The New Crie," which hits at those who think they know "councels,
projects, practices."
[14] In Schellhase, *Tacitus*, 150.
[15] See Bradford, "Stuart Absolutism," 136–37; and J. H. M. Salmon, "Seneca and
Tacitus in Jacobean England," in *The Mental World of the Jacobean Court*, ed. Linda
Levy Peck (1991), 186.

lated into English until after the fashion for melancholy in England had passed, Boccalini's dialogue demonstrates how firmly Tacitus was connected with both policy and equivocation.[16]

The duplicity of the emperors Tacitus investigated became hallmarks of his own style, its obscurity and doubtfulness. Tacitus seems to have provided a model both of a dangerous but attractive curiosity and of a style that conveys danger. The connection between these elements of his influence has not always been recognized, despite the similar combination of pragmatism and elliptical style in his most famous disciple, Francis Bacon. Richard Greneway pointed out the similarity between the styles of Tacitus and his imperial subjects in his translation of the *Annals* (1598): Tacitus has "no word not loaden with matter, and as himself speaketh of Galba, he useth *Imperatoria Brevitate*: which although it breed difficulty, yet carrieth great gravity" (*The Annales of Cornelius Tacitus*, fol. [*]3r). In the preface, Anthony Bacon likewise praises Tacitus' compression:

> . . . he hath written the most matter with best conceite in fewest words of any Historiographer ancient or moderne. But he is harde. *Difficilia quae pulchra*: the seconde reading over will please thee more then the first, and the third then the second. ("To the Reader," fol. ¶3r)

This is one of the most often cited defenses of obscure style in the 1590s, and the linchpin in Morris Croll's and George Williamson's classic arguments connecting the imitation of Tacitus and other silver age Latin stylists with the development of "strong lines." But the authorship of this preface may be just as significant: Anthony Bacon was the right-hand man of the Earl of Essex, the most notorious melancholic in Elizabethan England. As J. H. M. Salmon points out, other "followers of Essex who tended to stress Tacitus rather than Seneca" included Henry Savile, Francis Bacon, Henry Cuffe, John Hayward, and Henry Wotton. With Essex sponsoring Greneway's and Savile's translations of Tacitus as well as the projects of Bacon and other "politic historians," Essex House functioned as the gravitational core both for the intellectual qualities associated with cloaked style and for those posing as melancholic.[17] Even before his revolt, Essex's strategy was to represent himself as the

---

[16] Kenneth Schellhase points out that the most influential attack on Tacitus and his influence was that of the Jesuit Famiano Strada. Gasparo Scioppio, "a vitriolic hater of Strada and all Jesuits," responded by asserting, in Bradford's summary, that "Tacitus' history taught the evil Jesuits all they knew" (*Tacitus*, 150–51). See also Robert L. Bireley, S.J., *The Counter-Reformation Prince* (1990).

[17] Salmon, "Seneca and Tacitus," 172.

rightful locus of power, and his cloaking action illuminates the visible darkness of others making similar if lesser claims to power.

"Posing as melancholic" is of course far too simple a description for the madness of Essex. By reaching for his sword when Elizabeth cuffed his ear, invading her private chamber on his return from Ireland, and rebelling without a plan, he at the least manifested a dysfunctional practical intelligence. In an article on Hamlet's melancholy, Karin S. Coddon uses Sir John Harington's description of Essex before the insurrection to argue that "Essex's madness, whatever its precise pathological nature, was profoundly engaged in his transgressions as subject."[18] Her phrase "engaged in" is a deliberate hedge, designed to register the difficulty of separating cause from effect; his reason and his political fortunes spiraled downward in symmetry. For Harington, Essex's madness is unquestionably pathological, the result of his political frustration:

> It resteth wythe me in opynion, that ambition thwarted in its career, dothe speedilie leade on to madnesse; herein I am strengthened by what I learne in my lord of Essex, who shyftethe from sorrowe and repentaunce to rage and rebellion so suddenlie, as well provethe him devoide of good reason or righte mynde; in my last discourse, he uttered strange wordes borderinge on suche strange desygns, that made me hastene forthe, and leave his presence. Thank heaven! I am safe at home, and if I go in suche troubles againe, I deserve the gallowes for a meddlynge foole.[19]

Although an inveterate jester himself, Harington knew where strange words led. Coddon argues that Essex's disequilibrium (or internal disobedience) represents in itself—as much as in the desperate actions it precipitated—a casting off of the modes of obedience demanded by the state; "as the sinner was to the Church, now the disordered subjectivity is to the secular state" (" 'Suche Strange Desygns,' " 52). Pointing to Harington's phrase "such strange desygns," and to the ambiguity of Hamlet's words and actions, signs either of a deliberate "antic disposition" or of internal disruption, Coddon's analysis reveals the method in madness, the odd conjunction of what Thomas Walkington calls "stratagems" and "quirks" (53).

Yet because her purpose is to explore the internal disruptions of the subject interpellated by the structure of authority in Elizabethan England, Coddon underestimates this element of stratagem in Essex's be-

---

[18] Karin S. Coddon, " 'Suche Strange Desygns': Madness, Subjectivity, and Treason in *Hamlet* and Elizabethan Culture," *Renaissance Drama* n.s. 20 (1989): 52.
[19] John Harington, *Nugae Antiquae*, ed. Thomas Park (1804; 1966), 2:179.

havior. Precedent had been set by Ralegh's desperately theatrical displays of love melancholy in 1592. John Donne, writing to Henry Wotton
at Christmastide 1599–1600 from Lord Keeper Egerton's York House,
where Essex was confined, claims that "the worst accidents of his
sicknes are that he conspires with it & that it is not here beleeved."[20]
Despite quoting this passage, Coddon somehow claims that "Essex was
hardly suspected of putting on an antic disposition."[21] He was, and the
suspicion itself signifies how common the feigning of melancholy, melancholy as self-representation, had become by the turn of the century.
Coddon is no doubt right to say that his madness can be read as a sign of
his transgression against authority, but it can also be read as a sign of
his grasping for authority, his eagerness to rule. His distress at being a
subject, that is, was early modern rather than postmodern, political in a
personal rather than an ideological sense. Ironically, those questioning
Essex's madness were displaying their own mastery of the political
skills that study of Tacitus, Sallust, and Machiavelli would have helped
them cultivate, especially suspicion. Like any other form of behavior in
the courtly setting, madness was subject to dissimulation and suspicion:
courtiers demonstrated political talent both by dissimulating madness
and by suspecting anyone else displaying the symptoms.

Such suspicion, as Edwin B. Benjamin points out, was "the golden
plummet of the contemporary political drama": those who possess "the
ability to sound and measure accurately one's antagonist" succeed;
those who don't, fail.[22] If Polonius had a ghost, it would chant "Suspect." Paranoia may be unhealthy, but it comes in handy when everyone is out to get you; in the political sphere of the 1590s, with the paths
to patronage increasingly narrowing and the number of qualified seekers
widely increasing, suspicion seems to have been well-advised. This Tacitean ability to sound others' depths, however, also traditionally belongs
to those who suffer or benefit from melancholy; those who are not melancholic are gullible, though the failure their gullibility produces may
lead in turn to melancholy or the melancholy pose. From the perspective of Bright and Laurentius, suspicion haunts melancholics. Bright
says they "are doubtfull, suspitious, and thereby long in deliberation,
because those domesticall feares, or that internall obscuritie, causeth an
opinion of daunger in outwarde affaires, where there is no cause of
doubt" (*A Treatise of Melancholy*, 131). For Laurentius the nothings
that melancholics fear are "tirannous executioners" that "assayleth the
partie, with such an astonishment as that he is made afraide, and be-

---

[20] In R. C. Bald, *John Donne* (1970), 108.
[21] Coddon, "'Suche Strange Desygns,'" 55.
[22] Edwin B. Benjamin, "Bacon and Tacitus," *Classical Philology* 60 (1965): 104.

commeth a terror unto himselfe" (*A Discourse . . . of Melancolike Diseases*, 89).[23] As in the case of curiosity, a negative characteristic of melancholy becomes transformed into a positive virtue—or element of virtù—for the courtier. What might have seemed simply dangerous to Henry Sidney's generation now becomes, like wit, a weapon worth wielding, even if double-edged.

Marston's Duke Altofronto in *The Malcontent*, for example, blames his deposition on his failure to practice and recognize duplicity: "I wanted those old instruments of state, / Dissemblance and suspect" (1.4.9–10). After his fall, when he takes on the role of the melancholy Malevole, his plots effect his return to power. Hamlet's melancholy, similarly, prevents him from being "play'd on" by Guildenstern and others (3.2.350–372). For Altofronto and Hamlet melancholy is more a part of the plotting than its cause, but the association of wariness with melancholy contributes to the aesthetic logic of both characters. Bridget Lyons notes that Belleforest's "Historie of Hamblet" had implied a comparison between Hamlet's insight into the rottenness afoot in Denmark and the traditional powers of divination ascribed to saturnists.[24]

Suspicion, of course, feeds on itself. If courtiers believe success at court requires suspicion, they will be more suspicious, and display signs of suspicion as tokens of their political aptitude. They will carry themselves with suspicion, adopt a suspicious style. A cloaked style both insulates and intimates: its obscurity protects the writer against losing favor or the right hand, but also conveys the thrill of knowledge hidden. In a court of censorship, arbitrary power, and intrigue, to speak plainly might be to confirm one's status as an outsider. The most painful confession for an aspirant is the one Peregrine forces Sir Politic Would-Be to make in *Volpone*: that he has no plots, no secrets, nothing hidden that might arouse wonder or suspicion. The courtier's style, like the *charaktēr deinos* of Demetrius, always hints at something beyond, something too dangerous and wonderful to state clearly. Since courtiers can never admit that they are out of the loop, courts are the perfect breeding ground for such style.

As we have seen, suggestively obscure brevity is the hallmark of wonderful style, according to Demetrius in *On Style*. He considers the ability "to compress much thought in a little space, just as seeds contain potentially entire trees" to be "a mark of superior skill" (9). Such brevity acts as a catalyst, stimulating the inferences of the audience. Forced to imagine the logical consequences of a statement, each member of the

---

[23] See Greville's *Caelica*, 100, "In night, when colors all to black are cast," for a meditation on the products of the melancholy imagination.
[24] Lyons, *Voices of Melancholy*, 79.

audience becomes "not only your hearer but your witness, and a very friendly witness too," who "thinks himself intelligent because you have afforded him the means of showing his intelligence." Having engineered the train of thought that makes the orator's statement significant, the audience is both self-satisfied and grateful. To use Demetrius' metaphor of the seed, the audience, having nurtured the seed, is proud of the tree. Through elliptical style, employing *brachylogiai* ("brief utterances") and *emphasis* ("innuendo"), speakers get across to the audience that which they could not otherwise say: they manage to signify something beyond the capacity of the signifiers they employ. By doing so, they both make the veiled subject of their speech seem wonderful because inexpressible and make the audience marvel at its own powers of interpretation.

Such self-congratulation is exactly the response that Quintilian says stylists of his day counted on in their use of what he calls *suspicio*, which he describes as "similar, if not identical with" *emphasis* (*Institutio*, 9.2.65).[25] As a link between Greek and Roman characterizations of admirable style, *suspicio* is crucial. Quintilian complains that his contemporaries "regard allusion as better than directness of speech" and "regard it as a real sign of genius that it should require a genius to understand our meaning" (8.Pr.24–25). Associating cloaked expression with the schools of declamation, and saying it "is really not far removed from jesting," he claims it succeeds because "the hearer takes pleasure in detecting the speaker's concealed meaning, applauds his own penetration and regards another man's eloquence as a compliment to himself" (9.2.78–92). Quintilian describes a similar operation in the audience's reaction to riddles or "*adianoeta*":

> Such expressions are regarded as ingenious, daring and eloquent, simply because of their ambiguity, and quite a number of persons have become infected by the belief that a passage which requires a commentator must for that very reason be a masterpiece of elegance. Nay, there is even a class of hearer who find a special pleasure in such passages; for the fact that they can provide an answer to the riddle fills them with an ecstasy of self-congratulation, as if they had not merely heard the phrase, but invented it. (8.2.20–21)

Through *suspicio*, Quintilian explains, "we excite some suspicion to indicate that our meaning is other than our words would seem to imply," a meaning not "contrary to that which we express" as in simple irony "but rather a hidden meaning which is left to the hearer to discover."

[25] On *suspicio* and its relation to other forms of allusive style see Eden, "Hermeneutics."

Twice he points out that many rhetoricians consider *suspicio* the only true figure (Latin *figura*, Greek *schēma*), or the figure of figures.[26]

Quintilian provides no way of distinguishing *suspicio* from *emphasis*, which he includes among the necessary elements of amplification and which "requires the gift of signifying more than we say (*desiderat illam plus quam dixeris significationem*)" (9.2.3). Compared to *brachylogia*, "the brevity that says nothing more than what is absolutely necessary" (8.3.82–83), *emphasis* is "on a greater scale," more significant. Just as for Demetrius *brachylogiai* are wonderfully forceful because "we are left to infer (*hyponoēsai*) the chief of the meaning" (243), Quintilian aligns *emphasis* with forms of amplification that captivate the audience by requiring it to supply what seems to be missing (8.4.26). The more work the reader must do, the more credit the author deserves.

As Eden notes, "Longinus" and Seneca praise and blame cloaked style in similar terms, and reinforce Quintilian's assertion that *emphasis* or *suspicio* was especially popular in the first century A.D.[27] Despite his critique of overabundant figures (*schēmata*), "Longinus" finds true sublimity in concise passages that "leave behind . . . more food for thought than the mere words at first suggest" (*On the Sublime*, 7.3). Readers may claim, like Bacon's bee in *The New Organon*, to have produced something themselves through their rumination: "uplifted with a sense of proud possession, we are filled with joyful pride, as if we had ourselves produced the very thing we heard" (7.2). Although Seneca criticizes those who "cut the thoughts short, hoping to make a good impression by leaving the meaning in doubt and causing the hearer to suspect his own lack of wit" (*Epistulae Morales*, 114.11), he also congratulates Lucilius for his compact style: "You say all that you wish, and you mean still more than you say (*plus significas quam loqueris*)" (59.5).[28]

Quintilian attributes the appeal of obscure style to political conditions that made direct assaults on powerful figures dangerous (*Institutio*, 9.2.66–80), but he also admits that darkness makes speech vivid, impressive, amplified. The *Rhetorica ad Herennium*, the text considered most influential on rhetorical practice in the Renaissance, had earlier made a similar association between *emphasis* ("*significatio*") and liveliness. Emphasis, "the figure which leaves more to be suspected than has been actually asserted (*Significatio est res quae plus in suspicione relinquit quam positum est in oratione*)," is produced by "Hy-

---

[26] 9.1.14; 9.2.65. On Quintilian's contribution to the development of meanings for *figura* see Erich Auerbach, *Scenes From the Drama of European Literature* (1973), 25–28.

[27] "Hermeneutics," 81n39.

[28] Cf. Cicero, *Orator*, 139; Quintilian, *Institutio*, 9.1.45.

perbole, Ambiguity, Logical Consequence, Aposiopesis, and Analogy" (4.67). Each of these forms of emphasis, notably, also belong to Demetrius' *charaktēr deinos*.

The examples in the *Rhetorica ad Herennium* demonstrate that *emphasis* amplifies through concentrated forcefulness rather than copious dilation, providing qualitative rather than quantitative amplification. Through hyperbole "more is said than the truth warrants, so as to give greater force to the suspicion (*augendae suspicionis causa*), as follows: 'Out of so great a patrimony, in so short a time, this man has not laid by even an earthen pitcher wherewith to seek a fire for himself.'" The orator accentuates the point not by presenting a litany of the inheritor's indulgences, but by compressing them into a statement for the audience to unpack, imagining whatever indulgences they can. Emphasis through analogy, similarly, is "when we cite some analogue and do not amplify it (*cum aliqua re simili allata nihil amplius dicimus*), but by its means intimate what we are thinking, as follows: 'Do not, Saturninus, rely too much on the popular mob—unavenged lie the Gracchi.'" Here again, less is more. (Caplan's translation of "*nihil amplius dicimus*" as "do not amplify" is misleading, since the only sense in which these telling comparisons "do not amplify" is that they do not heap up examples.) To conclude his discussion of *significatio*, the author equates making speech lively with leaving something for the audience to puzzle out: "This figure sometimes possesses liveliness and distinction in the highest degree; indeed it permits the hearer himself to guess (*suspicari*) what the speaker has not mentioned." The various forms of this figure—including hyperbole, analogy, and ambiguity—give a speech life, force, *energeia*, and guarantee applause, even if the audience claps in part for itself.

Although Tudor rhetoricians do not consider *emphasis* the figure of figures, they repeat the assertions of the *ad Herennium* and Quintilian that compression makes speech wonderfully effective. Like their Greek and Roman predecessors, Tudor authorities see dark style as a means of simultaneously impressing readers and stimulating their intellects, of making speech strange and admirable. As demonstrated in chapter 1, Wilson, Peacham, Puttenham, Gascoigne, and Hoskyns incorporate the Greek insistence on distinctive strangeness into their treatments of amplification. Their comments on enigmatic style, appearing within general sections on amplifying speech or making it extraordinary and forceful, go even further in aligning suggestive brevity with wonder.

This connection is most explicit in Hoskyns' *Directions*; examining periphrasis and paraphrasis—long and short methods of making speech extraordinary—he restates the traditional assertion that the unusual arouses our wonder: "There is in the best writers sometymes a vaine of speech, wherein the vulgar conceipts are exceedingly pleased, ffor they admire this most, that there is some excellencie in it & yet they themselves suspect that it excells their admiracion." Although expressing difficulty believing that a speech in which "either the meaning or the wordes be obscure or unfamiliar" could "be much accepted," Hoskyns confesses that "it is impossible that there should be any extraordynarie delight in ordinarie wordes & plaine meaning." He recognizes, that is, the extremes of unintelligible distinctiveness and dull clarity between which Aristotle had advised speakers to pilot their style. The effect of either periphrasis or paraphrasis is that "though all the wordes of it by themselves, are most knowne & famylliar, yet the bringing in & fetch of it is strange & admyrable to the Ignorant" (160–61). Hoskyns further discusses suggestive style under the heading of "intimation," which includes hyperbole, puns, irony, and ambiguity (139). This "fashion of *Amplificacion*," Hoskyns states, "doth not directly Aggravate but by consequence & proporcion, & intimateth more to yor mynd then to yor eares" (140). "*Intimation*," he says, "leaves the collecion of greatnes to our understandinge, by expressing some marke of it, it exceedeth speech in silence, & makes our meaning more palpable by a touch, then by a direct handling." As an example of how the speaker leaves the heaping of examples—the "collecion of greatnes"—to the audience, Hoskyns explains that "he that should say (yow must live many years in his companie, whome yow shall accompt for yor friend) sayth well, but he that saith yow had need eate a bushell of sault with him, saith more, & gives yow to reckon more then many yeares." Like the earthen pitcher in the *ad Herennium*, Hoskyns's bushel of salt goes a long way, accomplishing swiftly what dilation of examples might do less effectively.

Wilson, Peacham, and Puttenham discuss obscure brevity in similar terms, but point less explicitly to the ulterior goal of provoking wonder. Wilson defines the figure of "close understanding" as "when more may be gathered than is openly exprest" (*Arte*, 203), supplying in the margin clear evidence of his debt to the Roman authors: "significatio plus ad intelligendum quam dixeris." Peacham, likewise, defines *Emphasis* as the name given "when there is more to be understood then the wordes by them selves do expresse, or thus, when there is a deeper understanding, or signifycation, then is declared by the wordes themselves" (*Garden*, H2r; cf. E3v). One of its relatives is "*Noema*" (U4r): "when we doe signify some thing so privily, that the hearers must be fayne to seeke out the meaning by long consideration." Another is "aenigma," which he considers more appropriate in poetry than oratory, because "every Aenigmaticall sentence is obscure, and every Oratour doth in speaking, flye obscurity, and darck speeches, in whome the facillity and perspecuity of the speech is a goodly vertue." Yet, he acknowledges: "sometime, darcknesse is delectable, as [that] which is understood of wyse and learned men, for when men fynde at last, by long consyderation, the meaning of some darcke riddle, they much delight and reioyce, that their capacity was able to compass so hard a matter, and commende highly the devysers wit" (D2r). When Puttenham discusses enigma, noema, and synecdoche—all species of *"Allegoria"*—he puts similar emphasis on the wit they require from both poet and audience: "We dissemble againe under covert and darke speaches, when we speake by way of riddle (*Enigma*), of which the sence can hardly be picked out, but by the parties owne assoile" (*Arte*, 188).[29] What better atmosphere for wonderfully obscure style than a discourse community whose members must prove themselves wits both by creating obscurity and by deciphering it?

"Short but Admirable Lines"

Few seventeenth-century references to "metaphysical" style exist, but the reactions of poet-critics demonstrate that Donne and others writing at the turn of the century intended to provoke wonder. These critical responses—whether favorable or caustic—also cement the connection between the practice of strong lines and the rhetorical tradition encouraging authors to astound audiences through *emphasis, suspicio, significatio,* and *hyponoia.* Seventeenth-century responses to strong lines match Quintilian's response to the style of his day surprisingly closely, particularly in specifying that obscurity allows members of the audience to exercise and show off their own powers of interpretation, or wit. As the verses praising the strong lines of Donne and William Cartwright attest, poets measured fellow poets by their ability to amaze through the darkness of strong lines.

[29] Because enigma's cousin synecdoche "seemeth to ask a good, quick, and pregnant capacitie, and is not for an ordinarie or dull wit so to do," he gives it the English name "quick conceit" (185; cf. 195). His distinction between quick and close conceit (*noema*) resembles Hoskyns's between periphrasis and paraphrasis: "Speaking before of the figure [*Synecdoche*] wee called him [*Quicke conceit*] because he inured in a single word onely by way of intendment or large meaning, but such as was speedily discovered by every quicke wit, as by the halfe to understand the whole, and many other waies appearing by the examples. But by this figure [*Noema*] the obscurity of the sence lieth not in a single word, but in an entier speech, whereof we do not so easily conceive the meaning, but as it were by conjecture, because it is wittie and subtile or darke, which makes me therefore call him in our vulgar the [*Close conceit*]" (230–31). Cf. Puttenham's treatment of allegory (*Arte*, 186–87), and Castiglione, *Courtier,* 159.

Jasper Mayne's lines on Donne's *First Anniversarie* are typical of contemporary praise for the poet Izaak Walton calls *"miraculous Donne."*
Through its ambitious obscurity, Donne's elegy serves as a trial of wit,
separating the fit from the dull. The poem is "so farre above its Reader,
good, / That wee are thought wits, when 'tis understood."[30] Even wits
"wonder" at it, but only temporarily: wonder stimulates their powers of
interpretation. The witless remain stupefied. The elegies printed with
the 1633 edition of Donne's *Poems* frequently focus on Donne's elevation, Arthur Wilson for example presenting him as more eagle than
dove:

> Thou dost not stoope unto the vulgar sight,
> But, hovering highly in the aire of Wit,
> Hold'st such a pitch, that few can follow it;
> Admire they may. . . .[31]

In Thomas Carew's more famous elegy, Donne's powerful eloquence
goes beyond mere persuasion to wonder, committing "holy Rapes upon
our will."[32] Carew identifies Donne's true poetic rage or furor, his "line /
Of masculine expression," as capable of producing such rapture that by
comparison "Old Orpheus" and "all the ancient Brood / Our super-
stitious fooles admire" pale. Like *deinotēs* for Demetrius or the sublime
for "Longinus," Donne's obscurity is more than eloquent, it is dreadfully potent.

Even those who praise strong lines handle the power relations between author and audience inconsistently, indicating the range of meanings for the kind of rapture identified with wonder. When critics stress
the element of coproduction in witty obscurity, they demand an active
audience. But when they draw like Carew on the association of force
with "manliness" in classical rhetoric, and stress the ability of elo-

---

[30] In A. J. Smith, ed., *John Donne: The Critical Heritage* (1975), 97; Arnold Stein
makes the connection between Quintilian, *Institutio*, 9.2.78 and Mayne in "Donne's
Obscurity and the Elizabethan Tradition," *ELH* 13 (1946): 112. In the poem prefixed
to the original publication of Donne's *The First and Second Anniversaries*, Joseph
Hall congratulates Elizabeth Drury on having had the good fortune to be praised by
one "that can relate / Thy worth so well to our last nephews eyne, / That they shall
wonder both at his, and thine" (in John Donne, *Epithalamions, Anniversaries, and
Epicedes*, ed. W. Milgate (1978), 20; I have dropped the italics).

[31] In Smith, ed., *Critical Heritage*, 99–100; cf. the concluding lines of Henry Valentine's elegy, 92.

[32] In Smith, ed., *Critical Heritage*, 93. On "manly" style and ravishment, see my
"Gender and Style in Seventeenth-Century Commendatory Verse," *Studies in En-
glish Literature, 1500–1900* 33 (1983): 507–22; and Fish, "Masculine Persuasive
Force," 223–52.

quence to overpower or ravish the will, then potency, virtù, belongs to author alone. It is not too much of a stretch to say that the first way of looking at strong lines fits with Castiglione's analysis of how meaning and value are produced at court, by courtiers, while the second fits better with Machiavelli's ideal of a prince's self-sufficiency. It is even less of a stretch to say that these two effects attested to by poet-critics in the seventeenth century—the capacity of strong lines to provoke the audience's inferences and to "ravish" the audience's will—are precisely the primary effects of Demetrius' *charaktēr deinos* and the sublime of "Longinus." The fluctuation between these two points of emphasis perhaps underscores the conflation of Greek and Roman terms of analysis in later discussions of force. Gorgias explicitly equates verbal persuasion with rape in the "Encomium of Helen" by arguing that it makes no difference whether Paris seized and assaulted her by physical violence or persuaded her through speech: in either case, he argues, she is blameless (6–14, esp. 12). He does not, however, use the term *deinotēs*, and *deinotēs* does not, to my knowledge, convey by itself the Greek analogy between verbal and sexual compulsion. The Latin term *vis*, however, does.[33] Also important is that in usage *vis* often shades into the etymologically distinct term *virtus*, which denotes specifically masculine power, or "manliness."[34]

Even critics of strong lines recognized that they were written in the tradition of *emphasis* and *suspicio*. In the preface to *Argalus and Parthenia* (1647), Francis Quarles disavows any intention "to set thy understanding on the Rack, by the tyranny of strong *Lines* . . . under the colour of which, many have ventured (trusting to the *Oedipean* conceit of their ingenious Reader) to write non sense, and felloniously [sic] fa-

[33] See the *Oxford Latin Dictionary*, ed. P. G. W. Glare (1968–82), sense 2a; and Thomas Cooper, *Thesaurus Linguae Romanae et Brittanicae* (1565; 1969).

[34] For a rhetorical example of this conflation, see Quintilian, *Institutio*, 9.4.142; see also Cooper's entries for *virilis*. Seneca and Quintilian gender as "manly" style that is harsh ("*durus*") or contains elements of unevenness ("*asperitas*") and vehemence ("*vehementia*"), juxtaposing it to continual smoothness and looseness. In his emphasis on boldness in the use of figures and in construction, Quintilian hints at an alignment between far-fetched analogy and harsh brevity. See Quintilian, *Institutio*, 8.6.16–17, 9.4.142, 10.2.12, 12.9.2, and 12.10.77; Seneca, *Ad Lucilium Epistulae Morales*, trans. Richard M. Gummere (1917–25), *Ep.* 114 (especially 4–5 and 20); and Ernesti, *Lexicon techologiae latinorum rhetoricae*, s.v. "*durus*," "*nervus*," "*asper*," and "*vis*." Although Quintilian says that if forced to choose "I should prefer my rhythm to be harsh and violent rather than nerveless and effeminate" (9.4.142), he frequently criticizes those who overuse Senecan methods of making style forcible; see 1.8.9, 2.11.6–2.12.8, 7.1.44, 8.5.13–14, 10.1.130. On the influence of Seneca, see Trimpi, *Ben Jonson's Poems*, 19–27, 242n27, and 251n77; Williamson, *Senecan Amble*; and Edinger, *Samuel Johnson*, 6–10 and 158–59.

ther the created expositions of other men; not unlike some Painters, who first make the Picture, then, from the opinion of better judgments, conclude whom it resembles" (A3r–v). For Quarles the questions of parentage that strong lines raise bring no credit to an author.[35] Dudley North, in the preface to *A Forest of Varieties* (1645), similarly disassociates himself from strong lines and admirable pitches, insisting that "These tormentors of their owne and their Readers braines I leave to bee admired in their high obscure flight."[36] By 1651, when William Cartwright's *Comedies, Tragi-comedies, With other Poems* were published, even Jasper Mayne had changed his tune, praising Cartwright for crystalline clarity rather than admirable wit:

> No cloud of Fancie, no mysterious stroke,
> No verse like those which antient *Sybils* spoke,
> No Oracle of Language, to amaze
> The Reader with a dark or Midnight phrase,
> Stands in thy Writings, which are all pure Day,
> A cleer, bright Sunshine, and the mist away.
> That which thou wrot'st was sense, and that sense good,
> Things not first written, and then understood.
> (Cartwright, *Comedies, Tragi-comedies*, b4v)

Obscurity continues to amaze, but is no longer a mark of praise. By the middle of the century the heyday of admirable style was over, as readers looked behind the curtain of obscurity and judged what they saw to be less than wonderful.

But if the elegies on Cartwright signal that the transition from wonderful obscurity toward what Mayne calls "Strength mix'd with Sweetness" had begun, they also signal that it was incomplete. Praise for Cartwright's ability to produce wonder appears throughout, and several elegists still see suggestive brevity as his primary means of producing it.[37]

---

[35] Quarles, *Argalus and Parthenia* (1647), A3r–v; cf. Endymion Porter's commendatory poem prefaced to William Davenant's *Madagascar* (no page):
  And that's the knowledge which belongs to mee;
  For by what's said I guesse at Poetrie:
  As when I heare them read strong-lines, I cry
  Th'are rare, but cannot tell you rightly why;
  And now I finde this quality was it,
  That made some Poet cite mee for a wit. . . .

[36] In *Literary Criticism*, ed. Tayler, 159.

[37] Nearly every elegist finds Cartwright's poems, plays, or sermons somehow admirable in the sense of evoking wonder. See, for example, the poems by Robert Stapleton (b2r), John Jeffryes (b3r), Jasper Mayne (b4v), Katherine Philips (πa6v), Edward

Thomas Cole warns all upstart "worms of *CARTWRIGHT'S* wit" that "His Lines are strong, you may a surfeit get," since "Each Page is here a Volume; *CARTWRIGHT'S* Pen / Speaks in one dash more than whole Books of Men" (***6r–v). John Berkenhead at first appears critical of strong lines:

> For thy Imperiall Muse at once desines
> Lawes to *arraign* and *brand* their weak *strong lines.*
> Unmask's [sic] the Goblin-Verse that fright's a page
> As when old time brought Devills on the Stage. (*8r)

His ultimate purpose, however, is to distinguish imperial Cartwright's true strong lines from flabbier impostors:

> Thine's the right Metall, Thine's still big with Sense,
> And stands as square as a good *Conscience.*
> No Traverse lines, all *written like a man:*
> *Their* Heights are but the *Chaff,* their Depths the *Bran*
> Gross, and not Great; which when it best does his
> Is not the *Strength* but *Corpulence* of Wit:
> Stuft, swoln, ungirt: but Thine's compact and bound
> Close as the Atomes of a *Diamond.*
> *Substance* and *Frame; Raptures* not *Phrensies* grown. . . . (*8v)

Berkenhead borrows the metaphoric language of Carew's elegy, pointing to both the pregnancy of Cartwright's wit and his strong, masculine line; just as Donne has "open'd Us a Mine / Of rich and pregnant phansie, drawne a line / Of masculine expression," so is Cartwright's eloquence of "the right Metall," "big with sense" though "*written like a man.*"[38] Miraculously, dreadfully, strong lines are hermaphroditic, both pregnant

---

Dering (πa8v), John Berkenhead (*8v), Joseph Howe (*15v), John Fell (¶1r–v), Henry Vaughan (*14r), and John (?) Cobbe (*8r) in Cartwright, *Comedies, Tragi-comedies.*

[38] According to Humphrey Moseley's preface, Ben Jonson is supposed to have said "with some passion, My son CARTWRIGHT writes all like a Man" (a5r). In a passage of the *Discoveries* that echoes Seneca's *Epistulae Morales*, 114, however, Jonson presents both exclusively rough and exclusively smooth styles as wrongheaded (*Ben Jonson*, 8:585; cf. 8:588, on the "true artificer"). On the one hand there are those who "in composition are nothing, but rough and broken," and who "if it would come gently," will "trouble it of purpose." "They would not have it run without rubs, as if that stile were more strong and manly, that stroke the eare with a kind of unevenness." On the other hand are those "that have no composition at all; but a kind of tuneing, and riming fall, in what they write. It runs and slides, and onely makes a sound. Womens-*Poets* they are call'd: as you have womens-*Taylors.*" Jonson aligns compositional and conceptual depth when he calls such poets "*Creame-bowle,* or but puddle deepe" (8:585).

with meaning and capable of committing violent rape upon the will of the audience. Ralph Bathurst, likewise echoing Carew on Donne, credits Cartwright with producing the sublimated rapture of powerful, sublime eloquence:

> But who could hear without an Extasie,
> When with a gracefull conquering presence He
> Stood forth, and, like Almighty Thunder, flung
> His numerous strains amongst th'amazed throng?
> A pleasing horror strook through every limb,
> And every ear was close chain'd up to Him:
> Such Masculine vigour ravish'd our assent;
> What He perswaded, was commandement. (**2r)

Even as strong lines passed out of fashion, readers measured authors' eloquence by their ability to amaze, to ravish the will.

For Jasper Mayne and Francis Quarles, the essence of witty strong lines lies in involving readers in the production of meaning, stimulating their efforts to understand. In Abraham Cowley's famous "Ode. Of Wit," similarly, the persona fails to find a satisfactory positive definition of wit, but demonstrates his understanding of wit by recognizing it in the lines of the fictional interlocutor.[39] After rejecting various provisional definitions, the narrating persona finally resorts to the experiential, displaying the addressee's poems and shouting "'*Tis this*." In the course of the poem Cowley rejects the equation of wit with jests, crowded figures, prurient tales, anagrams and acrostics, bombastic metaphors, or Senecan brevity: all are either misguided or incomplete versions of wit. What finally matters most for Cowley is that the reader knows wit on sight: it takes one to know one. The entire structure of the poem establishes this experiential definition, this participation of the reader in the production of witty writing, as the most viable definition of wit.

The poem begins with a request for a definition: "Tell me, O tell, what kind of thing is wit, / Thou who master art of it. . . ." The questioner, however, never gives the addressee a chance to present this requested definition, instead explaining why a definition is necessary (lines 3–20) and why various definitions are insufficient (20–54). In the eighth stanza the questioner at last presents a positive definition of wit, equating it with the divine perspective: it is that in which all things

---

[39] I have used the text of the poem in *Metaphysical Lyrics and Poems of the Seventeenth Century*, ed. Herbert J. C. Grierson, rev. Alastair Fowler (1995), 187–89.

"without discord or confusion lie / In that strange mirror of the Deity."
This definition, however unobjectionable, is so broad and vague that it
hardly sets limits (de-fines) to the subject.

Cowley builds the sense that this definition is not quite sufficient
into the poem: if the answer given by the eighth stanza were sufficient,
he could have made it the conclusion of the poem, even perhaps presenting it in the voice of the "master" of wit. Instead, having in the
course of the poem erased various possible poems or answers the "master" could have written, the questioner proceeds to apologize for this
presumption: "I took you for myself, sure, when I thought / That you in
anything were to be taught." The "master," who is both the addressee
within the poem and, significantly, the implied reader of the poem itself, knows all about wit. This reader, then, produces the required definition, but in a manner that enables the questioner also to demonstrate
a grasp of wit: in the master's lines (the reader writes as well as reads) all
discerning readers will find wit. If asked, then, what "right wit and
height of genius is," the questioner will not respond with a version of
stanza eight, or any other positive definition, but "only show your lines,
and say '*Tis this*." We, as readers of the fictional master's lines, will
ourselves be thought wits if we can understand that they are witty: in
reading these lines we simultaneously discover the meaning of wit and
display our own possession of it. Fit readers participate in creating the
meaning of the poem and may congratulate themselves as well as the
author for their wittiness.

The poem allows, though, for an even wittier interpretation, one in
which the reader actually does write, or at least rewrite the final stanza.
This interpretation has never, to my knowledge, been pointed out. In
stanza nine the questioner (who has never given the interlocutor a
chance to speak) apologizes:

> I took you for myself, sure, when I thought
> That you in anything were to be taught.
> Correct my error with thy pen;
> And if any ask me then,
> What thing right wit and height of genius is,
> I'll only show your lines, and say, '*Tis this*.

If we correct the questioner's error with our pens in a fairly literal way,
exchanging the second-person pronouns for the first-person (thus negat-
ing the effects of the "I" who "took *you* for *myself*"), the final lines of
the poem would read:

> And if any ask you then,
> What thing right wit and height of genius is,
> You'll only show my lines, and say, *'Tis this.*

These re-written lines, corrected by the master of wit's pen, would demonstrate the reader's involvement in producing wit. Only a witty reader would think of making the substitution, and thus be capable of showing the witty lines, nurtured by both author and reader.

By using *emphasis* or *suspicio*, the witty courtier displays the kind of natural, indeterminate, and audience-dependent wit that, as Frank Whigham notes, sets off an elite capable of maintaining the social and political order. Its dependence on audience verification—possibly connoting lack of self-sufficient virtù—is something of a problem for the courtier and especially for the prospective prince, but such style is also identified with dreadfully potent masculine control, with the ravishment beyond persuasion Ralph Bathurst credits Cartrwright with producing. Secrecy, in any event, craves an audience, though a small one, and Quintilian's much simpler pragmatic rationale for *emphasis* and *suspicio* in imperial Rome also applies to London in the 1590s. If, he says, "the danger" involved in speaking against a tyrant or powerful person "can be avoided by any ambiguity of expression, the speaker's cunning will meet with universal approbation" (*Institutio*, 9.2.68). *Suspicio* is therefore a cunning means of protecting oneself against the powerful, and especially against tyrants. But before we ascribe any particular political character to such style we need to remember that suspicion is also, paradoxically, a hallmark of the tyrant's own style of speaking and ruling, especially that of the worst of emperors, Tiberius.

"Obscurelie Doubtfull"

When Laurentius labels melancholics' groundless but astonishing fears "tirannous," he is referring to tyranny within the mind: the images produced by the imagination bypass the understanding and produce fear and wonder without proper cause, thus upsetting the mind's hierarchy.[40] But this fear, and the style it produces, might also belong to actual tyrants whose imaginations continually rehearse the plots that could bring them down. Melancholy may be the affliction (or disguise) of suspicious

---

[40] In an exchange between Richard and Buckingham at the beginning of act three, scene five of *Richard III*, tyrannous doubtfulness is also interestingly enough associated with the tragic hero experiencing wonder; see Cunningham, *Collected Essays*, 11.

tyrants as well as plotting malcontents, and of course the two categories
overlap in the case of tyrants by usurpation, who like Macbeth know
how much there is to fear.[41] Robert Johnson, insisting in his essay "Of
Wit" (1607) that wits "too pregnant and sharpe" are especially susceptible to this kind of doubtfulness, offers Tiberius as a case in point: "For a
working and craftie witte drawes commonly with it a doubtfull and wa-
vering judgement: Such was noted in Tiberius stirring up trifling regards
to containe him in suspense, rather increasing new doubts, then giving
any grounde to settle an opinion, being the true cause, why his speech
was commonlie obscurelie doubtfull, subject to a double interpretation,
dissolved in it selfe, and not knit to any constant end."[42] Tiberius, suspicious, writes obscurely, his tortuous style reflecting his constant need
to stir the roots around a problem. He is like Heraclitus, who "lived in
continuall teares, because (sayth *Theophrastus*) that he was possessed of
melancholie," and whose "writings altogether confused, and darkned
with obscurity doe sufficiently witnesse the same" (Laurentius, *A Discourse*, 93). For Laurentius fear and confusion are symptomatic of melancholy, but doubleness may be a function of policy as well as pathology, as Jonson suggests in *Sejanus*: according to Lepidus, Tiberius'
"subtilty hath chose this doubling line" (4.465). Francis Bacon points to
the value of such closeness in the essay "Of Negociating," where he
warns that "In dealing with cunning persons we must ever consider
their endes to interpret their speeches, and it is good to say little to
them, and that which they least looke for" (*Works*, 6:534). When he
wrote his history of Henry VII's reign, Bacon read Henry VII through the
filter of Roman histories of Tiberius, seeing the first Tudor as fitting the
melancholy mold: "he were a dark prince, and infinitely suspicious, and
his times full of secret conspiracies and troubles" (11:361). Bacon's
Henry was an anglicized *prince de tenèbres* who contrived through his
"inquiry" and "closeness" that those around him "stood in the light
towards him, and he stood in the dark to them" (11:359).

   When midcentury critics of admirable style refer to it as "tyrannous,"
they are probably conflating this identification of it as suspicious with
their recognition of its claim to power, its capacity to ravish the will.
Francis Quarles, for example, promises the reader not "to set thy understanding on the Rack, by the tyranny of strong *Lines*."[43] Milton connects
obscure brevity with tyranny in *Of Education* (1644), complaining that
learning insufficiently grounded in "vertue, and true generous breeding"

[41] On the tyrant by usurpation, see Julian H. Franklin, *Constitutionalism and Resistance in the Sixteenth Century* (1969), 197.
[42] Robert Johnson, "Of Wit," in *Essaies*, B5v–B6r.
[43] Quarles, *Argalus and Parthenia*, fol. A3r.

produces shallow courtiers who think "flattery, and court shifts and tyrannous aphorismes . . . the highest points of wisdom."[44] Strong lines
serve as the aesthetic equivalent of politic secrecy: they maintain
doubtfulness, avoid commitment to one position, allow speakers or
writers to avoid incriminating themselves, and provoke awe. From
within such darkness the speaker dazzles while retaining a clear view of
others, insuring that "all men wonder at him, and hee at no man."

Donne's *Satyre IV*: Suspicion of a Subtle Statesman

In *Satyre IV*, Donne performs in and on the court the satire of self-
advertisement rehearsed in and on the Inns of Court in *Satyre I*, and also
reveals it to be a place where paranoia breeds suspicious style. In place
of the fellow student there is the foppish courtier here, the stock fol-
lower of fashions, forms, and trashy "newes" that Jonson skewers in the
person of *Volpone*'s Sir Politic-Would-Be, Shakespeare in *Hamlet*'s Os-
ric. Compounding elements of the "malcontent, traveller, politician, in-
telligencer (informer), and even Jesuit in disguise," Donne's bore or boor
adds up to less than zero (*Satires*, 149). Razor-sharp in its irony, the
poem takes the court's deepest fears and turns them inside out, just as it
flips the Horatian pattern by making the bore the insider at court and
the satirist's persona the partially naive outsider. Donne exploits "the
court's xenophobia, its mistrust of 'strangers,' 'papist atheists,' and foreign intriguers, by intimating that the most preposterous enactments of
Ascham's proverbial 'Inglese italianato è diabolo incarnato' occur within
the court (and probably with the court's support)."[45] Not quite the
strangest "thing" at court, he is strange enough (17–29):

> Towards me did runne
> A thing more strange, then on Niles slime, the Sunne
> E'r bred; or all which into Noahs Arke came;
> A thing, which would have pos'd Adam to name;
> Stranger than seaven Antiquaries studies,
> Then Africks Monsters, Guianaes rarities.
> Stranger then strangers; One, who for a Dane,
> In the Danes Massacre had sure beene slaine,
> If he had liv'd then; And without helpe dies,

[44] In *Complete Prose Works of John Milton, vol. 2: 1643–1648*, ed. Ernest Sirluck
(1959), 2:375.
[45] M. Thomas Hester, *Kinde Pitty and Brave Scorn* (1982), 80. My debt to Hester's
study of *Satyre IV* is heavy.

> When next the Prentises 'gainst Strangers rise.
> One, whom the watch at noone lets scarce goe by,
> One to'whom th'examining Justice sure would cry,
> 'Sir, by your priesthood tell me what you are.'

As in *Satyre I*, this fool character allows Donne both to play the witty satirist exposing folly at court and to keep himself at least partially out of the dirt. Through him Donne is able to introduce the strange wonders so popular at court, satisfying the audience's demand for them even while conveying a sense of his own immunity from the craze.

Through the bore's gossip, Donne expresses Tacitean insight on the workings of power and place, knowledge of who and what is in and out, and how they got there (97–107):

> More then ten Hollensheads, or Halls, or Stowes,
> Of triviall houshold trash he knowes; He knowes
> When the Queene frown'd, or smil'd, and he knowes what
> A subtle States-man may gather of that;
> He knowes who loves; whom; and who by poyson
> Hasts to an Offices reversion;
> He knowes who'hath sold his land, and now doth beg
> A licence, old iron, bootes, shooes, and egge-
> shels to transport; Shortly boyes shall not play
> At span-counter, or blow-point, but they pay
> Toll to some Courtier;' . . .

Donne expresses detached disinterest here in precisely the kinds of court practices castigated in other satires, particularly the spread of monopolies, and his disdain for "household trash" is undercut by tacit recognition that in court no frown, smile, or wink is insignificant, that when the private body of the Queen frowns, the public sky darkens. Donne is a Teflon satirist in the first half of the poem, displacing onto the bore both the actual work of satirizing and the negative associations that go along with the job. The final item in this section—"Shortly boyes shall not play . . . but they pay / Toll to some Courtier"—is revealing. After a litany of what "He knowes" (and presumably what "He tells"), presented in indirect discourse, this critique of the absurd expansion of monopolies, tolls, and tariffs appears in the form of a declaration, its speaker uncertain. Milgate consistently emends his copy-text, the 1633 first printed edition, by supplying "terminal punctuation for direct speech," but in this instance the apostrophe after "Courtier;" implies more certainty about who is speaking than is warranted. Rapidly reducing all the previous examples to absurdity, the comment on taxing marbles displays more wit than the other comments attributed to the bore in the poem. Donne, of course, is not quite laying claim to the satirical stroke, but not quite giving the bore credit for it either. Here and throughout the poem he gets to maintain his own dignity even while indulging Juvenalian *indignatio*: after (if not during) a single visit to court, he proves himself to be neither naive about the real *arcana imperii*, the machinations there, nor as morally bankrupt as those totally immersed in its folly.

As in *Satyre I*, however, Donne wields wit at his own expense, or at the expense of wit itself. Just as the first satire takes a jab at "subtlewitted antique youth," *Satyre IV* blasts not only the overly neat Macrine, but "the other extreme," Glorius, who affects "a rough carelessnesse" and "keepes all in awe" with his frightening looks (220–21). Although exagerrated, a caricature borrowing features of the stock *miles gloriosus*, Glorius is also a fun-house mirror of Donne himself, one who "Jeasts like a licenc'd foole, commands like law" (228). But the self-accusatory quality of this poem that has rightly attracted the most critical attention, particularly in acute studies by M. Thomas Hester and James S. Baumlin, is Donne's daring use of allusions to Catholicism, to questions of recusancy and treason; "The satirist's own conduct, he admits, may be termed treasonous, just as the recusant was termed 'Traytor' (131) and 'Spie' (237) by the legal machinery and 'Giant Statutes' (132) of Elizabethan England" (Hester, *Kinde Pitty*, 75; cf. Baumlin, *John Donne*, 95–97). Representing himself as a melancholy satirist is daring enough. Representing himself as a recusant who fears exposure, which Hester and Baumlin persuasively argue is exactly what Donne does in *Satyre IV*, means leaping a line few would follow him across; like Hal crossing the symbolic border from Windsor into Eastcheap, Donne takes what looks like a one-way trip.

Opening with an abrupt comparison of the court he has just seen to "Purgatorie" (1–4) and a disclaimer that he went there on a whim (5–8), he likens his case to that of "Glaze," who paid a heavy fine for having gone "to'a Masse in jest" (8–16). His punishment was to meet the macaronic bore, that "thing more strange, then on Niles slime, the Sunne / E'r bred" (18–19), with dissolving clothes and motley tongue. Through line 154 the poem is loosely modeled, like *Satyre I*, on Horace's *Sat.* 1.9. But Donne's *adversarius* here is more threatening. Horace's bore is, after all, just a bore, but Donne's may well be a "priviledg'd spie" out to entrap him, which he realizes only late in the conversation when the bore's attacks sound less and less like satire, more and more like treason and libel. In good Aristotelian fashion, Donne's discovery or recognition is accompanied by wonder:

> I more amas'd then Circes prisoners, when
> They felt themselves turn beasts, felt my selfe then
> Becomming Traytor, and mee thought I saw
> One of our Giant Statutes ope his jaw
> To sucke me in; for hearing him, I found
> That as burnt venom'd Leachers doe grow sound
> By giving others their soares, I might growe
> Guilty, and he free. . . . (129–36)

Here Donne portrays the nadir of his initial visit to court, not only because he is in danger, but because he has flinched, "wondered at" this court nothing in just the sense that Castiglione enjoins him not to do.[46] Donne, like Glaze caught at Mass and forced to pay a fine, feels relieved to buy his escape from court with a small donation to the bore.

Yet the poem doesn't end there, and even in the course of this conversation with the "Makeron," Donne has displayed his wit, particularly his sly equivocation. Even before the danger dawns on him, Donne has been engaged in a duel of wit, responding craftily to the bore's invitations to implicate himself by expressing opinions on linguists (51–65), courts and kings (66–82), fashion (83–88), and, most dangerously, miscellaneous "newes" (93–128).[47] Donne's witty answers, which precede his conscious recognition of danger, display a seemingly intuitive and thus natural wariness about falling for the bore's feints, about lunging when he should parry (83–84):

> 'Are not your Frenchmen neate?' 'Mine? as you see,
> I'have but one Frenchman, looke, hee followes mee.'

Such responses display what Castiglione designates "the chiefe mattere" in wit, which is "to answere otherwise than the hearer looketh for" (*Courtier*, 168; cf. 148–49). They also show Donne heeding Bacon's warning that when "dealing with cunning persons we must ever consider their endes . . . and it is good to say little to them, and that which they least looke for."[48] Taking the abstract, indefinite "your" as the possessive adjective, Donne turns a national question into a personal question, but he also passes the loyalty test, since his dominance over his French servant contrasts with the sycophant's aping of French fashion. And yet Donne's wit throughout the conversation remains a double-edged sword, because what he is practicing is textbook-variety equivoca-

---

[46] Baumlin (*John Donne*, 109) picks up well on the powerlessness conveyed here, adducing Gorgias' comparison of powerful *logos* to a drug that controls, bewitches the listener ("Encomium on Helen," 8–14, in Freeman, *Ancilla*, 132–33).

[47] See Hester, *Kinde Pity*, 77n10; and Baumlin, *John Donne*, 107–10.

[48] See Marotti, *John Donne*, 29.

tion, which even in the 1590s carried slightly sinister undertones, if not
as pronounced as they would become after Garnet's treatise on equivocation became known and the Gunpowder Plot was uncovered. (If his
use of equivocation had been too dangerous, he would no doubt have
recast the poem when he removed the dangerous jests at the expense of
Richard Topsell and Protestant theologian John Sleidan.) Critics often
point to the failure of Donne's wit, since only "the prerogative of my
Crowne" is able to get rid of the bore, but Horace, too, was unable to get
rid of the bore in *Sat.* 1.9 until "saved by Apollo" in the form of the
bore's adversary in a lawsuit. However ineffective Donne's parrying
may be in getting rid of the fop, it insures that while the bore spews
libel after libel, he himself at least *says* nothing to incriminate himself
in the dialogue at court itself (as distinct from his editorializing report
on it).

Donne also rebounds from the depths of his fear simply by going back
to the court later. Unlike the melancholics described by Laurentius as
paralyzed by "tirannous executioners" or fears of nothing that "assayleth the partie, with such an astonishment as that he is made afraide,
and becommeth a terror unto himselfe" (89), Donne's return proves that
he has recovered from being "amas'd" and feeling himself "Becomming
Traytor" simply by listening to the [no]-"thing." His immunity from
fear is only partial, but he is stunned, not debilitated: as the poem proceeds he gets to express disgust for the atmosphere at court while seeming less and less suffocated by it.

Trying to account for such large divergences from the Horatian model
as Donne's reflection on his hellish first visit to court as well as the
entire description of his second visit (155–244), Hester adduces Juvenal's
third satire as "(at least) a significant analogue and (at most) a possible
source for the second half of *Satyre IV*" (*Kinde Pity*, 128). Admitting
that specific borrowings are difficult to demonstrate, Hester nevertheless argues persuasively that the poems take similar stances toward the
shaky social position of the satirist, "treading dangerously the borders of
illegality and sedition." In each poem a speaker represents himself as "a
patriotic expatriate alienated by his convictions about the moral and
ethical foundations of his civilization," one who sees the cultural center
as "a theatrical parody of national values" (*Kinde Pity*, 130). The Roman
model, however, affects the construction of more than the final ninety
lines of *Satyre IV*.[49]

In Juvenal's poem, the voice of the satirist's friend Umbricius domi-

[49] Hester explicitly at first compares Juvenal's poem only to lines 155–244 of *Satyre
IV*, but as his analysis proceeds it becomes clear that he too sees the Roman model
exerting influence nearly throughout.

nates, as he explains his decision to abandon "Greekified" Rome for, ironically enough, the Greek colony at Cumae. Umbricius, because he is presented as a friend, is far closer to Juvenal than the bore in *Satyre IV* is to Donne, yet he serves the similar purpose of allowing Juvenal to distance himself from the dangerously sharp indignation "his" satire nevertheless expresses, and from the role of satirist itself. Donne as author and Juvenal as author, that is, find ways to buffer themselves from the outlaw associations of the satiric role. Donne as satiric persona, however, himself bears comparison to Juvenal's Umbricius, who details his disgust at foreigners' success and influence in Rome, where Greeklings squeeze out poor honest Romans like himself. So, as in Donne's poem, what we have is a virtuous speaker bemoaning the foreign-bred deceit and treachery threatening him and denying him a place (Donne's speaker is not poor, an important distinction).

The prime targets for Umbricius—foreign influence, intrigue, and treachery—are Donne's prime targets, too, especially in his portrait of the bore, who is a walking, talking example of the insidious Greekified insider who so offends Umbricius. Donne's fastidious Macrine and rough Glorius also have their analogues in the third satire, but most of the indignation in both poems is directed at the foppish slave to foreign influence who craves gossip and secrets. "What man wins favour nowadays," Umbricius asks, "unless he be an accomplice—one whose soul seethes and burns with secrets that must never be disclosed?" (49–50).[50] By making his fop a court insider who knows all the secrets, Donne gives the expected answer to the rhetorical question. "Quick of wit (*ingenium velox*) and of unbounded impudence," Umbricius complains, these Greeklings "are as ready of speech as Isaeus, and more torrential" (73–74). Here what matters is the difference: whereas Umbricius blasts away ingenuously but not ingeniously, and has therefore often been read as "an ironic persona undercut by his own hyperbole, ineptitude, and unproductive nostalgia" (Hester, *John Donne*, 131), Donne's "I" never relinquishes the sword of wit. In *Satyre IV* Glorius, like Donne's first-person persona, "jeasts like a licens'd foole, commands like law," but not the bore: Donne may follow Juvenal in many ways, but he isn't about to present anyone else as a quicker wit.

This difference is coordinate with Donne's apparent disinterest in the economic issues so disturbing to Umbricius. As in *Satyre I*, the "I" of *Satyre IV* claims not to have a motive for going to court:

---

[50] In *Juvenal and Persius*, trans. G. G. Ramsay (1940). A line now considered spurious accentuates Umbricius' charge that such climbers exploit suspicion: "These men want to discover the secrets of the family, and so make themselves feared" (113).

My minde, neither with prides itch, nor yet hath ben
Poyson'd with love to see, or to bee seene,
I had no suit there, nor new suite to shew,
Yet went to court. . . . (5–8)

Donne presents himself here, somewhat disingenuously, as without ambition, but also as secure enough in his stature not to need the "brav-
ery" of a new suit. He poises himself between the overly pointed and
laced Macrine (197–210) and the rough Glorius (220–27), but never identifies himself as poor or sympathetic to the poor in the way Juvenal's
Umbricius does. Umbricius laments that "the poor man gives food and
occasion for jest if his cloak be torn and dirty" (147–48), but Donne
consumes these occasions with appetite, slamming the fop himself for the
sorry state of his fashionable suit (29–34). Donne is hypersensitive to the
issues of status that clothes raise, and willing to exploit the discrepancy
between the pretensions of the fop or Macrine and the condition of his
wardrobe, but his critique seems to have little egalitarian aim.

Nearly half of Juvenal's poem traces the plight of the honest poor in
Rome, how they do most of the suffering caused by urban crowding, a
topic Donne hardly touches. Donne points to practices likely to increase
poverty, but does not offer vivid portraits of deprivation, or identify himself with those who are suffering or about to suffer. This absence is
telling. My aim here is not to stress that Donne is less sympathetic to
the poor than Juvenal or the persona Umbricius, but that for Donne
such self-representation seems to be nearly unthinkable. Given what I
am arguing Donne hopes to achieve through the writing of the satires,
for him to follow Juvenal (or Sir Thomas More) in expressing indignation at increasing poverty is as unlikely as for Jonson to express soli-
darity with bricklayers. Unlike such very different court satire as, say,
Thomas Deloney offers in *Jack of Newbury*, Donne has little class soli-
darity or status-based agenda and little desire to replace aristocratic
values with bourgeois values, although he does insist that his own
"merit" should be known. Implicit in his critique is above all one kind
of transfer of power: he wants in. It is true that when he reflects on his
first retreat from court in amazement and fear, his moral dissatisfaction
is presented in terms of status:

Low feare
Becomes the guiltie, not th'accuser; Then,
Shall I, nones slave, of high borne, or rais'd men
Feare frownes? And my mistresse Truth, betray thee
To th'huffing braggart, puft Nobility?

The language of ethics and the language of status intermingle reveal-ingly here, even if this is a fairly standard version of the sixteenth-cen-tury debate whether birth or merit produces true nobility. Although the critique of the "high borne" seems to align Donne with the bourgeois position, he is tactfully silent about just what he considers his status to be, precisely because he wants it to be indeterminate, fluid. He is not base, and thus reminds himself with the again-bite of inwit that he should not behave "basely," showing "low feare," but he also claims not to be "rais'd," not a climber of the kind he satirizes here and in *Satyre I*. Or is he?

Juvenal's Umbricius has already given up: Rome is no place for poor Romans. But Donne's persona has not, as his second visit to the court signifies. True, he eventually leaves again, shaking "like a spyed Spie" in the presence of the guard (237). But as his final request indicates, he has hopes that his satire and his worth will be recognized, granted the kind of authority enjoyed by those he has presented as less worthy of it, such as the foppish "privileg'd spie" or the "licens'd" jester Glorius:

> Preachers which are
> Seas of Wit and Arts, you can, then dare,
> Drowne the sinnes of this place, for, for mee
> Which am but a scarce brooke, it enough shall bee
> To wash the staines away; Though I yet
> With *Macchabees* modestie, the knowne merit
> Of my worke lessen: yet some wise man shall,
> I hope, esteeme my writs Canonicall. (237–44)

As James Baumlin protests, Donne's request for authority undercuts the satirist's righteous posture of self-sufficiency: "Since the effect of this satire is thus made contingent upon its reception by a specific audience, the poet must turn outside of himself—pass the baton, as it were—to 'preachers' or 'some wise man' like Egerton, who holds power at court and could enact the changes the satirist himself is incapable of effect-ing" (115). By making such a request within his satire, he "admits its immediate powerlessness." Baumlin is precisely right, and the admis-sion is unquestionably painful for Donne, but Donne's analysis of the situation is also unquestionably accurate: he *is* generally powerless to effect the kinds of changes he claims to desire. If, however, he had more power. . . .

Throughout the poem Donne has slipped in and out of the satirist's role, shadow-boxing with its most dangerous associations, jumping back and forth over the line. At the end, pointing to the constraints on his power, he offers both a confession and a petition. At the midpoint of the poem he vows to press on with, notably, both the truth-telling role of satirist and his own presence at court. Donne's ideal would no doubt be to jest without license and to walk in court without fear, since fear implies a lack of self-sufficient power, virtù, but he is too savvy to expect this ideal to be realized without the assistance of a more powerful insider at court. As Annabel Patterson cautions, we need to beware of treating Donne's pragmatism as any more vicious, careerist, or ambitious than that of others in his cultural position, a caution I admit to having partially ignored by downplaying the element of conscience in the poem.[51] Dependent on audience ratification like any performer at court—which is where *Satyre IV* is "located" in more than one sense—Donne has the wit to know exactly who in the audience supplies the most important ratification. Recognition of his performance, his wit, will mean recognition of his worth not merely as satirist but as courtier. He also knows, and wants to convey that he knows, that "Suspitious boldnesse to this place belongs, / And to'have as many eares as all have tongues." Donne's fear is politic as well as satirical, and he wants it both ways. As satire, Donne's quaking signifies the ease with which the court misjudges; as Umbricius complains, he is at the mercy of the Greekling, "For when once he has dropped into a facile ear one particle of his own and his country's poison, I am thrust from the door" (122–24). His fear is politic in that both through his own witty equivocation in the duel with the Makeron and through his deflection onto the Makeron of the poem's most dangerous satire, Donne has accomplished precisely what Quintilian describes as the effect of *suspicio*: if "the danger" involved in speaking against the powerful "can be avoided by any ambiguity of expression, the speaker's cunning will meet with universal approbation" (*Institutio*, 9.2.68). If Donne draws back from the brink at the end of the poem, it is only after he has pushed the game as far as it can go.

For Donne to be truly secure against fear, truly licensed, and truly able to effect reform, he would need the kind of power located well above even the Lord Keeper's sphere. Total freedom from judgment once belonged only, as Ernst H. Kantorowicz explains, to the Pope, who claimed sanction from 1 Corinthians 2:15: "The spiritual man judges all, but himself is judged by none." Kantorowicz traces how this maxim later became attributed to those at the height of secular power, to kings and to emperors, as in the declaration by Mattheus de Afflictus that "The emperor commands the others, but he is commanded by no one."

---

[51] See Patterson, "All Donne," 37–50, which takes aim especially at John Carey's biography. For the reading most sensitive to the author's conscience see Hester, *Kinde Pity*, 73–97.

James I, in what Kantorowicz calls a "pivotal" move in the development of absolutism, acknowledges in his "Speech to the Lords and Commons" of March 21, 1609, that God has this power "to judge all and be judged by none," but insists that "Kings are justly called Gods, for that they exercise a manner or resemblance of Divine Power on earth."[52] Kantorowicz (much less James) does not, however, point to Castiglione's injunction that courtiers astonish all and remain astonished by none as a scaled-down version of this maxim, an imitation at two removes of the most awful presence. Cloaking themselves in admirable style, courtier-poets were at the same time invoking for themselves the reflected aura of the divine.

In *James I and the Politics of Literature*, Jonathan Goldberg detailed the ways Jacobean writers appropriated to themselves the "stile of *Gods*" that James I claimed for himself, and threw it back at him with a vengeance.[53] Rightly, one of Goldberg's prime examples of how poets treated Stuart preoccupation with secrets, monsters, prodigies, and assorted "household trash" is *Volpone's* Sir Politic Would-Be (*James I*, 72–81), but like the airy nothing denied either a local habitation or a name in Jonson's Epigram 11, "On Some-Thing, That Walkes Some-Where," Sir Pol would seem to be heavily indebted to Donne's portrait of the strange thing in *Satyre IV*. Goldberg treats poets as reacting to James, but the interchange between king and court was reciprocal. The emphasis on suspicion as a hallmark of power was already established before James arrived, and precisely in that satellite of the court that he resuscitated, the Essex faction that had contributed so much to the dissemination of Tacitus. The lesson that obscurity preserves reverence was not exclusive to absolute monarchs, politic historians, or would-be courtiers. The most significant source for this lesson, paradoxically, was not political theory but religious discourse; there, embedded within defenses of divine obscurity, was the most sophisticated analysis of the psychology of wonder available. In this shared discourse were the roots of the cloaking strategy adopted by both courtiers and kings. The recognized appropriateness of admirable style for representing the divine also helps to explain why paradox, enigma, and conceits remained features of the seventeenth-century religious lyric long after the crush of competing aspirants that produced the shift in style had dissipated.

[52] Ernst H. Kantorowicz, *Selected Studies* (1965), 387, 388.
[53] The phrase "stile of *Gods*" is from the poem to Prince Henry prefaced to *Basilikon Doron*. See James I, *Political Works*, 3; Goldberg, *James I and the Politics of Literature* (1989), esp. 26–32 and 65–112.

4 Powerful Insinuations: Obscurity as Catalyst and Veil

Manuals for the overlapping activities of rhetoric, poetry, and conduct pointed late Renaissance poets to methods of evoking wonder, but texts investigating divine obscurity gave them at least as much reason to pursue it. By investigating obscurity both in concepts of the divine and in divinely authored scripture, philosophers and theologians in the mainstream and in eccentric, esoteric traditions fueled the later pursuit of signs of wonder, especially because they offered acute examinations of the psychology of wonder. In particular, they connected obscurity to reverence. Christian examinations of the *deus absconditus*, unsurprisingly, often harmonize with the central insight concerning obscurity offered by the Greek rhetorical tradition, that, in the words of Demetrius, "obscurity often produces force, since what is distantly hinted is more forcible, while what is plainly stated is held cheap" (*On Style*, 254). Through opaque style, according to Augustine and Aquinas as well as Clement of Alexandria, Pseudo-Dionysius, and Nicholas of Cusa, authors could discourage the profane multitude from investigating divine matters and also stimulate the intellects of worthy students, whose interpretive ability was proof of their distinction, or even of their election.[1]

---

[1] On Christian defenses of obscurity and metaphor, see Jean Pépin, "Saint Augustin et la fonction protreptique de l'allégorie," *Recherches Augustiniennes* 1 (1958): 243–86; H.-I. Marrou, *Saint Augustin et la fin de la culture antique* (1938), 299–327 and 469–94; Kathy Eden, "The Rhetorical Tradition and Augustinian Hermeneutics in *De doctrina christiana*," *Rhetorica* 8 (1990): 45–63; Mazzeo, *Renaissance and Seventeenth-Century Studies*, 1–28; Marcia L. Colish, "St. Augustine's Rhetoric of Silence

In his discussion of "Poesie Allusive, or Parabolical" in *De Dignitate et Augmentis Scientiarum*, 2.13, Francis Bacon neatly points to these two functions of obscurity—obscurity as catalyst and veil. This "sacred and venerable" kind of poetry, which "excels the rest," is according to Bacon "of ambiguous use, and applied to contrary ends": "For it serves for *Obscuration*; and it serveth also for *Illustration*: in this it seems, there was sought a way how to teach; in that an Art how to conceal."[2] Both of these functions, teaching and concealing, depend on wonder.

Obscurity promotes learning by increasing our wonder about that which we do not understand. Augustine in particular emphasizes that obscurity provides an opportunity for *exercitatio*, or stimulating mental and spiritual exercise. By remaining veiled, however, an object of representation remains remote, unfamiliar. This strangeness, as Aristotle, Demetrius, and "Longinus" insist in antiquity and Boccaccio, among others, repeats in the Renaissance, provokes and preserves wonder. In Christian thought, with its view of the human intellect as limited and divine nature as incomprehensible, obscurity may be a stimulus less to knowledge than to faith. Yet the road from obscurity through Augustinian *exercitatio* to faith passes invariably through wonder. In order to understand Christian treatments of astonishing obscurity as both catalyst and veil, however, we must turn again to Aristotle.

For Aristotle, philosophy begins in wonder. Here, as in his identification of wonder as an effect of epic and tragedy, he follows the lead of Plato. In the *Theaetetus* Socrates assures the frustrated student that there is good reason to boggle at the paradoxes of being and becoming: "This sense of wonder is the mark of the philosopher" (155d). "Philosophy," Socrates continues, "indeed has no other origin, and he was a good genealogist who made Iris [philosophy] the daughter of Thaumas

---

Revisited," *Augustinian Studies* 9 (1978): 15–24, and *The Mirror of Language* (1968), 7–54; R. A. Markus, "St. Augustine on Signs," in *Augustine: A Collection of Critical Essays*, ed. Markus (1972), 61–91; B. Darrell Jackson, "The Theory of Signs in St. Augustine's *De Doctrina Christiana*," ibid., 92–147; and Valerie Laporte, "John Donne and the Esoteric Tradition" (Ph.D. diss., Columbia University, 1986). On the relationship between Neoplatonism and the Christian emphasis on obscurity, see James A. Coulter, *The Literary Microcosm* (1976), 49–72 and 105–30; Kustas, *Byzantine Rhetoric*, 63–100 and 159–99; Trimpi, *Muses*, 164–240; and the essays in Dominic J. O'Meara, ed., *Neoplatonism and Christian Thought* (1982). For obscurity in the Renaissance especially, see Gombrich, *Symbolic Images*, 123–95; Wind, *Pagan Mysteries in the Renaissance*, esp. 1–25 and 218–35; and James V. Mirollo, *Mannerism and Renaissance Poetry* (1984), 99–124.

[2] In *Literary Criticism*, ed. Tayler, 148–49.

[wonder]."³ In the *Metaphysics*, similarly, Aristotle credits wonder with initiating philosophy:

> For it is owing to their wonder that men both now begin and first began to philosophize; they wondered originally at the obvious difficulties, then advanced little by little and stated difficulties about the greater matters, e.g. about the phenomena of the moon and those of the sun and the stars, and about the genesis of the universe. And a man who is puzzled and wonders thinks himself ignorant (whence even the lover of myth is a lover of wisdom, for myth is composed of wonders); therefore since they philosophized in order to escape from ignorance, evidently they were pursuing science in order to know, and not for any utilitarian end. (982b11–20)⁴

Wonder is in part the recognition of ignorance that must precede the acquisition of knowledge. Wonder is necessary because it increases our desire to know: "the object of wonder is an object of desire" (*Rhetoric*, 1.11;1371a31–34). Aristotle describes this movement from ignorance to knowledge in terms derived from his physics, as a physical disruption that necessitates a subsequent attempt to return to a natural state: wonder is an itch knowledge must scratch.

In his *Commentary on the Metaphysics of Aristotle*, Albertus Magnus amplifies this physical quality by making it more graphic:

> Now, wonder (*Admirationem*) is defined as a constriction and suspension of the heart caused by amazement at the sensible appearance of something so portentous, great, and unusual, that the heart suffers a systole. Hence wonder is something like fear in its effect on the heart. This effect of wonder . . . springs from an unfulfilled but felt desire to know the cause of that which appears portentous and unusual: so it was in the beginning when men, up to that time unskilled, began to philosophize—they marvelled at certain difficulties, which were, as a matter of fact, fairly easy to solve. (*In I Met.*, Tr. 2, ch. 6; *Opera Omnia* 6:30; trans. Cunningham, *Collected Essays*, 70–71)

³ See *Plato's Theory of Knowledge (The Theaetetus and the Sophist of Plato)*, trans. Francis M. Cornford (1957), 43. As Cornford notes, this genealogy (and etymology) is presented in *Cratylus*, 398d. Iris is also the rainbow, messenger of the gods, and the scientific investigations of the rainbow by Descartes and Newton earned praise from poets in the eighteenth century but blame from poets in the Romantic period who regretted that such demystification decreased their opportunities for wonder. See chapter 5 below.

⁴ On Aristotle's comparison of the lover of myth to the lover of wisdom, cf. *Republic*, 475c. At *Rhetoric*, 1371b27, Aristotle defines "scientific wisdom (*sophia*)" as "the knowledge of many wonderful (*thaumaston*) things."

Like the Greek rhetoricians, Albertus treats wonder as akin to fear: it has a powerful physical effect, and is produced by that for which we feel compelled to find an explanation, but cannot. (When James advises Henry in *Basilikon Doron* to "admire reverently such obscure places [in scripture] as ye understand not," what he neglects is precisely this element of wonder, wonder as Marlovian thirst that feeds the desire to know.)

Albertus, significantly, continues his gloss by adducing Aristotle's treatment of wonder in the *Poetics* as the *telos* of poetry:

Now the man who is puzzled and wonders apparently does not know. Hence wonder (*admiratio*) is the movement of the man who does not know on his way to finding out, to get at the bottom of that at which he wonders and to determine its cause. A token in proof is that the famous Philomithes according to this way of looking at the matter is a philosopher, for he constructed his stories out of wonderful events. . . . Thus Aristotle shows in that branch of logic which is called poetic that the poet fashions his story for the purpose of exciting wonder, and that the further effect of wonder is to excite inquiry. . . .

Hence poetry offers a method of philosophizing, just as do the other sciences of logic. But the other sciences or branches offer a method of proving a proposition by reasoning, that is, by conclusive or probable argument; poetry, however, offers no method of proof but rather a method of wonder by which we are incited to inquiry.[5]

Wonder incites inquiry, and poetry offers a method of wonder. The goal of poetry is therefore the production of "an unfulfilled but felt desire to know the cause of that which appears portentous and unusual"; like the *charaktēr deinos* of Demetrius, poetry in general thus aims to provoke the audience to make inferences, to move from perplexity toward knowledge.

For Aquinas, this incitement to inquiry and hope of eventual knowledge is pleasurable. In explaining why, Aquinas emphasizes, as Theophrastus and Demetrius had, that we congratulate ourselves for seeing through obscurity. He admits that contemplating what we know is "in itself more pleasurable than inquiry into things unknown," but insists that sometimes "inquiry is more pleasurable in that it has more drive

---

[5] "The poet Philomithes," Cunningham explains, "is a character that grew from a misreading of the Greek text in the passage in which Aristotle states that 'the lover of myth (*philomuthos*) is in a sense a lover of Wisdom, for the myth is composed of wonders' (*Metaphysics* 1.2. 982b18–19)" (*Collected Essays*, 71–72).

and springs from a greater desire" (*Summa Theologiae*, 1–2.32.8).[6] "But wonder (*admiratio*)," he continues, "is a kind of desire for knowledge"; this desire begins "when one sees an effect and does not know its cause, or when the cause of the particular effect is one that exceeds his power of understanding." The process of inquiry by which we overcome ignorance is therefore pleasurable, "and consequently a man takes the greatest pleasure in those things which he discovers for himself or learns from the ground up." If we can overcome perplexity by ourselves, we will especially enjoy the movement from ignorance through wonder to knowledge. Aquinas notes that any event or representation that causes us to wonder offers an opportunity for us to make this pleasurable transition, planting a seed that we nourish through our attempts to understand.

In his answer to another objection to the idea that wonder is pleasurable, Aquinas offers the other main justification of obscurity: that it keeps us from becoming overly familiar with divine things, and therefore preserves our sense of them as exalted. Aquinas first points out that the usual and habitual are pleasant, and cites Augustine's opinion (*In Joan.*, tr. 24) that "what one is used to is not wonderful"; "therefore," he initially concludes, "wonder is precisely not a cause of pleasure." Yet he responds that "what is unusual can be pleasurable, either with respect to the process of learning, since our desire for knowledge is proportional to the marvellousness of the subject, or with respect to the actual doing, since the mind is strongly impelled by desire to that which is felt intensely because of novelty." That which is wonderful is unusual, but the pleasure we feel at responding to our desire to learn about it compensates for the absence of the pleasure that accompanies what is familiar.

In saying that "our desire for knowledge is proportional to the marvellousness of the subject," Aquinas points to what Wesley Trimpi has called "the ancient dilemma of knowledge and representation" (*Muses*, 98). This dilemma arises from our different ways of evaluating knowledge, a dilemma Aristotle presents in the opening sentence of *De anima*: "While knowledge of any kind is a thing to be honoured and prized, one kind of it may, either by reason of its greater exactness or of a higher dignity and greater wonderfulness in its objects, be more hon-

---

[6] I use Cunningham's translation (*Collected Essays*, 72–74) of this article from the *Summa Theologiae*, in which Aquinas draws on Aristotle for authority throughout, citing the passages on wonder from the *Metaphysics*, *Rhetoric*, and *Poetics* examined in chapter 1 and above. In the first passage I have quoted in this sentence, Aquinas is quoting Aristotle's *Ethics*, 10.7: "Sed *delectabilius est contemplari iam cognita, quam inquirere ignota*, ut Philosophus dicit" (*Summa Theologiae*, 1a2ae.32, 8).

ourable and precious than another" (402a1–3). Although we are glad to know much about things that we do not consider especially important, we also rate highly even slight knowledge of objects that are more excellent or more wonderful ("*thaumasiōterōn*"). By saying in the *Metaphysics* that the wondering mind moves from the "obvious difficulties" to "difficulties about greater matters," Aristotle suggests that there is a correlation between the degree of excellence inherent in an object of knowledge and the degree of desire with which we pursue it.[7] Our wonder increases according to how unusual, distant, or excellent an object appears to be, but according to Aristotle such objects are knowable in inverse proportion to their marvelousness: the greater the object the more obscure our knowledge of it, and the more accurate our knowledge of an object, the less wonderful and excellent we tend to find it.

To illustrate how this ancient dilemma influenced ideas about representation, Trimpi cites a debate in Philostratus' *Life of Apollonius of Tyana* over Greek and Egyptian methods of expressing the nature of the gods through sculpture. Thespesion supports the Egyptian method of representation, Apollonius the Greek method. Their positions, Trimpi argues, exemplify the most common responses to the dilemma: (1) to "assume the incompatibility of its two opposing terms—the excellence of an object as opposed to the accuracy of an inquiry into it—and pursue these two terms separately," or (2) to "attempt to relate one to the other in order to relax the tension between them" (*Muses*, 102). Thespesion chooses the first method, the Egyptian: he prefers to represent the gods through exact, lifelike statues of birds and animals, which arbitrarily symbolize divine excellence. Apollonius defends the Greek practice of representing gods in human form, through "an imaginative conception which expresses at least some of the divine superiority" (104).

Apollonius finds the accurate but arbitrary representations of gods in animal form used by Egyptian artists likely to lower the dignity of the gods themselves, but Thespesion disagrees. "I think," he argues, "that you criticise our religion very superficially; for if the Egyptians have any wisdom, they show it by their deep respect and reverence in the representation of the gods, and by the circumstance that they fashion their forms as symbols of a profound inner meaning, so as to enhance their solemnity and august character." For Thespesion, the animal forms preserve reverence for the gods' marvelousness. Apollonius questions whether these images are as "august or awe-inspiring (*semnon de dē ē emphobon*)" as the Egyptians would wish, and proposes that "if they are to be held august for the hidden meanings which they convey, surely

[7] See Trimpi, *Muses*, 130–31.

the gods in Egypt would have met with much greater reverence, if no images of them had ever been set up at all." As Apollonius implies, the extreme form of the Egyptian position would be to shrink completely from representation. For Thespesion, however, the Greek practice is less likely than the Egyptian to inspire awe, and any attempt to capture divine excellence robs it of its wonderfulness.

As Trimpi points out, Thespesion's position "is articulated with increasing conviction and detail by the Christian and Neoplatonic mystical traditions" (105). For Plotinus the beautiful object is a place to start, not rest: "For he who contemplates physical beauty must not lose himself therein, but he must recognize that it is an image and a vestige and a shadow, and he must flee to that of which it is a likeness" (*Enn.*1.6.8). In his *Commentary on the Republic of Plato*, Proclus praises the inventors of mythology on similar grounds, for having created fictions about the gods that, by treating them as monstrous, force us to intuit their true excellence:

> [Mythmakers] imitate the surpassing quality of the models by rendering the creations of the divine by means of expressions as antithetical as possible to the divine. Those who go furthest in this direction reveal by those things which [in us] are contrary to nature (*para phusin*) the very things which, in the gods, are superior to nature (*huper phusin*), by failures of rational calculation (*paralogois*) what is more divine than reason itself, and by objects which appear ugly to us what transcends in its simple wholeness the beauty of any individual part [which remains of necessity incomplete]. In this way, these fathers are likely to put us in mind again of the surpassing eminence of the gods. (*Comm. Rep.* 1.77.13–30)[8]

Monstrous images arouse wonder both directly, because of their disparity from what is accepted as natural, and indirectly, because they maintain our sense of the incomprehensibility, and thus the wonderful excellence, of what they symbolize. The unnatural hints at the supernatural, the monstrous at the miraculous. For Plotinus brevity serves a coordinate function: like paradoxical representation, it points to the inexpressible. So the "wise of Egypt," he says

> . . . left aside the writing forms that take in the detail of words and sentences—those characters that . . . convey the propositions of reasoning—and drew pictures instead, engraving in the temple-inscrip-

---

[8] Quoted in Trimpi, *Muses*, 217; see also Coulter, *Literary Microcosm*, 49–57 and 107–26.

tions a separate image for every separate item: thus they exhibited the absence of discursiveness in the Intellectual Realm. . . . Later from this wisdom in unity there appears, in another form of being, an image, already less compact, which announces the original in terms of discourse and unravels the causes by which things are such that the wonder rises how a generated world can be so excellent. (*Enneads* 5.8.6).[9]

The less compact the image, Plotinus implies, the less wonderful the object of representation will seem.

From Clement of Alexandria through Pseudo-Dionysius to Nicholas of Cusa, Christian advocates of negative theology likewise encouraged visual hieroglyphics and verbal enigmas. Just as the impulse to conceal that motivates hieroglyphs reaches its vanishing point in the complete avoidance of visual images, so brevity in speech ends in silence. In discussions such as Clement's the two primary rationales for obscurity—as shield to astound the profane and as goad to prompt inquiry—are often presented simultaneously.

Clement draws most often on the authority of Paul in 1 Corinthians 2, arguing that the limited mental and spiritual capacities of the crowd dictate that "prophecies and oracles are spoken in enigmas." Brief, enigmatic utterances are intended, like the sphinxes in front of Egyptian temples, "to signify that the doctrine respecting God is enigmatical and obscure."[10] They serve the function, that is, of the warning James gives to Henry: they "tell" the crowd to "admire reverently" what should be seen as beyond their capacity. Yet, at the same time, Clement emphasizes the pedagogical value of obscurity. In an earlier book of the *Stromata* he had reaffirmed Plato's statement in the *Theaetetus* that knowledge begins with wonder, and had defined philosophy as desire for the true being and of knowledge pertaining to it (2.45.4–6.).[11] Here he treats concise Greek proverbs such as "Know thyself" as examples of the "wisdom, hidden, dark" that the Holy Spirit promises to give us (Isaiah xlv.3). As a rule, "Dreams and signs are all more or less obscure to men . . . in order that research, introducing to the understanding of

[9] Quoted in Trimpi, *Muses*, 184–85.
[10] Clement of Alexandria, *Stromata*, ed. The Rev. Alexander Roberts and James Donaldson (1951), 5.4, 5.5. Clement's interpretation of the sphinxes, however, contrasts with Thespesion's insistence on symbols that inspire fearful awe (cf. Trimpi, *Muses*, 234): the sphinxes signify "perhaps also that we ought both to love and fear the Divine Being: to love Him as gentle and benign to the pious; to fear Him as inexorably just to the impious; for the sphinx shows the image of a wild beast and of a man together."
[11] I have paraphrased the editor's French translation of Clement's Greek text.

enigmas, may haste to the discovery of truth." Enigmatic brevity in speech has the same twin effects as visual representations of the gods in animal form, concealing and provoking.

Dissimilar images and concise statements are likewise coordinate in the writings of Pseudo-Dionysius, whose influence in the Renaissance is easier to demonstrate than Clement's.[12] Dionysius takes pains to make clear that sensible images of God are not to be taken literally, but are rather intended "to uplift our mind in a manner suitable to our nature" (*Celestial Hierarchy*, 2.1; 137B). Like the Egyptian Thespesion, Pseudo-Dionysius explicitly rejects images that might seem more fitting in favor of "dissimilar similarities":

> Indeed, it could be argued that if the theologians wanted to give corporeal form to what is purely incorporeal, they should have resorted to a more appropriate and related fashioning, that they should have begun with what we would hold to be noblest, immaterial and transcendent beings, instead of drawing on a multiplicity of the earthiest forms and applying these to godlike realities which are utterly simple and heavenly. Now perhaps this intends to lead us upward and not lead the celestial appearances down into incongruous dissimilarities. But in fact it illicitly defies the divine powers and also misleads our mind, entangling it in profane compositions. (2.2; 137C)

In short, "Since the way of negation appears to be more suitable to the realm of the divine and since positive affirmations are always unfitting to the hiddenness of the inexpressible, a manifestation through dissimilar shapes is more correctly to be applied to the invisible" (2.3; 141A).[13] When confronted by scriptural representations of angels with an eagle's wings or ox's feet, he says, his mind "was not permitted to dwell on imagery so inadequate, but was provoked to get behind the material show, to get accustomed to the idea of going beyond appearances to

[12] See the introductory essays in *Pseudo-Dionysius: The Complete Works*, trans. Colm Luibheid (1987), especially Karlfried Froehlich's "Pseudo-Dionysius and the Reformation of the Sixteenth Century." All texts of Pseudo-Dionysius cited are those in this edition unless otherwise specified. According to Froehlich, "Except for the Bible and perhaps the works of Boethius, no writing of the early Christian era received similar attention in terms of translations, excerpts, commentaries, and . . . cumulative corpora" (33). He notes that Torquato Tasso cites Pseudo-Dionysius when arguing that poetic images serve a function beyond logical demonstration: "Now to lead to the contemplation of divine things and thus awaken the mind with images (*con l'imagini*), as the mystical theologian and the poet do, is a far nobler work than to instruct by demonstration, the function of the scholastic theologian" (32).

[13] Cf. Julian the Apostate on incongruous myths (II.119; cited in LaPorte, "John Donne," 195).

those upliftings which are not of this world" (2.5; 145B).[14] Dionysius
explains why we use shapes at all by pointing to their twin purposes:
presenting to our limited minds "the permitted forms of the marvelous
and unformed sights," and concealing truth from "the *hoi polloi.*"[15]

If these images promote human understanding of the divine, it is an
understanding beyond the capacity of images or language to convey: it is
apprehension that is not comprehensible. As Paul states in the text that
Bottom in *MND* garbles when referring to his strange and admirable
dream, "Eye hath not seen, nor ear heard" the heavenly blessings (1 Cor.
2.9).[16] Reverence for the divine requires brevity, and the approach to the
divine involves moving closer and closer to silence: "The higher we rise,
the more concise our language becomes, for the Intelligibles present
themselves in increasingly condensed fashion. When we shall advance
into the Darkness beyond the Intelligible it will no longer be a matter of
conciseness, for the words and thought cease altogether. When our discourse descends from the higher to the lower, its volume increases, the
further we move from these heights" (*Mystical Theology*, 3; 1033B–C).[17]
Pseudo-Dionysius thus perhaps offers a theological equivalent of Demetrius' combination within the *charaktēr deinos* of both obscure brevity and far-fetched metaphor: he finds that "dissimilar images" and conciseness fading into silence incite wonder. His "dissimilar similarities,"
admittedly, are visual images rather than metaphors, but they operate
on the same principle, "telling" what the signified is not, in order to
drive us toward knowledge of what it is. Even those without direct access to the texts of Pseudo-Dionysius could easily have been exposed to

[14] Compare Montaigne at his most skeptical, in the *Apology for Raymond Sebond*:
"We can not worthily conceive of these high, mysterious, and divine promises; if wee
can but in any sort conceive them, and so imagine them aright; they must be thought
to be inimaginable, unspeakable and incomprehensible, and absolutely and perfectly
other than those of our miserable experience. No eye can behold, (saith Saint *Paul*)
The hap that God prepareth for his elect, nor can it possibly enter the heart of man (I
Cor.ii.9)" (*Essayes*, 2.12, trans. Florio, 463). Because of the human mind's inability to
frame adequate images of the divine, Montaigne prefers distant and arbitrary symbols:
"Things most unknowne are fittest to bee deified. Wherefore, to make gods of our
selves (as antiquitie hath done,) it exceeds the extreme weakness of discourse. I
would rather have folowed those that worshipped the Serpent, the Dogge and the
Oxe, forsomuch as their Nature, and being is least knowne to us; and we may more
lawfully imagine what we list of those beasts and ascribe extraordinarie faculties
unto them" (461).
[15] Cf. Pseudo-Dionysius, *The Ecclesiastical Hierarchy*, 1, 377A; and Epistle 9,
1105C and 1108A–C.
[16] Cf. Isaiah 64.4, and 2 Cor. 12.2–4, where Paul, rapt into the third heaven, "was
caught up into paradise, and heard unspeakable words, which it is not lawful for man
to utter."
[17] Quoted in and trans. Gombrich, 168.

his ideas about representation, since Aquinas uses his argument for dissimilar similarities to defend metaphor in scripture.[18] Since "what He is *not* is clearer to us than what He is," "similitudes drawn from things farthest away from God form within us a truer estimate that God is above whatsoever we may say or think of Him" (*Summa Theologiae* I.Q.1,a9,r.3). Like concise but weighty statements, symbols reflect the depth of both our ignorance and our desire to know.

Pseudo-Dionysius also underpins the mystical theology of Nicholas of Cusa, who acknowledges him as source of the idea of God as a coincidence of what to us seem opposites, *discordia concors* (*De docta ignorantia*, 1.16). His influence also makes itself felt in *De visione dei*, where Cusa paradoxically attributes our shadowy apprehension of the divine face to its overwhelming brilliance (6.22), "dark with excessive bright":

> O Face exceedingly lovely! All the things which have received the gift of looking thereupon do not suffice for admiring (*admirari*) its beauty.
>
> In all faces the Face of faces is seen in a veiled and symbolic manner (*velate et in aenigmate*). But it is not seen in an unveiled manner as long as the seeker does not enter, above all faces, into a certain secret and hidden silence (*occultum silentium*) wherein there is no knowledge or concept of a face.[19]

Silence and obscurity accompany the Face of faces, seen as Paul says "per aenigmate in speculum." As when looking into the sun, blindness means sight: "For that obscuring mist arises in his eye as a result of the excellence of the light of the sun. Therefore, the more dense he knows the obscuring mist to be, the more truly he attains, within that mist, unto the invisible light." The looker's blindness here, like that of the soul emerging from Plato's cave, occurred because "the passage from the deeper dark of ignorance into a more luminous world and the greater brightness had dazzled its vision" (*Republic* 7, 518a; cf. *De docta ignorantia*, 3.11).[20] Since, according to Milton, even the seraphim are dazzled by God's "glorious brightness," the human soul should not be surprised to find wonder alongside even at the heights of its contemplative flight, or to see deepening murk as evidence of approaching light.

---

[18] See Trimpi, *Muses*, 105.

[19] On the influence of Pseudo-Dionysius here, see *Nicholas of Cusa's Dialectical Mysticism*, trans. Jasper Hopkins (1985), 19.

[20] On blindness as caused by an excess of either darkness or light for both Aristotle and Plato, and the effect of their analyses on later ideas of style, see Trimpi, "HASD," 49n24.

Movement toward the divine is for Cusa a function of appetite, which "cannot cease from desiring but is directed toward infinity" (*De visione dei*, 16.72). Just as for Aquinas "our desire for knowledge is proportional to the marvellousness of the subject," Cusa insists that desire for God exceeds all other desires because God is "incomprehensible and infinite." For Aquinas, however, we especially desire knowledge of God because God *is* most marvelous; for Cusa, God *must be* especially marvelous, in order to be the object of greatest desire. According to Cusa, paradoxically, "the more incomprehensible I comprehend You-my-God to be, the more I attain unto you, because the more I attain the End of my desire" (16.73). "The intellect," he argues, "can be fully satisfied only by an intelligible object which it knows to be so intelligible that this object can never fully be understood" (16.74). All attempts to comprehend God fail therefore, but feed a desire that leads ultimately to apprehension of God "by means of a certain mental rapture." This rapture or *O! altitudo*, which in *De sapientia* Cusa associates explicitly with admiration, requires incomprehensibility.

Less fervent but more influential in aligning obscurity with silence and desire is Augustine, who shares with Cusa and Pseudo-Dionysius a heritage of Neoplatonism and whom Aquinas also draws on to defend obscure metaphors in scripture. The "darkness of figures," Aquinas argues, "serves to exercise those eager to learn (*utilis est ad exercitium studiosorum*)" (*Summa Theologiae* I.Q.1,a9,r.2). *Exercitatio*, the catalytic function of obscurity, is key for Augustine, but seemingly compatible with its cloaking function; the authors of scripture wrote "with a useful and healthful obscurity for the purpose of exercising and sharpening, as it were, the minds of the readers and of destroying fastidiousness and stimulating the desire to learn" (*On Christian Doctrine*, 4.8.22).[21] Despite cautioning preachers against imitating scriptural obscurity, Augustine points out that metaphorical language pleases the audience (2.6.7–8; cf. 4.7.15). He claims to have difficulty explaining why he prefers to receive what he considers the same lesson in metaphorical rather than literal form, but feels safe in concluding that "no one doubts that things are perceived more readily through similitudes and that what is sought with difficulty is discovered with more pleasure." With characteristic insight, Augustine captures the psychology of wonderful obscurity: "Those who do not find what they seek directly stated labor in hunger; those who do not seek because they have what they wish at

---

[21] See Pépin, "La fonction protreptique," 254–56; and Marrou, *Saint Augustin*, 299–327.

once frequently become indolent in disdain." Again, obscurity preserves reverence for the holy while prompting the desire to learn.[22]

Joseph Mazzeo finds in Augustine "the germ of a new sensibility based on the positive evaluation of obscurity, or at least of what later developed into a new sensibility."[23] Although Augustine's view represents a much later stage in the development of this sensibility than his statement indicates, Mazzeo is certainly right to emphasize Augustine's influence on literature, rhetoric, and interpretation. When combined with his reevaluation of the Ciceronian levels of style—his rejection of a scale of styles proportional to the relative importance of various subjects, and his defense of the scriptural *sermo humilis*, or humble style— Augustine's position on obscurity bears comparison to that of Demetrius. Both authors find the essence of sublimity in passion rather than in impressive artistic patterning (*On Christian Doctrine*, 4.42; *On Style*, 7–9, e.g.), and both find obscurity and brevity forceful. Although, as Shuger argues, Augustine's ideas concerning excellence of style are likely to have influenced Renaissance practice more pervasively than Demetrius', together Demetrius and Augustine made the rough, obscure, or strong-lined style seem not plain, but grand.[24]

Augustine's attempt to see eloquence in the simplicity of the Bible and to defend difficulty as a cause of spiritual exercise had an incalculable effect on methods of scriptural exegesis, on apologies for poetry,

[22] Cf. Augustine, *Letters*, 120.5: "Of certain of His wonderful works it is better sometimes for the reason to be hidden; otherwise, our minds, weighed down with weariness, might hold them cheap if we had knowledge of their causes. There are others, and they are many, who are more impressed by wonder at the objects than by a knowledge of their causes (qui plus tenentur admiratione rerum quam cognitione causarum), and when miracles cease to be wonderful, they have to be roused to faith in the invisible by visible wonders."

[23] Mazzeo, *Renaissance and Seventeenth-Century Studies*, 17; see also Erich Auerbach, *Literary Language and Its Public in Late Latin Antiquity and in the Middle Ages*, trans. Ralph Manheim (1965), esp. 36–81; and *Mimesis*, trans. Willard R. Trask (1953), 66–74; Marrou, *Saint Augustin*, 489–91; Shuger, *Sacred Rhetoric*, 41–117. Shuger asserts that "the decisive influence on Renaissance rhetoric was neither hellenism nor Ciceronianism but Christianity," and that Augustine "is the principal figure in the adaptation of Classical rhetoric to Christian purposes" (41–42).

[24] Shuger, *Sacred Rhetoric*, 41; see also Ruth Wallerstein, *Studies in Seventeenth-Century Poetic* (1965), 72–81. Marcia Colish, reexamining what Mazzeo calls Augustine's Platonic "rhetoric of silence," has demonstrated that Augustine frequently views silence as imbedded within systems of signification—speech, music—rather than transcendent; she has made clear that Augustine drew on Aristotelian, Stoic, and Ciceronian sources—as well as Platonic—in developing his understanding of silence ("St. Augustine's Rhetoric of Silence Revisited"). Colish has not, however, refuted Mazzeo's thesis that in *On Christian Doctrine* Augustine adopts a Platonic or Neoplatonic view of signification, in which the inevitable failure of any sign to represent the divine adequately leads ultimately to silence.

myth, and parable (including those of Boccaccio and Bacon), and on poetic practice from the *trobar clus* of the troubadours, through Dante, to well into the seventeenth century. Most notably here, his view of metaphor as cause of continued wonder at the doctrine it conceals and reveals, and of scripture as wonderful in both its simplicity and its profundity, is championed by John Donne.

In the *Devotions*, Donne identifies God as "a figurative, a metaphorical God" as well as "a direct God . . . a literal God" (124). In God's words Donne finds:

> such a height of figures, such voyages, such peregrinations to fetch remote and precious metaphors, such extensions, such spreadings, such curtains of allegories, such third heavens of hyperboles, so harmonious elocutions, so retired and so reserved expressions, so commanding persuasions, so persuading commandments, such sinews even in thy milk, and such things in thy words, as all profane authors seem of the seed of the serpent that creeps, thou art the Dove that flies.

Like Augustine, Donne contrasts scripture, which as a teacher of rhetoric Saint Augustine had felt needed defense in light of its differences from the Ciceronian mode of eloquence, to secular works. He also, like Augustine, insists that scriptural style has value for its simplicity and majesty: "O, what words but thine can express the inexpressible texture and composition of thy word, in which to one man that argument that binds his faith to believe that to be the word of God, is the reverent simplicity of the word, and to another the majesty of the word; and in which two men equally pious may meet, and one wonder that all should not understand it, and the other as much that any man should" (124–25).[25] For Donne scripture both appeals to various audiences and performs various functions: "so, Lord, thou givest us the same word for our satisfaction and for our inquisition, for our instruction and for our admiration too. . . ." Satisfaction and instruction are functions of clarity and ease of interpretation, inquisition and admiration of obscurity and challenge. Donne treats metaphor and obscurity as methods of inquisition most fully in the *Essays in Divinity*, and as methods of admiration in

[25] Cf. Augustine, *Confessions*, Book 12: "I would then, had I . . . been enjoined by Thee to write the book of Genesis, have desired such a power of expression and such a style to be given me, that neither they who cannot yet understand how God created, might reject the sayings, as beyond their capacity; and they who had attained thereto, might find what true opinion soever they had by thought arrived at, not passed over in those few words of that Thy servant" (*Confessions*, trans. Edward B. Pusey, D.D. (1961), 224).

the fourth Prebend sermon, on *Psalms* 65.5. In both texts, however, the underlying association of obscurity with wonder should be borne in mind.

In the *Essays in Divinity*, which also contain Donne's lengthiest examination of miracles, Donne treats obscurity as an antidote to the human tendency to "slumber in a lazy faith" (16). John L. Klause has recently demonstrated that Donne habitually attacks spiritual laziness, slowness, or stupidity. He has shown that Donne feels compelled to seek "the experience of miracles" out of fear that an excess of "familiarity with greatnesse" would lead him to such slumber.[26] Miracles, which Augustine defines as "whatever appears that is difficult or unusual above the hope or power of them who wonder" (*De Utilitate Credendi*, 16.34), find their verbal equivalent in strange and admirable style. Our work at puzzling out the mysteries of scripture will have the effect that Donne attributes to our inquiries into mysteries in the book of creation: "God will be glorified both in our searching these Mysteries, because it testifies our liveliness towards him, and in our not finding them" (27). Inquiry into the mysteries of God must begin and end in wonder, but interpretations of scripture often end in at least the conviction of having found a solution.

In such cases, Donne notes, the expositor is proud to have risen to the challenge. Such expositors even, as in the ancient rhetorical tradition of emphasis (not to mention the modern profession of scholarship), feel proprietal about their readings. Donne remarks that Francis George, for example, became angry when he found out that Augustine had noticed before him that "*the Ark of Noah*, and *our body* had the same proportion and correspondency in their parts" (*Essays in Divinity*, 32). "So natural is the disease of *Meum et Teum* to us," Donne concludes, "that even contemplative men, which have abandon'd temporall propriety, are delighted, and have their *Complacentiam*, in having their spirituall Meditations and inventions knowne to be theirs: for, *qui velit ingenio cedere, rarus erit* [rare is the one who would be willing to relinquish a claim to genius]."[27] Although Donne criticizes allegorical readings that convert the "strong toyles" of scripture into "fine cobwebs to catch flies," he also gives credit to those who solve apparent difficulties of interpretation. Such readers, Donne's language implies, breathe life into passages prematurely buried in darkness. In explaining the specific problem of inconsistent numbering in the Bible, Donne offers a general apology for scriptural difficulty:

[26] Klause, "Donne and the Wonderful," 53.
[27] My translation.

To make men sharpe and industrious in the inquisition of truth, he withdrawes it from present apprehension, and obviousness. For naturally great wits affect the reading of obscure books, wrastle and sweat in the explication of prophesies, digg and thresh out the words of unlegible hands, resuscitate and bring to life again the mangled, and lame fragmentary images and characters in Marbles and Medals, because they have a joy and complacency in the victory and atchievement thereof. (56)

As in Donne's *Satyre III*, where it is "a huge hill / Cragged and steep," truth is here won only with great effort, an effort that serves first as inquisition and then—if successful—as a source of proprietary joy. The reader, though not creating meaning ex nihilo, performs the miraculous act of resuscitation.

This act is perhaps comparable to the miracles Donne describes in the previous section of the *Essays*, in which "a mighty People is miraculously made, not of Nothing, (upon which Consideration can take no hold) but of a disproportionall, and incompetent littlenesse" (54). In such miracles "the smallnesse of the root, or seed, is a degree of the miracle." Just as God miraculously repropagates the world after the flood, readers expand brief, obscure passages into fully developed interpretations.[28] Although the source of Donne's seed image here is impossible to determine, his association of difficulty with miracle and joy indicates his familiarity with Augustinian ideas of *exercitatio* and with Aquinas' argument concerning wonder as a cause of pleasure.

Yet wonder is also, according to Albertus Magnus and Aquinas (*Summa Theologiae* 1.2. 41.4), a species of fear. Donne acknowledges the less benign aspects of obscurity in his Prebend sermon on Psalms 65.5: "By terrible things in righteousnesse wilt thou answer us, O God of our salvation, Who art the confidence of all the ends of the earth, and of them that are a far off, upon the sea." Explicating this text, Donne connects the admiration that obscurity produces to the terror inspired by holy power.

---

[28] Compare the treatment of Genesis I in Books 12 and 13 of the *Confessions*, where Augustine expounds at length the miraculous spiritual nourishment provided by the Books of Scripture and Creation, through which God makes all things increase and multiply. Augustine frequently emphasizes the fruits that grow from our attention to what God has provided, and attests to the miraculous compression of the Word: "For as a fountain within a narrow compass, is more plentiful, and supplies a tide for more streams over larger spaces, than any one of those streams, which, after a wide interval, is derived from the same fountain; so the relation of that dispenser of Thine, which was to benefit many who were to discourse thereon, does out of a narrow scantling of language, overflow into streams of clearest truth, whence every man may draw out for himself such truth as he can upon these subjects" (*Confessions*, 224).

Donne begins the sermon in a manner that reinforces my argument
that he considers miracles of propagation and sustenance comparable to
the richness of metaphorical speech; he adduces the preaching of sermons as an example of God's miracles since creation: "God makes nothing of nothing now. . . . But God makes great things of little still; And in
that kinde hee workes most upon the Sabbath; when by the foolishnesse
of Preaching hee infatuates the wisedome of the world, and by the word,
in the mouth of a weake man, he enfeebles the power of sinne, and
Satan in the world. . . . And this worke of his, to make much of little,
and to doe much by little, is most properly a Miracle" (*Sermons*, 7:300).
Donne compares his own preaching to an audience of thousands through
the texts of his five Psalms to Christ's "miraculous feeding of a great
multitude" with five loaves (7:301). Donne continues his "Metaphore,
and miracle of feeding" by explaining that the three senses of the text
that he will bring out correspond to three meals. The first sense, "what
he [God] hath done for man, in the light and law of nature," "works as a
break-fast." The second, "that which God did for the Jewes in their Law,
and Sacrifices, and Types, and Ceremonies, is as that Dinner . . . spoken
of in the Gospel . . . prepared for some certaine guests, that were bidden,
and no more." The third sense, "what he had reserved for man after, in
the establishing of the Christian Church," corresponds to "*the marriage
Supper of the Lambe*" for the blessed "in the Kingdome of heaven." Here
Donne's unfolding of the text by reference to "What God hath done in
Nature, what in the Law, what in the Gospel" feeds his audience miraculously: both the method of interpretation and the text that contains
within itself the seeds of such interpretation are miraculous, wonderful.[29]

In the third section of the sermon Donne makes the connection between obscurity and wonder more explicit. Glossing the psalm's phrase
"terrible things in righteousnesse," Donne explains that these "*Terribilia*, Terrible, fearefull things" are God's judgments, and "by terrible
Judgments he will answer, that is, satisfie our expectation" (7:314). But
these terrible things are not simple acts of justice like those carried out
by civil authorities; they testify to God's incomprehensibility as well as
power. Thus Donne finds the translation of the phrase "terrible things
in righteousnesse" to be "convenient," but potentially misleading:

---

[29] Donne specifies Nature, Law, and Gospel as the three "parts" of his sermon (*Sermons*, 7:302). Although his method is three-fold rather than four, Donne's division of
the sermon into parts matching the levels of interpretation confirms Harry Caplan's
argument that "As a means of *dilatatio* . . . the principle of employing the kinds of
explication may be considered to belong in a theory of rhetorical *inventio*" (*Of Eloquence*, ed. Anne King and Helen North [1970], 93). Caplan's example of this kind of
organization is considerably less solemn than Donne's sermon (127–28).

But, the word, which we translate *Righteousnesse* here, is *Tzadok*, and *Tzadok* is not faithfulnesse, but holinesse; and these *Terrible things* are Reverend things; and so *Tremellius* translates it, and well; *Per res Reverendas, By Reverend things*, things to which there belongs a Reverence, *thou shalt answer us*. And thus, the sense of this place will be, That the God of our salvation . . . calls us to Holinesse, to Righteousnesse, by Terrible things; not Terrible, in the way and nature of revenge; but Terrible, that is stupendious, reverend, mysterious: That so we should not make Religion too homely a thing, but come alwayes to all Acts, and Exercises of Religion, with reverence, with feare, and trembling, and make a difference, between Religious, and Civill Actions. (7:314)

Terribilia shield the divine from excessive familiarity, which would make it "homely," or inappropriately low on the scale of wonder: like the sphinx, then, God's judgments preserve his majesty. Donne proceeds with his argument by presenting obscure forms of expression as examples of *terribilia*.

Like Clement of Alexandria, who insists that "All . . . who have spoken of divine things, both Barbarians and Greeks, have veiled the first principles of things, and delivered the truth in enigmas, and symbols, and allegories, and metaphors, and such like tropes" (*Stromata* 5.4), Donne considers *terribilia* a universal feature of religion: "In the frame and constitution of al Religions, these Materials, these Elements have ever entred; Some words of a remote signification, not vulgarly understood, some actions of a kinde of halfe-horror and amazement, some places of reservation and retirednesse, and appropriation to some sacred persons, and inaccessible to all others" (7:314). Donne sees parallels between the "sacrifices of the Gentiles," the "self-manglings and lacerations of the priests of *Isis* and of *Baal*," and "that very discipline which was delivered from God, by *Moses*," in which "the service was full of mysterie, and horror, and reservation" (7:315). Just as "*By terrible things*, (Sacrifices of blood in manifold effusions) *God answered them.* . . . So," Donne says, "the matter of Doctrine was delivered mysteriously, and with much reservation, and in-intelligiblenesse, as *Tertullian* speaks." God's obscure method of inscribing human history, foreshadowing the Messiah's arrival and sacrifice through the events—or "Types and Sacrifices"—of the Old Testament, is thus for Donne a prime example of the terrible things through which God provokes reverence.

Teachers who imitated in their speech God's method of revelation through "Visions" and "Similitudes," Donne explains, wielded similar power. There was, he notes, "an Order of Doctors amongst the Jews that professed that way, To teach the people by Parables and darke sayings; and these were the powerfullest Teachers amongst them, for they had their very name (*Mosselim*) from power and dominion." These teachers "had a power, a dominion over the affections of their Disciples, because teaching them by an obscure way, they created an admiration, and a reverence in their hearers, and laid a necessity upon them of returning againe to them, for the interpretation and signification of those darke Parables." Donne demonstrates that Moses, David in Psalms, and Solomon in Proverbs explicitly adopt this method of teaching through parable. Christ, however, is the supreme example for Donne of one who teaches powerfully through darkness:

> For when it is said, *He taught them as one having authority* [Matthew 7.29], And when it is said, *They were astonished at his Doctrine, for his word was with Power* [Luke 4.32], they refer that to this manner of teaching, that hee astonished them with these reserved and darke sayings, and by the subsequent interpretation thereof, gained a reverend estimation amongst them, that he onely could lead them to a desire to know, (that darke way encreased their desire) and then he onely satisfie them with the knowledge of those things which concerned their salvation. For these Parables, and comparisons of a remote signification, were called by the Jews, *Potestates*, Powers, Powerfull insinuations, as, amongst the Grecians, the same things were called *Axiomata*, Dignities; And of Christ it is said, *Without a Parable spake he not* [Matthew 13.34]. (7:315–16)

Christ's dark way of speaking astonishes: it simultaneously veils doctrine and stimulates the desire to know. For Donne the veiling function of Christ's speech is especially requisite.

"God in the Old, and Christ in the New Testament," has presented doctrine in a manner insuring that "evermore there should be preserved a Majesty, and a reverentiall feare . . ." (7:316). Donne considers "that Majesty, and that holy amazement" at the divine to be more important to Christians than to members of other religions, "because we have a nearer approximation, and vicinity to God in Christ, then any others had, in any representations of their Gods" (7:316). Even though it is "a more dazeling thing to looke upon the Sun, in a direct, then in an oblique or side line," this nearness runs the risk of rendering the Christian God incarnate "over-homely." Admiration is therefore all the more important for Christians to preserve: "And therefore, the love of God, which is so often proposed unto us, is as often seasoned with the feare of God." In style, obscurity preserves this dread.

Donne, of course, has left no explanation of his poetic practice, and his awareness of the power accruing to admirable style is circumstantial. This is not a smoking gun. Donne's recognition of the advantages of "powerfull insinuations" does not conclusively demonstrate that he practiced obscurity in his own poetry with the specific intention of gaining admiration, but certainly makes this supposition extremely probable. His explicit treatment of his own sermon as performing a function comparable to Christ's "miraculous feeding" shows that he felt little compunction about trying to produce miraculous effects. And as we have seen, his contemporaries had no doubt about his intentions, treating the strong-lined verse he and others wrote as designed specifically to arouse wonder through obscurity that acts as catalyst or veil.

The ease with which Donne acknowledges that the prose of his sermon is designed to imitate Christ's miraculous feeding also suggests how amenable the subjects of religious lyrics by Donne, George Herbert, Andrew Marvell, Richard Crashaw, and Henry Vaughan were to treatment in admirable style. When the desperate conditions for advancement at court eased very early in the reign of James, and equivocation became more than suspect in the wake of the Gunpowder Plot, the religious lyric became the primary residence for admirable style, and finally its last refuge. Conceits, paradoxes, and enigmas needed little apology in poems celebrating the Christian mysteries, such as Richard Crashaw's choric praise of the incarnation ("In the Holy Nativity of Our Lord God," 79–84):

> Welcome, all wonders in one sight!
>   Eternity shut in a span,
> Summer in winter, day in night,
>   Heaven in Earth, and God in man!
> Great little one, whose all-embracing birth
> Lifts Earth to heaven, stoops heav'n to Earth.[30]

In a sense the devotional lyric reappropriates the methods and material Donne had snatched when he went over the top with the Petrarchan doctrine of sublimation through love.[31] The mature Donne may have sincerely wished to preserve with reverence the distinction between "Religious, and Civill Actions," but crossing this divide had been the master trade of Jack Donne, displayed again and again in his jauntily

---

[30] In *Metaphysical Lyrics*, ed. Grierson, 151.
[31] On Donne's religious lyrics of wonder, see Klause, "Donne and the Wonderful."

blasphemous love poetry. The dangerous dance I have traced in the satires found its well-known equivalent in the conflation of love's mysteries with God's in such poems as "The Flea," with its invocation of the Passion, and "The Canonization," which in a single stanza arrogates to Donne and his beloved co-presence, the mingled attributes of the eagle and the dove, and Christ-the-phoenix's resurrection. "Admyring her my mind did whett / To seeke thee God," Donne writes in "Since she whome I lovd," the poem thought to have been written about the death of his wife in 1617 and his subsequent attempt to renounce the secular for the divine.[32] In his love poetry, whatever its precise degree of biographical reference, Donne had already exercised the strategies for provoking admiration that he knew were all the more sanctioned in religious verse.

Yet when employing these methods—conceits, paradoxes, enigmas—religious poets are under special obligation to direct the wonder they produce away from themselves and toward the divine. If Donne in his secular lyrics, particularly his satires, must negotiate between the desire to evoke awe and the danger of aligning himself too closely with the people and forces his culture most fears, the authors of seventeenth-century religious poems must take care to avoid arrogating to themselves the kind of power that secular conceits imply.[33] This is the anxiety rehearsed and rehearsed in the devotional lyric; it provides the device, for example, informing Donne's "*La Corona*" 1, Herbert's "The Wreath," Marvell's "The Coronet," and Carew's "To My Worthy Friend, Master George Sandys." As Crashaw's hymn "In the Holy Nativity of Our Lord God" expresses most memorably, poetic praise is superfluous to "the mighty babe" (45–47):

> The phoenix builds the phoenix' nest.
> Love's architecture is his own.

When George Herbert nevertheless builds *The Temple*, he thus devotes much of it to exploring how he may create wonder without claiming credit for it, and his awareness of the bright shoot of pride engrafted in

---

[32] See *The Divine Poems*, ed. Helen Gardner, 78.

[33] In the preface to *Silex Scintillans* (1654), Henry Vaughan confesses that in his early poems—mostly satires and imitations of Donne—he was guilty of "wallowing in *impure thoughts* and *scurrilous conceits*" (*Complete Poems*, ed. Alan Radran (1981), 140), a disease he says was once epidemic: "That this kingdom hath abounded with those ingenious persons, which in the late notion are termed *wits*, is too well known. Many of them having cast away all their fair portion of time, in no better employments, than a deliberate search, or excogitation of *idle words*, and a most vain, insatiable desire to be reputed *poets*" (*Complete Poems*, 138).

every display of ingenuity becomes a predominant subject not only in the "The Wreath" and the "Jordan" poems but throughout.

And yet despite his fervent defense of plainness, or search for it, Herbert also acknowledges in "Thanksgiving" that even if representing the Passion is beyond him, "If thou shalt give me wit, it shall appear, / If thou hast giv'n it me, 'tis here" (43–44).[34] Like all divine gifts, Herbert suggests, the talent for metaphor must not be neglected. He exercises this wit in "Prayer (I)" by piling conceit on conceit à la Sir Thomas Browne's later pursuit of *O! altitudo*; in "The Pulley" by drawing the central conceit from a humble mechanism and by indulging in wordplay on "rest"; in the dusty heraldry of "Church Monuments"; in the acrostics of "Paradise"; and in the various shaped poems. In the epigram on the anagram of "Mary" and "Army" he makes his boldest (if worst) display of the gift he must neither deny nor vaunt:

> How well her name an *Army* doth present,
> In whom the *Lord of Hosts* did pitch his tent!

Wit of this kind is admittedly rare in Herbert (though less rare in the sacred epigrams of Richard Crashaw), and this poem would pass few imaginable tests of excellence, but by violently yoking opposites it signals Herbert's awareness that what seems least divine may still figure it forth. The epigram can be saved by the argument that its insufficiency and indecorum are exactly the point—that the feebleness of its wit deflects glory from the author even while the poem conveys the theme of human insufficiency in comparison to the divine. Once the squinting Herbert had gained the aperçu, had recognized the anagram, to deny it in silence would have been to squander the gift of insight. Such bold indiscretions in pursuit of the audience's astonishment are rare in Herbert; by the middle of the century, when a heightened sense of decorum had begun to toll the bell for wit, they are all but extinct everywhere.

If the defense of Herbert's small anagram seems forced (as would a defense of Vaughan's "The Ass" or Robert Herrick's circumcision poem "To his Saviour. The New yeers gift"), it depends on logic similar to that by which Donne is reported at second hand to have justified his most ambitious poems, *The Anniversaries*. As the story retold by William Drummond of Hawthornden goes, Ben Jonson judged the first poem "prophane and full of Blasphemies," indecorously hyperbolic in its description of Elizabeth Drury and the effects of her death. Jonson claimed to have "told Mr Donne, if it had been written of the Virgin

[34] All quotations of Herbert are from *English Poems of George Herbert*, ed. C. A. Patrides (1974).

Marie it had been something," and to have received the answer that "he described the Idea of a Woman and not as she was."[35] Jonson wants the praise to be appropriate, commensurate with its object. His standard is based on the classical desire for mimetic accuracy, and the logic of his complaint, as Edward W. Tayler argues in *Donne's Idea of a Woman*, underlies the multitude of allegorical readings claiming to unmask the *true* subject of the *Anniversaries*, whether Christ, the Virgin Mary, or Elizabeth Tudor.[36] Donne's reputed reply to Jonson, however, abjures the mimetic standard in favor of the kind of "representation" that seeks not to depict the world of sense but to direct the audience toward the intelligible, the Platonic "idea." Donne's subject may be secular, that is, but his principle of representation is that explored in the defenses of religious obscurity: his goal is to drive the reader beyond Elizabeth Drury to the knowledge of perfect virtue. Such knowledge, Donne seems to imply, is divine, whatever its stimulus. That his praise is egregiously inappropriate is of no importance from this point of view: Donne approaches Drury not as an immanent subject to limn but as a transcendent soul on which to ascend. If all roads can and should lead to God—a premise accepted by Donne, Herbert, Vaughan, and Sir Thomas Browne—there are no wrong turns. Instead, those who fail to see the divine element in even the most seemingly insignificant object repeat the error that led to the Sacrifice. Conversely, in the words of hermetic Henry Vaughan, "*the seeds of foul sorrows be / The finest things that are, to see*" ("Fair and young light!" 33–34).[37]

---

[35] *Ben Jonson*, 1:133; see Edward W. Tayler, *Donne's Idea of a Woman* (1991), which explores Donne's rationale in detail, tracing precisely what "Idea" meant to Donne. Explaining the thorny wonder of Shakespeare's bizarre elegy "The Phoenix and the Turtle," J. V. Cunningham illuminates the manuever of making the beloved into God, a manuever that involves distilling the Neoplatonic element out of "the scholastic doctrine of the Christian God" and then transfusing it into the human object of love. The lover (Cunningham's example is Valentine in *Two Gentlemen of Verona*, 3.1.170–84) "locates the infinite Idea in the finite beloved" ("Idea as Structure," in *Collected Essays*, 200). As Cunningham emphasizes, however, the wonder generated by the love of the phoenix and turtle derives primarily from the Christian concept of indivisible yet separate essences in the Trinity, a concept without a Neoplatonic equivalent. Donne, of course, does not even claim Elizabeth Drury as beloved. Wesley Trimpi notes in *Ben Jonson's Poems* (279n12) that Jonson's critique of the first *Anniversary* as "profane and full of Blasphemies" might be applied to his own funeral elegies "On the Lady Jane Pawlet" and "Elegie on my Muse" (on Lady Venetia Digby).

[36] Tayler takes most seriously, even while disputing, Barbara K. Lewalski's influential argument in *Donne's "Annniversaries" and the Poetry of Praise* (1973) that Elizabeth represents the regenerate Protestant soul (9–18).

[37] All quotations of Vaughan are from *Complete Poems*; cf. "The Seed Growing Secretly," 33–40. On Vaughan's poetic principles see Wanamaker, *Discordia Concors*, 55–70.

The value of the obscure—despite human blindness to humble majesty, to the jewel in the mud—preoccupies Vaughan most of all. His meditation on the flower underground in "I walked the other day," inspired by Herbert's "The Flower," makes the point (36–42):

> . . . how few believe such doctrine springs
> From a poor root
> Which all the winter sleeps here under foot
> And hath no wings
> To raise it to the truth and light of things,
> But is still trod
> By every wandering clod.

Truth may lie hid in his book as in the world, but in the preface to *Silex Scintillans* he justifies such obscurity as beneficial to the reader (143):

> In the *perusal* of it, you will (peradventure) observe some *passages*, whose *history* or *reason* may seem something *remote*; but were they brought *nearer*, and plainly exposed to your view, (though that (perhaps) might quiet your *curiosity*) yet would it not conduce much to your greater *advantage*.

Yet Vaughan's poetry is among the cloudiest in English not because it employs obscure methods, but because it so often takes obscurity as its topic. For Vaughan, to be obscure is divine, to err by failing to see, human. Only grace relieves this blindness ("I walked," 48–54):

> Grant I may so
> Thy steps track here below,
>
> That in these masques and shadows I may see
> Thy sacred way,
> And by those hid ascents climb to that day
> Which breaks from thee
> Who art in all things, though invisibly. . . .

As Vaughan explains with crystalline clarity in "The Incarnation, and Passion," Christ is the model, figure, or type of all "hid ascents" (1–8):

> Lord! when thou didst thyself undress
> Laying by thy robes of glory,
> To make us more, thou wouldst be less,
> And becam'st a woeful story.

To put on clouds instead of light,
And clothe the morning-star with dust,
Was a translation of such height
As, but in thee, was ne'er expressed.

God, wrapped in "Brave worms, and Earth!" on behalf of "impure, rebellious clay," is translation of translations, and deepest height of "strange wonders." Recognizing and expressing astonishment at these mysterious shroudings is Vaughan's poetic vocation; poem after poem invites the reader to share his passion for wonder:

There is in God (some say)
A deep, but dazzling darkness; as men here
Say it is late and dusky, because they
See not all clear;
O for that night! where I in him
Might live invisible and dim. ("The Night" 49–54)

Even at his most allusively hermetic, Vaughan seems uninterested in making himself or his poems objects of wonder, although he does lay claim to having greater than average skill in interpretation, or at least to knowing there is more than darkness in the dark.

Because Vaughan follows Herbert in largely abjuring wonder for himself, it is all the more significant when he does pay poetic tribute to one act of human shrouding, Charles I's escape from Oxford in April 1646, disguised as a servant.[38] "The King Disguised" steals generously from Vaughan's description of Christ's "undressing" at the Incarnation, taking every opportunity to conflate the divine example with the royal, and many readers familiar with *Silex Scintillans*—printed if not written earlier—must have mistaken the poem's subject until reaching the name "Charles" in line 28:

A King and no King! Is he gone from us,
And stol'n alive into his coffin thus?
This was to ravish death, and so prevent
The rebels' treason and their punishment.
He would not have them damned, and therefore he
Himself deposèd his own Majesty. . . .
Poor, obscure shelter! if that shelter be

---

[38] Cf. John Cleveland, "The King Disguised," in *The Poems of John Cleveland*; Cleveland dwells far more than Vaughan on the negative judgment of the king's "Renegado form," but ultimately acknowledges its appropriateness.

> Obscure, which harbours so much Majesty.
> Hence profane eyes! the mystery's so deep,
> Like *Esdras'* books, the vulgar must not see't. (1–12)

Beyond listing biblical analogues, Vaughan uses the *discordia concors* of the event as an occasion to worry once again his favorite question: how the humble elevates, ironically preserving reverence most effectively. Charles in his disguise, like Hal in Eastcheap, suffers at most a brief eclipse:

> But all these clouds cannot thy light confine,
> The sun in storms and after them, will shine.
>
> . . . .
>
> But I am vexed, that we at all can guess
> This change, and trust great *Charles* to such a dress.
> When he was first obscured with this coarse thing,
> He graced *plebians*, but profaned the King.
> Like some fair Church, which zeal to charcoals burned,
> Or his own Court now to an ale-house turned. (23–32)[39]

Vaughan recognizes the danger—that in violating social and political decorum (not to mention bravely running away), the king risks diminishing the *dignitas* and *maiestas* of the King—yet proceeds to put such questioning of royal strategy out of bounds:

> But full as well may we blame night, and chide
> His wisdom, who doth light with darkness hide:
> Or deny curtains to thy Royal bed,
> As take this sacred covering from thy head.
> Secrets of State are points we must not know;
> Thy vizard is thy privy council now,
>   Thou Royal Riddle, and in every thing
>   The true white Prince, our hieroglyphic King! (33–40)

[39] Cf. Cleveland, "The King Disguised," lines 10–12, 39–50, and 111–22; and the prefatory poem "To my Worthy Friend, Mr. Henry Vaughan, the Silurist" by "I. W." (John Williams?) (11–18):

> And first thy manual opening gives to see
> Eclipse and sufferings burnish Majesty,
> Where thou so artfully the draught hast made
> That we best read the lustre in the shade,
> And find our Sovereign greater in that shroud:
> So lightning dazzles from its night and cloud;
> So the *first Light himself* has for his Throne
> Blackness, and Darkness his Pavilion.

By deferring to the royal will, Vaughan shows how successful the first Stuart had been in establishing the absolutist tenet that kings are not to be judged, even if the second Stuart was soon to learn, keenly, that such deference was something less than universal. In tracing the decline of admirable style, especially its exit from secular poetry, the Stuart mystification of royal prerogative demands particularly close attention. Royal policy and royal interest did not encourage the proliferation of phoenixes.

5 Passing Wonder or Wonder Passing?

The introduction of clearness was attended also by a revolution in belief, which underwent a change along with everything else. And this was the result: in days of old what was not familiar or common, but was expressed altogether indirectly and through circumlocution, the mass of people imputed to an assumed manifestation of divine power, and held it in awe and reverence; but in later times, being well satisfied to apprehend all these various things clearly and easily without the attendant grandiloquence . . . , they blamed the poetic language with which the oracles were clothed, not only for obstructing the understanding of these in their true meaning and for combining vagueness and obscurity with the communication, but already they were coming to look with suspicion upon metaphors, riddles, and ambiguous statements. . . .
—Plutarch, *Moralia*, 407A–B, "The Oracles at Delphi No Longer Given in Verse"

The incentives driving poets of the late sixteenth century to produce wonder through style were varied, powerful, and interrelated, often in subterranean ways. But when lyric wonder went out of fashion, it went way out: by the early 1650s it was nearly dead in poetic practice, and its critics, who had begun to dance on its grave even before it was fully buried, kept dancing through the middle of the next century to keep it down.[1] Just as the development of admirable style was overdetermined in late Renaissance culture, so was its decay attributable to no single cause. And uneven. Some strands of the matrix of rhetorical, political, aesthetic, and philosophical causes that led to the use of rough and ob-

[1] In *From Donne to Dryden* (57–61), R. L. Sharp notes that verse featuring conceits, although increasingly rare, continued to be printed through the early 1660s (not to mention the posthumous publication of Marvell's poetry in 1678).

scure style had shorter half-lives than others, and in nearly all spheres of the culture wonder continued to hold prestige, although frequently in new forms.

New forms and appraisals of the wonderful killed admirable lyric style, but not immediately: the reputations of assorted quick wits, Donne above all, kept the movement alive despite the disappearance of the conditions that gave rise to it, and in religious verse paradoxes wound up into mysteries found a new home. Both Arthur Marotti and Ernest W. Sullivan, II, have recently argued that printed miscellanies and manuscript collections indicate that Donne's verse was widely available and—even in the strict sense—popular much later than study of the printed editions alone had led us to believe.[2] Jonson, temporarily not in the mood to hang Donne for his roughness or doom him to obsolescence for his obscurity, writes in *Epigram* 23 that Donne's "most early wit / Came forth example, and remains so yet." The epigram's judgment of Donne's influence was no doubt most true when first printed in Jonson's *Works* in 1616 (seven years before he railed in "An Execration upon Vulcan" at "strong lines, that so the time doe catch"), yet it was passed as current by inclusion in the printed editions of Donne's poetry in 1650, 1654, and 1669.[3] Wit's fall, then, was erratic, incomplete, and coruscating, but fall it did. Even though the young Dryden and Milton mined what Carew described in his elegy on Donne as the vein of wit, its ore was ultimately judged fool's gold, and Andrew the Marvelous inherited a bankrupt kingdom from the Monarch of Wit.

Positing a single gravitational force responsible for wit's fall would make for an elegant theory, but instead I will offer condensed speculations about the intricately related forces that brought it down. The decreasing prestige of admirable style is best reflected in the increasing tendency to redefine "wit" or "true wit," with Dryden, as "a propriety of thoughts and words"; judgment's rise is wit and fancy's fall.[4] This qualified movement toward propriety and away from far-fetched com-

---

[2] See Arthur F. Marotti, *Manuscript, Print, and the English Renaissance Lyric* (1995); and Ernest W. Sullivan, II, *The Influence of John Donne* (1993).

[3] All of Jonson's epigrams, according to Herford and Simpson, were written by the end of 1612. On the reprinting of Jonson's poem in editions of Donne's poetry, see *Ben Jonson*, ed. Ian Donaldson (1985), 650.

[4] *Essays of John Dryden*, ed. Ker, 1:190. Extensive studies of the shifts in artistic taste during the seventeenth century include: Sharp, *From Donne to Dryden*; George Williamson, *The Proper Wit of Poetry* (1961); J. W. H. Atkins, *English Literary Criticism* (1966); Earl Miner, *The Metaphysical Mode from Donne to Cowley* (1969), and *The Cavalier Mode from Jonson to Cotton* (1971); A. J. Smith, *Metaphysical Wit* (1991). See also the introductions to *Critical Essays of the Seventeenth Century*, ed. J. E. Spingarn (1908–9; 1957); and *Literary Criticism*, ed. Tayler. None of these

parisons—qualified above all by the continuing use of the poetic of correspondence by Marvell and by religious poets such as Vaughan and Traherne, and of hyperbole in courtly compliment—was accompanied by a movement in verse technique toward smoothness and *facilitas*, the "easy" style credited to Waller and Denham.[5] Denham epitomizes this easy style in the apostrophe to the Thames first included in the 1655 text of *Cooper's Hill* (189–92):

> O could I flow like thee, and make thy stream
> My great example, as it is my theme!
> Though deep, yet clear, though gentle, yet not dull,
> Strong without rage, without ore-flowing full.[6]

Denham's qualifying antitheses express anxiety about defending a style lacking the rough power, obscure depth, and *furor poeticus* associated with strong lines, but his manifesto signals the move toward smoothness, order, and regularity that indisputably gathered momentum during the course of the century. But why? Here the waters murk.

David Summers notes that when attempting "to explain deep stylistic change, we must not only describe what takes place, and offer reasons for it, we must also explain why changes compel more or less universal assent."[7] The contrapositive is also true: when, as in the case of wit's fall from grace, so many seem to cheer it down, we need to ask why it failed to secure or maintain universal assent. In the provisional explanation that follows, I will point first to the changes within court culture that made a desperately rough and obscure style no longer seem worth the risk it had always involved, then to broader, although related, shifts in the episteme, reverberations of the new rationalism in philosophy

---

studies treats the decline of wit as a strictly aesthetic phenomenon, but all of them examine critical developments in more detail than is possible here, and plot the decline of admirable wit.

[5] When critics after the Restoration assess pointed, sententious, or conceited style, they often lump poets now categorized as Cavaliers—Sir John Suckling, Sir John Denham, and even Edmund Waller—with Donne and Cowley. See, for example, William Walsh's preface to *Letters and Poems, Amorous and Gallant* (1692), printed in [John Dryden,] *Miscellany Poems* (1716), 4:338–39; and Charles Gildon's reply in *Miscellaneous Letters and Essays* (1694) (in *Literary Criticism*, ed. Tayler, 398–406). Both Sharp, in *From Donne to Dryden*, and Williamson, in *The Proper Wit of Poetry*, take pains not to exaggerate the shift from Donne to Waller; as Sharp argues, "the revolt was completed during Dryden's lifetime [1631–1700], not before" (176).

[6] I have used the "B" text in Brendan O Hehir, *Expans'd Hieroglyphicks: A Study of Sir John Denham's Coopers Hill with a Critical Edition of the Poem* (1969); O Hehir provides a full textual history and argues that Denham invented the notion that earlier versions of the poem had been pirated.

[7] David Summers, *The Language of Sense* (1987), 12.

and natural philosophy, and finally to elements of the critique of wit that seem to look backward rather than forward—to forms of resistance to wit that threatened its efflorescence from the beginning, and became increasingly deadly.

Clarity and vividness were, both in the rhetorical and poetic manuals of the sixteenth century and in the Aristotelian treatises that so influenced them, the requirements insisted upon most emphatically, and the failure of admirable style to fulfill them—although deliberate—was always the primary threat to its ability to pass muster. When poets sacrificed clarity for abrupt, obscure brevity, they sought to project, as Ben Jonson claimed, an image of "manly," martial toughness, and mysterious danger. Given James's embrace of the image of himself as a peaceful Solomon, and his active discouragement of belligerence toward Spain, Italy, and France, only the satellite court of Prince Henry sustained the martial spirit connected to abruptness. His death in 1612 helped make the martial and melancholic pose obsolete, although the Gunpowder Plot certainly had a more appreciable effect, demonizing equivocation. If the Stuart court expected clarity, it adored vividness. Although the rise of the new Spenserians, the mania for collecting and sponsoring painters and paintings, and the increasing reliance on spectacle in the masque may have been coincidental developments, they all underscore the prestige of the image as distinct from the verbal symbol, *enargeia* as distinct from *energeia*.

If it seems paradoxical that wonderful lyric obscurity became obsolete during the century in which renewed interest in *On the Sublime* raised the capital of wonder to a new high—and it should—this process becomes more understandable in light of the context in which "Longinus'"s treatise was received. When read in conjunction with Horace and Quintilian—both of whom offer strong critiques of the fragmentation and bloat that rough obscurity can produce—and with the French criticism that stressed distinctions among the genres, small wonder that *On the Sublime* seemed more an indictment than a defense of small wonder.

"The Vertue of a Regal Eye"

Employing wonderful style had always been a desperate strategy (it would not have been so astonishing if it had not been), but the incentives for risky self-promotion decreased rapidly in James's reign with the expansion of opportunities for advancement. Intense competition at court in the 1590s helped inaugurate the style, pushing amateur poets to wild acts of self-display in an attempt to prove their worthiness, but the well-documented proliferation of titles in the Stuart court made such acts hardly worth the risk. (The most telling evidence of this proliferation appears in Appendix 3 of Lawrence Stone's *Crisis of the Aristocracy*, which shows that more knights, baronets, and Irish and English peers were created in the first year of James's reign than in *all* of Elizabeth's.)[8] Combined with the reaction to the Gunpowder Plot and the absolutist attempt to consolidate power in the person of the monarch throughout the first half of the century, this disincentive to desperate verbal behavior proved powerful. As Linda Levy Peck, Graham Parry, R. Malcolm Smuts, and Kevin Sharpe have recently explored in detail, the Stuart court moved decisively—if not uniformly or exclusively—in the direction of neoclassicism, pacifism, and order; after the death of Prince Henry in 1612, this movement swerved less.[9] The court's aesthetic values, as epitomized by the orderly machinery and wonderful visual effects designed by Inigo Jones for the Stuart masque, left little place for the rough verbal wonder practiced in the 1590s. Jones described his own style as "solid, proportionable, according to the rules, masculine and unaffected": against this Augustan foil, admirable style looked increasingly outlandish and fantastic.[10]

The ban on satire in 1599 had eliminated a crucial early outlet for the display of quick wit, especially in its rougher varieties. Wit's disappearance from secular verse also had more occult causes. When James advocated the absolute concentration of power in the person of the king, he also laid sole claim to the attributes that political theorists ancient and modern had identified as bulwarks of power. Simply put, James arrogated to himself more wonder, leaving less for courtiers; Stephen Greenblatt's succinct comment on the inelasticity of power applies also to wonder: "the gain of one party is inevitably the loss of another."[11] This contraction of power reaches its ultimate point only during the decade of personal rule by Charles beginning in 1629, but is the Stuart goal from the accession of James, or even before. James laid claim not only to wonder generally, but also to the admirable skills in employing

---

[8] Lawrence Stone, *The Crisis of the Aristocracy 1558–1641* (1965), 755; see chapter III, "The Inflation of Honours" (65–128).
[9] See Linda Levy Peck, "Court Patronage and Government Policy: The Jacobean Dilemma," in *Patronage in the Renaissance*, ed. Guy Fitch Lytle and Stephen Orgel, 27–46; Graham Parry, *The Golden Age Restor'd* (1981); R. Malcolm Smuts, "The Political Failure of Stuart Cultural Patronage," in *Patronage in the Renaissance*, ed. Lytle and Orgel, 165–87, and *Court Culture and the Origins of a Royalist Tradition in Early Stuart England* (1987); and Kevin Sharpe, *Criticism and Compliment* (1987).
[10] Quoted in Smuts, *Court Culture*, 101.
[11] Greenblatt, *Renaissance Self-Fashioning*, 141.

and decoding secrecy that I have argued were intricately bound up in the use of witty style by courtier-poets. He raised more than money for the crown by selling titles, because he was simultaneously emptying them of their symbolic capital, their mystery. Older aristocratic families might complain that by floating more titles, the crown was devaluing them all (and they were right), but by relieving the pressure on prospective courtiers to astound in order to merit promotion, James's dispersion inflicted a less obvious wound. He sold titles, of course, not because he had a genius for ideological strategy but because he needed cash. Still, his willingness to lessen the value of nobility was characteristic, telling. Uninterested (in both senses) in how courtiers impressed those below them on the social scale (and blind to the failures of his favorites to impress in a way that Elizabeth had never been in regard to Leicester and Ralegh), for James the political scale of wonder contained a mirror for princes, but a glass ceiling for everyone else. In the infamous "Speech to the Lords and Commons" of March 21, 1609, he posits that kings "exercise a manner or resemblance of Divine Power on earth," and are therefore not to be judged; his implicit model of the relationship between kings and subalterns, by contrast, is one of absolute difference rather than resemblance.[12]

It was beyond the power of James to deny courtiers all opportunities to astonish, and skill in political intrigue was as much a part of the courtier's uniform in his reign (and after) as in Elizabeth's, but there is abundant evidence that he succeeded in representing himself, and in encouraging others to represent him, as most politic of all. One factor here is the rise of the masque, subsidized by the court, which replaced the lyric as the primary literary form of courtly wonder; another, related factor is the treatment of James, especially because of the Gunpowder Plot, as the best disciple of Tacitus or diviner of secrets. These phenomena are tied together by the feature of courtly staging that Stephen Orgel highlights in *The Illusion of Power*: the masque is a form designed to create a spectacle of wonder, but one that only the royal spectator sees in perfect perspective. The Stuart masque simultaneously endows royal sight and celebrates royal perception, quite literally directing wonder at the king. This celebration of royal scrutiny dovetails neatly with *Volpone*'s parody of courtiers' pretensions to such sight in the person of Sir Politic-Would-Be (1606).

As noted in chapter 3, the plotting of Sir Pol bears sharp comparison with that of the "thing" in Donne's earlier *Satyre IV*, but the differences

---

[12] *The Political Works of James I*, ed. Charles Howard McIlwain (1965), 307.

also tell: both are preoccupied with secret wonders, but Donne's "thing"
is an insider at court, capable of endangering Donne's persona, whereas
Sir Pol is less than marginal. He is immediately and perpetually, as he
confesses to Peregrine, "astonished" (2.1.42). That Jonson could make a
plotter seem so ridiculous so soon after the Gunpowder Plot, and rele-
gate him to a subplot, should surprise us; no doubt some of the laughter
he generated in the Globe was nervous. But as Jonson shrinks the
courtly plotter, he and other Stuart authors amplify James, whose vision
burns through such plots. The standard mode of praising James's miraculous interception and interpretation of the letter that revealed the Gunpowder Plot was to adopt Proverbs 16:10, as Joseph Hall did in his *Holy
Panegyrick* (1613) on the tenth anniversary of the accession: "If there
had not been a divination in the lips of the King, wee had all been in the
jawes of death."[13] Applied to James, the text from Proverbs underscores
the verbal quality of his seemingly miraculous powers of interpretation.

Foresight is easy to praise in hindsight, but Jonson had praised the
king's power to prophesy even before the Gunpowder Plot (James had, of
course, survived numerous plots before, most notably the Gowrie Plot
of 1600). During the plague-delayed progress through London on 15
March 1604 to celebrate the accession, Jonson and Thomas Dekker paid
elaborate tribute to James's interpretive powers, his eagle eye, in the
immensely complicated iconography of the triumphal arches through
which the royal retinue passed.[14] The texts of the entertainments stress
wonder as the effect of majesty, as was entirely commonplace, but put
special emphasis on the sight of James and James's sight as cause for
admiration.

Dekker's portions, recorded in *The Magnificent Entertainment* (1604),
play up the equation of royal sight with the sun, emphasizing simultaneously the rays it attracts and the rays it sends forth; according to
Dekker's character "*Genius Loci,*" as London awaits James its "Streets

---

[13] Quoted in Parry, *The Golden Age Restor'd*, 234. See also Lancelot Andrewes' first
sermon on the Gunpowder Plot, delivered before James at Whitehall in 1606; Andrewes cites and quotes Proverbs 16:10, locating "a very 'divination,' a very oracle 'in
the King's lips,' and his mouth missed not the matter; made him, as Joseph, 'the
revealer of secrets,' to read the riddle, giving him wisdom to make both explication
what they would do, and application where it was they would do it" (*The Works of
Lancelot Andrewes* (1841–54; 1967), 4:214). The next sentence, significantly, reads,
"This was God certainly." Ben Jonson similarly finds God's hand in the king's survival of the pre-Gunpowder plots: see *Epigram* 35, "To King James."
[14] See Parry, *The Golden Age Restor'd*, 6–8. Dekker and Jonson were, as Herford
and Simpson report, "hostile collaborators," each printing his own version of the
entertainment and slighting the contributions of the other (*Ben Jonson*, 10:386).

(like Gardens) are perfum'd with Flowers: / And Windows glazde onely with wondring eyes; / (In a *Kings* looke such admiration lyes!)."[15] Dekker recycles several times this conceit of royal splendor reflected in the wondering gaze of the people, always treating the royal "look" as the prime source of power. In the device at Soper-lane End, a boy from St. Paul's hailed James as the new Phoenix, who has rescued England from *"Detraction"* and *"Oblivion"* with "Beames from thine eyes / So vertually shining, that they bring, / To *Englands* new *Arabia*, a new Spring."[16] At the sixth arch *Zeale* offers similar praise of the king whose miraculous sight has healed the damage Elizabeth's death has inflicted on the four kingdoms (England, Ireland, France, and Scotland), the four cardinal virtues, even the four elements:

> But see, the vertue of a Regall eye,
> Th'attractive wonder of mans Majestie,
> Our Globe is drawne in a right line agen,
> And now appear new faces, and new men. (2:297)

Praising royal sight for its dazzling power was anything but avant-garde flattery in 1604, but James and Charles both treated such standard metaphors for royal power with a new seriousness, consistently encouraging their subjects to understand the royal eye's "vertue" as real, rather than a poetic virtual reality. As countless analysts of the royal collapse have stated more eloquently, the Stuarts seem to have believed their own hype.

Jonson's texts of the entertainments for the progress and for the king's entrance to Parliament on 19 March 1604, printed together as a quarto in 1604, credit James even more specifically for his interpretive power. Describing the arches' symbols of royal virtue and virtù as hybrids containing "Hieroglyphickes, Emblemes, or Impreses," Jonson declares that he wanted them "so to be presented, as upon the view, they might without cloud, or obscuritie, declare themselves to the sharpe and learned: And for the multitude, no doubt but their grounded judgements did gaze, said it was fine, and were satisfied" (*Ben Jonson*, 7:90–91). It is

---

[15] *The Dramatic Works of Thomas Dekker*, ed. Fredson Bowers (1964), 2:255; cf. the lines spoken by Jonson's "Genius": "set with sparkling eyes / Thy spacious windows; and in every street, / Let thronging joy, love, and amazement meet" (279–81; *Ben Jonson*, 7:91).

[16] *Dramatic Works*, 2:279; cf. 2:283, where Sylvanus says that Peace, *Eirene*, had been unable to find a kingdom in which to settle until James's arrival: "from them all, shee hath beene most churlishly banished: not that her beautie did deserve such unkindnes, but that (like the eye of Heaven) hers were too bright, and there were no Eagles breeding in those nests, that could truly beholde them."

doubtful that even the learned king could have fully appreciated their iconography (as Jonson's explications after the fact indicate), even if he had lingered to study them, but the intent was clearly to hold up James as fit to dispel mysteries at which the multitude would only wonder. And like the Stuart masque, with its marvelous scenes of transformation, the entertainments Jonson staged at the arches enacted the marvelous power of the king, the magic of his presence.

Thus the frame containing Jonson's Latin panegyric poem for James at the first arch:

> was covered with a curtaine of silke, painted like a thicke cloud, and at the approach of the K. was instantly to be drawne. The Allegorie being, that these clouds were gathered upon the face of the Citie, through their long want of his most wished sight: but now, as at the rising of the Sunne, all mists were dispersed and fled. When sodainely, upon silence made to the Musickes, a voyce was heard to utter this verse;
> *Totus adest oculis, aderat qui mentibus olim,*
> Signifying, that he now was really objected to their eyes, who before had beene onely, but still, present in their minds. (7:90)

Making literal the emblem *hinc clarior* that Shakespeare's Hal adopted as his credo and that I have associated with admirable style, Jonson reappropriates it for royal wonder. Jonson takes advantage of the delay in welcoming James to declare, through the mouth of the "Genius Loci" of London (336–37):

> Never came man, more long'd for, more desir'd:
> And being come, more reverenc'd, lov'd, admir'd. (7:93)

By representing this royal power to evoke admiration visually, through the show of drawing the silk curtain, Jonson presages the shift from verbal to scenic wonder that he himself would come to lament in "An Expostulation with Inigo Jones" (1631):

> O Showes! Showes! Mighty Showes!
> The Eloquence of Masques! What need of prose
> Or Verse, or Sense, t'express Immortall you?
> You are the Spectacles of State! 'Tis true
> Court Hieroglyphicks, & all Artes affoord
> In the mere perspective of an Inch board!
> You aske noe more then certeyne politique Eyes,

> Eyes that can pierce into the Misteryes
> Of many Colours! read them! & reveale
> Mythology there painted on slit deale! (39–48; 8:403–4)

Jonson's later critique seems somewhat disingenuous given the obscurity of his own designs for the Entertainment, and their implicit claim for himself as producer of "court hieroglyphics," but his position is consistent at least in the sense that what the drawn curtain reveals is poetry, which he claims Jones was trying to make irrelevant to the masque form. In 1604, however, Jonson was positioning himself as "spectacles of state," trying to win a place on the most powerful politic eyes.

The contest between visual and verbal representation is absent in the poem Jonson wrote to commemorate James's first visit to Parliament four days later, but the note of *hinc clarior* rings even louder; here James *is* the sun (3–18):

> Againe, the glory of our Westerne world
> Unfolds himself: & from his eyes are hoorl'd
> (To day) a thousand radiant lights, that stream
> To every nooke and angle of his realme.
> His former rayes did onely cleare the skie;
> But these his searching beams are cast, to prie
> Into those darke and deepe concealed vaults,
> Where men commit blacke incest with their faults;
> And snore supinely in the stall of sin:
> Where *Murder, Rapine, Lust* doe sit within,
> Carowsing humane bloud in yron bowles,
> And make their denne the slaughter-house of soules:
> From whose foule reeking cavernes first arise
> Those dampes, that so offend all good mens eyes;
> And would (if not dispers'd) infect the Crowne,
> And in their vapor her bright metall drowne. (7:113)

Like Hal "breaking through the foul and ugly mists / Of vapors" to appear "like bright metal on a sullen ground," James's "searching beams" insure continued wonder for the crown. (That Jonson collapses Hal's analogies seems to indicate far more than coincidence; whether or not James would have appreciated the comparison is another question). Jonson's interest, however, is in both the gaze the king attracts—which the remainder of the poem stresses—and the power of the gaze itself: in the king's dazzling and undazzled sight.[17] Indeed the searching power of his beams produces, in part, the wonder Jonson attributes to him.

After the discovery of the Plot, such treatment of James as all eye of course intensified, beginning with his own speech to Parliament on the following day in which he points to "three wonderfull, or rather miraculous events": the scope of the target, the plotters' lack of recognizable motive, and his own ability to ferret out the danger hinted at in the letter to Lord Monteagle (*Political Works*, 282). Careful to note first that he "ever did hold Suspition to be the sicknes of a Tyrant," James is able to claim that his suspicion in this instance, because unusual, deserves special wonder. He sees for once, then, something:

> When the Letter was shewed to me by my Secretary, wherein a general obscure advertisement was given of some dangerous blow at this time, I did upon the instant interpret and apprehend some darke phrases therein, contrary to the ordinary Grammer construction of them, (and in an other sort then I am sure any Divine, or Lawyer in any Universitie would have taken them) to be meant by this horrible forme of blowing us up all by Powder; And thereupon ordered that search to be made, whereby the matter was discovered, and the man apprehended: whereas if I had apprehended or interpreted it to any other sort of danger, no worldly provision or prevention could have made us escape our utter destruction. (283-84)

James grabs opportunity by the forelock, using the discovery and especially his own miraculous act to underscore his unique capacity to preserve "the weale, both of your King and of your Countrey, whose weales cannot be separated" (288). His demonstration of his interpretive powers supports his claim to have sounded "the particular mysteries of this State" in the two short years since his accession, a claim that in turn allows him to instruct Parliament to see their function as conciliar rather than legislative (287). This definition of the role of Parliament, central to his agenda, continues to be the royal position throughout the crises of his reign and that of Charles. Having established that "the end for which the Parliament is ordeined" is "only for the advancement of Gods glory, and the establishment and wealth of the King and his people," James condemns those who would instead "utter there their private conceipts," seek "satisfaction of their curiosities" concerning royal

---

[17] Jonson characteristically mixes advice in with his praise, and his advice consists mostly in reminding James to prefer the love to the fear of his people, and to be aware that his own acts are under public scrutiny.

behavior, and "make shew of their eloquence" (288).[18] Convened, James
says, "by your lawfull King to give him your best advises, in the matters
proposed by him unto you" (288), members of Parliament: "should bee
ashamed to make shew of the quicknesse of their wits here, either in
taunting, scoffing, or detracting the Prince or State in any point, or yet
in breaking jests upon their fellowes" (289). Without pushing the causa-
tive argument for the fall of wit too far here, it is apparent that James, at
least, aligns private wit with private interest—that is, with any interest
distinct from the royal interest that he declares to be indistinguishable
from public interest—and considers them equally wrongheaded depar-
tures from the proper function of his courtiers. Not simply errant, such
behavior is superfluous: his all-sufficient power to preserve himself and
the state, implicitly demonstrated by his quick-witted discovery of the
Plot, makes Parliamentary investigation, debate, and sanction unneces-
sary.

James began the speech, admittedly, by crediting God for "the great
and miraculous Delivery," and Lancelot Andrewes, when delivering his
annual Gunpowder Plot sermons to the King in Whitehall, stands out as
especially scrupulous in reminding the King repeatedly where the ultimate credit for his interpretive insight lies.[19] Yet the discovery seems
most often to have been viewed as bringing special credit to James. Particularly salient is John Donne's characteristically complex 1622 sermon on the anniversary of the Plot, complex especially because it magnifies the institution of monarchy without limit even while alluding
cautiously but repeatedly to the causes of widespread discontent with
the court, including James's "intemperate hunting" and the "perversenesse and obliquity" of his subalterns. The frame of the sermon is entirely laudatory, but within it Donne catalogues the popular charges
against the king, and fails to exonerate him.

Donne uses the miraculous delivery as an occasion to liken kings to
God in the manner of his Whitsunday sermon of 1623, where he declares that "The Kings of the earth are faire and glorious resemblances
of the King of heaven; they are beames of that Sun, Tapers of that Torch,
they are like gods, they are gods" (*Sermons*, 5:85). Like James, Donne
treats kingship as uniquely reflective of divinity, the divine image so
thoroughly represented in the earthly institution that resemblance, find-

---

[18] Cf. his critiques of subaltern "curiousity" concerning mysteries of state in *Basilikon Doron* and in the "Speech to Parliament of 1607" (*Political Works*, 27, 291).

[19] Andrewes consistently emphasizes God as first cause of the discovery, which he
terms "a miracle consummate" (*Works*, 4:216), both in this sermon and throughout
the series (see, for example, 4:259 and 4:269). His text in the first sermon is Psalms
118.23, 24: "This is the Lord's doing, and it is marvellous in our eyes. / This is the
day which the Lord hath made; let us rejoice and be glad in it." See also n. 13 above.

ing its vanishing point, blurs into identity: "Of all things that are, there *was* an *Idea* in God; there was a modell, a platform, an exemplar of everything, which God produced and created in Time, in the mind and purpose of God before: Of all things God *had* an *Idea*, a preconception; but of Monarchy, of Kingdome, God who is but one, *is* the *Idea*; God himselfe, in his Unity, *is* the Modell, He *is* the Type of *Monarchy*" (4:241). Yet throughout the sermon there is a palpable air of urgency: a not quite tacit recognition of extreme discontent with James and Buckingham, and of extreme fear that the old religion is on the wing. With James still pursuing a Spanish match for Charles despite the Spanish invasion of the Palatinate, and with a sudden economic depression underway, the king's judgment was subject to increasing doubt.[20] Because Donne keeps veering *toward* these issues, and toward recognition of "the dangerous declination of the Kingdome" (4:239), his exact purpose is difficult to gauge. Invoking what Ernst Kantorowicz identifies as the crucial tenet of absolutism—the notion that no one is qualified to judge the actions of the king, any more than those of God—Donne discourages such judgment by treating the plotters' actions as an instance of it: they arrogated to themselves powers of judgment reserved for God and kings. Donne has unquestionably reviewed James's speech to Parliament of 1605 in preparing this sermon, reaffirming its central arguments even while obliquely responding to them.[21] Donne himself keeps raising the issues on which the negative judgments of James are based, and seems far less committed to defending James than to denying that the king's critics can pluck the heart out of his mystery.

Donne's text for the sermon is Lamentations 4.20: "The breath of our nostrils, The anointed of the Lord, was taken in their pits." Because he explicitly notes that the text had been read as encouraging support of kings both good (Josiah) and bad (Zedekiah) when they encounter tribulations, Donne defers the question of whether or not he himself would sanction all of James's actions:

> We imbrace that which arises from both [applications], That both good Kings, and bad Kings, *Josiah*, and *Zedekiah*, are the *anointed* of the Lord, and the *breath of the nostrils*, that is, The Life of the people; and

[20] For a solid overview of the converging causes of discontent with James between 1614 and the fall of 1622, see Derek Hirst, *Authority and Conflict* (1986), 118–33.
[21] On standard responses to the Plot, see Richard F. Hardin, "The Early Poetry of the Gunpowder Plot," *ELR* 22 (1992): 62–79; and John N. Wall, Jr., and Terry Bunce Burgin, "'This sermon . . . upon the Gun-powder day': The *Book of Homilies* of 1547 and Donne's Sermon in Commemoration of Guy Fawkes' Day, 1622," *South Atlantic Review* 49 (1984): 19–29. Although I find Donne's sermon to be less supportive of James than Wall and Burgin do, and see James's speech of 1605 rather than the *Book of Homilies* as Donne's point of departure, their article provides valuable context.

therefore to be lamented, when they fall into dangers, and consequently both to be preserved by all means, by *Prayer* from them who
are private persons, by *counsell* from them, who have that great honour and that great charge, to be near them in that kinde, and by *support* and *supply*, from all, of all sorts, from falling into such dangers.
(4:239)

Having established that the goal of all subjects should be to support the
king, good or evil, Donne in a sense licenses his own references to the
failings of James, even while denying in general the right of any but
kings to judge kings: "That man must have a large comprehension, that
shall adventure to say of any King, *He is an ill King*; he must know his
Office well, and the actions of *other Princes* too, who have correspondence with him, before he can say so" (4:249). Perhaps drawing on
James's own treatment of his interpretation of the letter to Monteagle as
appropriately but uncharacteristically suspicious, Donne claims that
"Many times a Prince departs from the exact rule of his duty, not out of
his own indisposition to truth, and clearnesse, but to countermine un-
derminers"; "with crafty neighbours," in sum, "a Prince will be crafty,
and perchance false with the false" (4:249). Unlike Catholic plotters in
1605 (and, implicitly, Puritan critics in 1622), who consider kings to be
"subject to their censures, and corrections":

> We say, with St. *Cyrill, Impium est dicere Regi, Inique agis: It is an
> impious thing,* (in him, who is onely a private man, and hath no other
> obligations upon him) *to say to the King,* or *of the King, He governs
> not as a King is bound to do*: we remit the judgement of those their
> actions, which are secret[,] to God; and when they are evident, and
> bad, yet we must endevour to preserve their persons; for there is a
> danger in the losse, and a lamentation due to the losse, even of
> *Zedekiah,* for even such are *uncti Domini, The anoynted of the Lord,
> and the breath of our nostrils.* (4:250)[22]

The parenthesis here is a curious but significant hedge, and one which
hints at Donne's purpose in including so much implicit criticism of
James: Donne sees his own function as that of a counselor. In taking on
"that great honour and that great charge," Donne knows the risk, which
he presents as a risk of misinterpretation.
   By chastising those who would presume to criticize the king while

---

[22] This passage demonstrates as well as any the slipperiness of the text: were Donne
interested in wholly defending James, the reference to actions that are "evident, and
bad" would be counterproductive.

pretending to praise him or pray for him, Donne points to the equivocal
nature of speech, and insists on the primacy of intention:

> But then, beloved, a man may convey a *Satir* into a *Prayer;* a man may
> make a prayer a *Libell;* If the intention of the prayer be not so much,
> to incline God to give those graces to the King, as to tell the world,
> that the King wants those graces, it is a Libell. We say sometimes in
> scorn to a man, *God help you,* and *God send you wit;* and therein,
> though it have the sound of a prayer, wee call him foole. So wee have
> seen of late, some in obscure Conventicles, institute certain prayers,
> *That God would keep the King, and the Prince in the true Religion;*
> The prayer is always good, always usefull; but when that prayer is
> accompanied with circumstances, as though the King and the Prince
> were declining from that Religion, then even the prayer it selfe is li-
> bellous, and seditious. (4:253)

What Donne accomplishes here is a brilliant stroke of dissimulation.
His purpose is double: by blasting equivocal prayers he of course equates
contemporary critics with the equivocating Jesuits responsible for the
plot, but he also clears the ground for his own declaration (or prayer),
which immediately follows and which provides the emotional climax of
the sermon:

> Let our prayers bee for continuance of the blessings, which wee have,
> and let our acknowledgement of present blessings, bee an inducement
> for future: pray, and praise together; pray thankfully, pray not sus-
> piciously: for, beloved in the bowels of Christ Jesus, before whose face
> I stand now, and before whose face, I shall not be able to stand among
> the righteous, at the last day, if I lie now, and make this Pulpit my
> Shop, to vent sophisticate Wares, in the presence of you, a holy part, I
> hope, of the Militant Church, of which I am, In the presence of the
> whole Triumphant Church, of which, by him, by whom I am that I
> am, I hope to bee, In the presence of the Head of the whole Church,
> who is All in all, I *(and I think I have the Spirit of God,)* (I am sure I
> have not resisted it in this point) I, (and I may bee allowed to know
> something in Civill affaires) (I am sure I have not been stupefied in
> this point) doe deliver that, which upon the truth of a Morall man, and
> a Christian man, and a Church man, beleeve to be true, That hee, who
> is *the Breath of our nostrils,* is in his heart, as farre from submitting us
> to that Idolatry, and superstition, which did heretofore oppresse us, as
> his immediate Predecessor, whose memory is justly precious to you,
> was: Their wayes may bee divers, and yet their end the same, that is,

The glory of God; And to a higher Comparison, then to her, I know
not how to carry it. (4:253–54)

Throwing the passionate weight of his moral, Christian, *and civil* authority into the oath, Donne preaches to a dual audience, addressing
both the audience in the church and the royal audience. He is exercising
the skill he had mastered in erotic poems such as "The Bait," addressed
both to an imagined mistress and to a predominantly male coterie. No
one could accuse him of failing to do his best to quell the congregation's
fears, since he puts his own soul on the line, but he has also satisfied his
own conscience by performing the function Castiglione (and James himself in the speech of 1605) had treated as primary: counseling the prince.
James of course is not bound by Donne's oath, but neither can he question it, or any of Donne's references to behavior and circumstances he
would prefer not to acknowledge: Donne insures that his sermon can
only be interpreted as prayer, not satire, even while he repeats phrases
in themselves potentially libelous. In case the act of embedding his
counsel within a passionate oath is not a sufficient shield from the
charge, Donne later in the sermon makes the point explicit: "a man that
flattereth, spreadeth a net, and a Prince that discerns not a flatterer,
from a Counsellor, is taken in *a net*" (259).

It seems no accident that the paragraph containing Donne's oath immediately follows one where Donne claims, without naming names,
that when a monarch's actions "will not admit a good interpretation,"
subjects "must be apt to remove the perversenesse and obliquity of the
act from him, who is the first mover to those who are *inferiour instruments*" (252).[23] In order to transfer to these inferiors (read "Buckingham") the blame for what he three times calls "perversenesse," Donne
revises his sheer equation of God with monarchs:

> God does work in every Organ, and in every particular action; but yet
> though he doe work in all, yet hee is no cause of the obliquity, of the
> perversenesse of any action. Now, earthly princes are not equall to
> God; They doe not so much as work in particular actions of instru-
> ments; many times, they communicate power to others, and rest
> wholly themselves; and then, the *power* is from them, but the *per-
> versenesse* of the action is not. God does work in ill actions, and yet is
> not guilty, but Princes doe not so much as worke therein, and so may

[23] Donne's own forbearance to accuse any subalterns by name implicitly resembles
the Holy Ghost's forbearance to name the persecutors of Josiah or Zedekiah and
James's forbearance to name other possible conspirators in the Gunpowder Plot,
which Donne attributes to "his naturall sweetnesse" (259).

bee excusable; at least for any cooperation in the evill of the action,
though not for countenancing, and authorising an evill instrument;
but that is another case. (252–53)

Donne's politic distance from particular events, actions, and people here
is notable, as is his seeming unwillingness to offer a blanket defense of
James, epitomized in the paragraph's concluding deferral.

Presenting himself as unstupefied by royal awe, and proudly expert in
civil matters, Donne has traveled far from the naive persona of *Satyre
IV*. Admittedly, my analysis of Donne's strategy—which gives him far
more credit for questioning James, if not absolutism, than is usual—
seems to demonstrate that wit is alive and well, despite the Stuart
consolidation of power. Yet for Donne to exercise a form of equivocal
wittiness seems only to be expected, and even if he presents himself as
qualified to offer judgmental if subtle counsel to the king (as though he
were still, even in 1622, showing James how fit he was for highest trust),
the bulk of the sermon denies this power, again and again, to others.
Donne is our best example of an admirable wit inventing (as he admits)
the grounds for satire in order to get noticed, but in the Gunpowder Plot
sermon he rejects satire and judgment of kings even when, as he shows,
the grounds for such satire are ready-made. And he reinforces, finally,
James's own argument that the miraculous discovery proves the king
all-sufficient: "And by making his servant, and our Soveraigne, the
blessed means of that discovery, and that deliverance, he hath directed
us, in all apprehensions of dangers, to rely upon that *Wisdome*, in civill
affaires, affaires of state, and upon that *Zeale*, in causes of Religion,
which he hath imprinted in that soule" (260). Here, and in his repeated
unequivocal references in the concluding section of the sermon to James
as "our Josiah," Donne declares that (himself and God excepted) no one
can or should generate such wonder as the king. His argument here offers retrospective support for my claim that in *Satyre IV* Donne aims to
demonstrate his fitness for a position of civil authority by showing that
he is able to sniff out and avoid danger: the absolutist argument with
which Donne concludes the Gunpowder sermon is that James has demonstrated his fitness to reign supreme because he has sniffed out and
prevented the plot.

Unsurprisingly, Donne's participation in the ceding of politic wonder
to the king is both uniquely clever and, finally, standard: when he sings
the praises of the self-sufficient royal sight, he joins a choir of contemporaries who follow the score laid out in James's own speech to Parliament of 1605. Yet James was given credit for keen sight into the mysteries of nature as well as state. Quoting Proverbs 25.2 in the preface to

The Great Instauration (1620), which he dedicated to James, Bacon writes that "it is the glory of God to conceal a thing, but it is the glory of the King to find a thing out" (*Works*, 4:20). Bacon applies the text of Proverbs 25.2 loosely here, encouraging the king to support scientific experiment but not, admittedly, expecting the king to lend an eye to the enterprise. In the context of such praise of the royal gaze as Jonson and others offer, however, Bacon seems to be implying that the natural world is an appropriate arena for the exercise of the eagle eye, a fit challenge by which it may show its strength: "the universe to the eye of the human understanding is framed like a labyrinth; presenting as it does on every side so many ambiguities of way, such deceitful resemblances of objects and signs, natures so irregular in their lines, and so knotted and entangled" (4:18).

As Stephen Orgel accentuates, Bacon advertises his project as a means of extending royal dominion: the discovery of hidden knowledge increases the "glory of the *king*, not of the scientist" (*Illusion of Power*, 55).[24] Glory, majesty, wonder, and power seem all to have been viewed as inelastic: for the king to have more, someone must have less. Stuart proclamations explicitly appropriate wonder from courtiers below, but Stuart cultural and scientific projects, especially the royal sponsorship of a Promethean natural philosophy unbound, also pull from God above. More than the Stuart court led to the new epistemology and the new methods of scientific inquiry in the seventeenth century, without doubt, but advocates of science from Bacon on repeatedly invoked the court as protector and exemplar of this new rage for order, and the Stuart masque increasingly represented royal dominion as dominion over nature, as nature made orderly. In the earliest masques of Jonson and Jones, Orgel explains, wild nature is transformed, astonishingly, into an orderly example of royal civility; the wild antimasque evaporates at the entrance of the spectacularly sophisticated masque proper, and art trumps nature (*Illusion of Power*, 49). After 1616, however, the natural world itself becomes the symbol and locus of order:

> When pastoral settings appear they come at the end, and embody the ultimate ideal that the masque asserts. For the earlier sequence we might take as the normative masque Jonson's *Oberon*, which opens with "a dark rock with trees beyond it and all wildness that could be presented," then moves to a rusticated castle, and concludes with a Palladian interior. For the later sequence, a good example is Jonson's *Vision of Delight*, which opens with a perspective of fair buildings,

---

[24] Compare George Herbert's quite different use of the biblical text in the sonnet "Sure, Lord, there is enough."

changes to mist and cloud, and concludes with the Bower of Spring.
(50)

What Orgel records is the process by which the transcendence of disorder in the natural world—a transcendence effected by the king—comes
to replace the simple substitution of civil order for natural disorder.
This harmonizing of discordant elements resembles that practiced by
Donne and Marvell, but is modeled on the harmonic power attributed
above all to God, who is in Cowley's phrase "that strange *Mirror*" where
all things "without *Discord* or *Confusion* lie" ("Ode. Of Wit," 71–72).
But there are crucial differences. In his secular verse Donne employs
discordia concors as a method, designed to renew his audience's wonder
at the poet; in religious poetry he and others employ the method to
renew the audience's wonder at creation and the creator; but in the
Stuart masque, and in royalist poems such as Denham's *Cooper's Hill*,
or Pope's *Windsor Forest*, *discordia concors* is a poetic theme rather
than a poetic method, and the wonder devolves more to the king than
the poet. As Orgel further argues, noting that "Jones's pastoral visions
become most elaborate during the 1630s, the decade of prerogative
rule," the masques above all "express the developing movement toward
autocracy," presenting the monarch as sufficient alone to endow nature
with the order and abundance Bacon dreamed his study of the elements
might produce: "If we can really see the king as the tamer of nature . . .
there will be no problems about Puritans or Ireland or Ship Money.
Thus the ruler gradually redefines himself through the illusionist's art,
from a hero, the center of a court and a culture, to the god of power, the
center of a universe. Annually he transforms winter to spring, renders
the savage wilderness benign, makes earth fruitful, restores the golden
age" (*Illusion of Power*, 50). Equating scientific rationalism with royalist
ideology would be naively reductive, would in a sense be to buy what
the masques are selling, but to ignore their rough fit would also leave
a distorted impression, and the fitful growth of both absolutism and
rationalism over the course of the century helped to squeeze out admirable style.

To exemplify how the development toward a vision of "creation
which is ordered by regular physical laws and harmoniously manageable
by mind" becomes embodied in poetic style, A. J. Smith quotes lines
37–42 of Pope's *Windsor Forest*, lines written in 1704:

> See Pan with flocks, with fruits Pomona crowned,
> Here blushing Flora paints th'enamelled ground,
> Here Ceres' gifts in waving prospect stand,

And nodding tempt the joyful reaper's hand,
Rich Industry sits smiling on the plains,
And peace and plenty tell, a STUART reigns.

In their neat employment of heroic couplet, chiastic order and balanced epithet, these lines demonstrate the subtle shift from a rougher *discordia concors*, where the violence of the yoking is undisguised, to a milder, smoother harmonizing of opposites. Yet they also draw explicit attention to what they share with many other pronouncements on order and regularity in style: a view of the order in nature as bringing credit not to the divine first mover, but to the royal house of Stuart. Certainly we need to distinguish, say, Pope's royalism from Denham's, a tribute to Anne from a tribute to Charles, but both poets draw on a tradition of treating wonderful natural abundance and beauty as proof of royal efficacy; this tradition, as Stephen Orgel forcefully argues, begins during the reign of James I, in the masques of Jonson and Jones.

Candid Style

A. J. Smith, Edward W. Tayler, and others place little emphasis on the court's image of itself as endowing nature with order, but they argue convincingly that the stylistic shifts away from roughness and obscurity harmonize with new conceptions both of the working of human faculties and of the proper methods of investigating the natural world—with the "rationalist" philosophy of Bacon, Descartes, Hobbes, Locke, and, at least in his optics and physics, Newton. The spirit of Descartes inspires Thomas Sprat's call in *The History of the Royal Society* (1667) for a language filled with "positive expressions; clear senses; a native easiness: bringing all things as near the Mathematical plainness, as they can" (*Literary Criticism*, ed. Tayler, 318), and Abraham Cowley's ode to the Society presents Bacon as the exemplar of this style:

> His candid Stile like a clean Stream does slide,
>   And his bright Fancy all the way
>   Does like the Sun-shine in it play;
> It does like *Thames*, the best of Rivers, glide,
> Where the God does not rudely overturn,
>   But gently pour the Crystal Urn. . . .
> ("To the Royal Society," 176–81)

Cowley's tribute affirms the values he finds dominant soon after the Restoration—clarity, smoothness, and regularity—and it aligns these

values with the goals and methods of the Society envisioned by Bacon
(however dubious it is as a description of Bacon's own style). Cowley
seems notably less defensive about the easy style modeled on the gliding
Thames than Denham had been even in 1655, reflecting the increasing
weakness of strong lines and admirable wit.

More equivocal is the judgment of admirable style Hobbes delivers in
his "Answer . . . to Sir William Davenant's preface before *Gondibert*,"
printed in the *Discourse upon Gondibert* (1650). "Equivocal" might be
too generous: Hobbes's treatment of figurative obscurity, pointing both
to its philosophic rationale and to its growing incompatibility with the
new philosophy, is divided against itself.[25] Beauty of poetic expression,
he begins: "consisteth in two things, which are, *To know well*; that is,
to have images of nature in the memory distinct and clear; and *To know
much*. A sign of the first is perspicuity, property, and decency. . . . A
sign of the later is novelty of expression, and pleaseth by excitation of
the mind; for novelty causeth admiration; and admiration, curiosity;
which is a delightfull appetite of knowledge" (*Literary Criticism*, ed.
Tayler, 286–87). Hobbes tries to stand both on Cartesian epistemology
("images . . . distinct and clear") and on the primarily Aristotelian notion of distinctive strangeness as a catalyst to the pursuit of knowledge,
but these are the divergent legs of a pair of stilts, not a compass. Want-
ing to credit Davenant for his original metaphors, and, as a translator of
Aristotle himself, aware that the Philosopher had designated the capacity for metaphor a crucial sign of philosophical intellect, he has to praise
"the admirable variety of metaphors and similitudes," particularly the
"new (and withall, significant) translation" of familiar words and "farre
fetch't (but withall, apt, instructive, and comely) similitudes" (288).
Like the mixed attitude toward strong lines displayed in the elegies on
Cartwright examined in chapter 3, Hobbes's position at midcentury
seems poised, recognizing the claims both of wit and fancy on one side,
and judgment on the other. But his comments on strong lines, which
immediately follow his critique of obscure and bombastic terms, show
where he and the century lean: "To this palpable darknesse, I may also
add the ambitious obscurity of expressing more then is perfectly conceived; or perfect conception in fewer words then it requires. Which
Expressions, though they have had the honour to be called strong lines,
are indeed no better then Riddles, and not onely to the Reader, but also
(after a little time) to the Writer himself, dark and troublesome" (287).
Hobbes here echoes Dudley North's criticism of "strong appearing

---

[25] I have used the text in *Literary Criticism*, ed. Tayler. On Hobbes's inconsistency
see Williamson, *Proper Wit*, 67–70.

lines," printed in *A Forest of Varieties* (1645) but perhaps written as early as 1610, as unpersuasive:

> Some proceed in a stuttering confused obliquity, groping as in a mist or darknesse; some goe more directly, and exhibit their Idea's [sic] and conceptions with so cleare and distinct a light, illustrations, instances, demonstrations, enforcements, and arguments so perspicuous and concluding, that the understanding and assent are captivate beyond evasion or subterfuge. Sophistry and figures may appear fine and witty, but prevaile little upon the best judgements: Reason must convince the intellectuall soule.[26]

Both Hobbes and North reject the emphatic, suggestive mode of amplification in favor of full, methodical demonstration. If strong lines are incompatible with Descartes' model of intellection, puzzling both author and reader, they are also, as Cowley's ode implies, incompatible with the Baconian approach to the interaction between the natural world and the divine.

"Rest in Nature, not the God of Nature"

When Bacon defends his interest in secondary causes in the *The Great Instauration* and the first book of *The Advancement of Learning*, he denies that by excluding consideration of a divine prime mover and *telos* he is contributing to atheism. Yet the inductive, mechanistic procedures of Baconian science encase for observation the landscape that metaphysical poems by Donne, Herbert, Marvell, Vaughan, and Traherne had treated as opening, everywhere, vistas on another world. In items eleven and twelve of the "Catalogue of Particular Histories by Titles" Bacon appends to *The New Organon*, he indicates interest in "Dew" and evaporation (or "all other things that descend from above, and that are generated in the upper region") (*Works*, 4:265). But for devotional poets from Donne ("The Primrose") to Herbert ("Grace," "Virtue," "The Bunch of Grapes," and most beautifully, "The Flower") to Marvell ("On a drop of dew") to Vaughan ("The Search," "The Morning Watch," "Unprofitableness," "Love, and Discipline," "The Timber," "The Seed Growing Secretly," "The Night," "The Waterfall"), dew is

---

[26] In *Literary Criticism*, ed. Tayler, 165; for an argument that North's essay was written much earlier, see L. A. Beaurline, "Dudley North's Criticism of Metaphysical Poetry," *Huntington Library Quarterly* 25 (1962): 299–313. Cf. Samuel Johnson on demonstration in lyric, *Rambler* no. 158 (*Works*, 6:108–9).

the image of images, the type of types; dropped down to raise (like manna) and to be raised up (like Christ), it embodies the possibility— and the means—of regeneration for every human soul.

For Bacon, poets celebrating dew worship an Idol of the Tribe, both in approaching a natural substance through its relation to human concerns and in devising, for a possibly unique phenomenon, "parallels and conjugates and relatives." The entire poetic of correspondence also exemplifies one of the Idols of the Cave, errors due to the warp or "peculiar constitution" of the individual character: "The steady and acute mind can fix its contemplations and dwell and fasten on the subtlest distinctions; the lofty and discursive mind recognizes and puts together the finest and most general resemblances. Both kinds, however, easily err in excess, by catching the one at gradations, the other at shadows."[27] For Bacon these "shadows" are literally nothings, images without substance; for the devotional poets they are dim reflections of God, or fingerprints on the book of creation:

> For the bright firmament
> Shoots forth no flame
> So silent but is eloquent
> In speaking the creator's name.
>
> No unregarded star
> Contracts its light
> Into so small a character,
> Removed far from our human sight:
>
> But if we steadfast looke,
> We shall discern
> In it, as in some holy book,
> How man may heavenly knowledge learn.
> (William Habington, "Nox Nocti Indicat Scientiam. DAVID," 9–20)[28]

God, as Sir Thomas Browne says, is seen "asquint upon reflex or shadow" (*Religio Medici*, 1.13). In "The Retreat," Henry Vaughan, for one, pleads

---

[27] *New Organon*, XLV, LV; cf. LVII (in *Works*: 4:55–60), where Bacon distinguishes atomists from natural philosophers "so lost in admiration of the structure of nature that they do not penetrate to the simplicity of nature." The metaphysicals' preoccupation with dew would also fall into this category of error simply because it flaunts Bacon's rule that the "student of nature" should suspect "whatever his mind seizes and dwells upon with particular satisfaction" (LVIII).

[28] In *Metaphysical Lyrics*, 144.

happily guilty to Bacon's charge of chasing shadows, praising this habit of his "Angel-infancy":

> When yet I had not walked above
> A mile, or two, from my first love,
> And looking back (at that short space,)
> Could see a glimpse of his bright-face;
> When on some *gilded cloud*, or *flower*
> My gazing soul would dwell an hour,
> And in those weaker glories spy
> Some shadows of eternity. (7–14)[29]

Not sharing Bacon's evaluation of practical knowledge, the devotional poets look at natural phenomena with different eyes. The Baconian method, lingering on the study of secondary causation, is for Sidney Godolphin ultimately vain, no more valuable than simple reverence:

> Wisemen in tracing natures lawes
> Ascend unto the highest cause,
> Shepheards with humble fearfulnesse
> Walke safely, though their light be lesse:
> Though wisemen better know the way
> It seemes noe honest heart can stray.
>
> There is no merit in the wise
> But love, (the shepheards sacrifice).
> Wisemen all wayes of knowledge past,
> To th'shepheards wonder come at last,
> To know can only wonder breede,
> And not to know, is wonder's seede.
> ("Lord when the wisemen came from far," 7–18)[30]

In Marvell's "Dialogue Between the Resolved Soul and Created Pleasure," the Baconian desire to understand each substance well enough to

---

[29] Vaughan, *Complete Poems*, 172.

[30] In *Metaphysical Lyrics*, 145; cf. Sir William Davenant, "The Christian's Reply to the Philosopher" (ibid., 177) and George Herbert, "Vanity (I)." Browne, however, rejects the equation of ignorant and learned wonder at creation: "The wisedome of God receives small honour from those vulgar heads, that rudely stare about, and with a grosse rusticity admire his workes; those highly magnifie him whose judicious enquiry into his acts, and deliberate research of his creatures, returne the duty of a devout and learned admiration" (*Religio Medici*, 1.13).

manipulate nature becomes more than futile: it is the last temptation. When the Soul declines Pleasure's invitation to "know each hidden cause; / And see the future time: / Try what depth the centre draws; / And then to heaven climb" (69–72), the Chorus immediately hails the Soul's triumph.[31]

The corpus of religious poetry by Marvell, Vaughan, and Traherne (as well as Browne's *Garden of Cyrus* and *Hydriotaphia*), demonstrates that the poetic of correspondence was alive even late in the century, but it was not well. Marvell's "The Mower Against Gardens," dating from the poet's stay at Nun Appleton from 1650 to 1652, already treats the gods as chased from the landscape, the world's rotundity struck flat.[32] Describing horticulture as having reduced "wild and fragrant innocence" (34) to a "dead and standing pool of air" (6), Marvell expresses a simmering hint of the nostalgia for the mysterious world that would boil over in 1817 when Keats and Wordsworth drank a toast to "Newton's health, and confusion to mathematics," blaming Newton for having "destroyed all the poetry of the rainbow by reducing it to its prismatic colours."[33] Kill the rainbow (Iris), and wonder (Thaumas), her mother, suffers. As Marjorie Hope Nicolson notes, Keats's animus against Newton resurfaces in *Lamia* (2.229–37):

> Do not all charms fly
> At the mere touch of cold philosophy?
> There was an awful rainbow once in heaven:
> We know her woof, her texture; she is given
> In the dull catalogue of common things.
> Philosophy will clip an Angel's wings,
> Conquer all mysteries by rule and line,
> Empty the haunted air, and gnomed mine—
> Unweave a rainbow. . . .[34]

---

[31] *Andrew Marvell: The Complete Poems*, ed. Elizabeth Story Donno (1972), 27–28.

[32] For the dating, see ibid., 260. I have overstated the incompatibility of the poetic of correspondence and the interest in scientific learning: Browne manages to combine them, although he demonstrates how insufficient exclusive investigation of the natural world is for him. For more nuanced handling of the effect of scientific discovery and method on wit, see A. J. Smith, *Metaphysical Wit*, 235–52.

[33] Benjamin Haydon hosted the dinner and recorded the conversation: quoted in Marjorie Hope Nicolson, *Newton Demands the Muse* (1946), 1; see also M. H. Abrams, *The Mirror and the Lamp* (1953), 303–12. For the rainbow as a cause of wonder in the seventeenth century, see Henry Vaughan, "The Rain-bow," in *Complete Poems*, 275.

[34] In John Keats, *John Keats*, ed. Elizabeth Cook (1994), 208–9.

No longer the wonder it had been for Henry Vaughan, or even a sign, Newton's rainbow has drooped like Bacon's dew to the indifferent status of an item in a catalogue.

The new science ahead might have been sufficient to undercut the poetic of correspondence, but old rhetoric also loomed: as I previewed in the first chapter, one threat that lurked even within wit rising was its association with *deinotēs*, the quality itself often associated with the sophistic legacy. As wit declined, its most noticeable features, especially conceits, became prey to attacks by critics who simply would not buy the idea that rough, bold, and obscure epigrams, satires, and other lyrics could be viewed as miniature equivalents of epic and tragedy, and that their hyperbole was wonderful. Instead, critics even early in the seventeenth century found such features pseudotragic, borrowing their terms of judgment from Hermogenes and "Longinus," as read in harmony with Horace and Quintilian. Over the course of the century, these voices of dissent grew deafening. Wonder remained an important goal of poetry, largely because of the enormous influence of *On the Sublime*, but critics refused to accept the methods that Donne and others had used to provoke such wonder, and poets gave them up.

Miracle or Monster

In poetic practice, roughness was the quality of admirable style that disappeared most quickly, ushered out by such developments as the pacifism of James, the attempt by both James and Charles to give the English court a more cosmopolitan air, and the French influence of Henrietta Maria. Conceits lingered not only in the verse of Marvell, John Cleveland, and Katherine Philips, but in that of the young Milton and Dryden. Hyperbole, especially hyperbolic compliment, is not exclusive to admirable style, and continues to be a feature of fashionable, courtly verse throughout the century. Cavalier lyrics sling as much hyperbole as Donne ever did, but even poems such as Edmund Waller's "On a Girdle" bring less attention to their own exaggeration than do Donne's "The Bait" or "The Sunne Rising" (to which "On a Girdle" is too seldom compared); Waller, Lovelace, Suckling, and Denham more frequently display their wit through the opposite extreme: exaggerated understatement, the infinite *sprezzatura* exemplified in Lovelace's dismissal of the dangers of warfare in "To Lucasta, Going to the Wars."[35]

[35] Just as "On a Girdle" compares to "The Sunne Rising" in its treatment of the speaker's beloved as "all states," even the universe, "To Lucasta" is slightly compara-

Andrew Marvell's ability to wield both tones so effectively, especially in
his tours de force of tonal variation—"To His Coy Mistress" and "An
Horatian Ode Upon Cromwell's Return from Ireland"—mark him as in
step with contemporary developments yet the true heir to Donne's
crown. Yet even Marvell largely abandons the roughness of Donne,
adopting the regularity of meter, couplet, and stanza form that would
lead critics in the eighteenth century to look back on the verse of the
midcentury as "easy."

In poetic theory, conceits drew the most fire (in part because roughness had few defenders). Examining admirable style through a composite
lens of Horace, Quintilian, and "Longinus," critics saw a style too affected to be sublime, too ingenious to be passionate, and too rough to be
correct. They therefore pronounced its effect to be admiration but not
rational admiration, wonder that passes rather than passing wonder. For
them, admirable style as practiced in the seventeenth century exhibits
the *deinotēs* of the Sophists, not the *deinotēs* that marks the height of
excellence in Greek oratory, transporting the audience and commanding
their assent. Lyric wonder was primarily rejected because it occurred
within lyric. Although sixteenth-century critics of course showed concern for the expectations of various genres (though devoting much less
attention to lyric than to tragedy, comedy, or epic), this concern rigidi-
fied considerably in seventeenth-century criticism, as did resistance to
lyric appropriation of the wonder reserved for tragedy and epic. Critics
who embraced what they believed to be classical standards—which will
be my working definition here of neoclassical critics—did not approach
particular styles in a vacuum or as discrete phenomena: they considered
their place in a hierarchy of styles considered appropriate for various
purposes yet usually ranked in order either of the kind and degree of
emotion they elicited, or the importance of the subject they handled.
Over the course of the seventeenth century this hierarchy consisted less
and less of the three Roman *genera dicendi*, or grand, middle, and plain
styles; instead, as William Wimsatt and Cleanth Brooks acknowledge,

---

ble to Donne's "A Valediction: Forbidding Mourning," if only as a farewell poem. In
both cases the cavalier poems are especially unlike Donne in their regularity of form
and meter. Although Lovelace's poem features the conceit of the enemy as "a new
mistress," which no doubt earned the poem its place in Grierson's anthology of *Metaphysical Lyrics*, it makes little attempt to "hammer out" or exploit the conceits,
unlike Donne's treatment of the gold leaf and the compasses in the "Valediction."
Lovelace's only departure from strict metrical regularity in the poem is the not very
unusual (but very Donnean) inversion of the first foot. Lovelace's meter is less regular
in "To Lucasta, Going Beyond the Seas," which lacks a surprising conceit but is even
closer in theme and diction to Donne's "Valediction" (with an admixture of "The
Ecstasy").

eighteenth-century critics tended to simplify the three levels into "the polar concepts of the lofty and the low."[36] But even "lofty" and "low" very weakly describe the contrasted styles that come to dominate treatments of style after the middle of the seventeenth century, which are more precisely the sublime, bold style and the correct, accurate style.

This shift from the Roman tripartite system to the Greek binary system of classifying styles leaves admirable style between Scylla and Charybdis. Seen as neither passionate enough to be sublime, nor smooth, regular, and easy enough to be correct, admirable style loses out. As *On the Sublime* became increasingly popular, such style even lost much of its claim to be admirable, because critics associated wonder-provoking sublimity with passion, and usually found epigrammatic style too ingenious to be sincere; in leveling this charge they often drew on Horace's recommendation that "If you would have me weep, you must first feel grief yourself (*si vis me flere, dolendum est / primum ipsi tibi*)" (*Art of Poetry*, 102–3). Quintilian's critique of overly epigrammatic style helped to shape neoclassical reaction to admirable style, and also sums it up: "where eloquence seeks to secure elevation by frequent small efforts, it merely produces an uneven and broken surface which fails to win the admiration (*admirationem*) due to outstanding objects and lacks the charm that may be found in a smooth surface" (8.5.29).[37] Ancient critiques of epigrammatic style jumped out at critics in the later seventeenth century in part because these critiques fit neatly with the sharp distinctions among genres that French critics, especially, had recently sought to enforce.

These more rigid distinctions brought into focus the divergence between the two primary kinds of *deinotēs* recognized in ancient Greek rhetoric: (1) the rough, oral style identified by Demetrius as the *charaktēr deinos* and by Hermogenes as his first category of *deinotēs* and (2) the elaborate written style used by the Sophists for epideictic display, which features paradox, carefully balanced antitheses, and conceits. Even though Demetrius juxtaposes this sophistic style to his *charaktēr deinos*, and Hermogenes expresses regret that the paradoxical style, his third category of *deinotēs*, has come to be considered wonderful, confusion between these meanings seems to have reigned supreme (further complicated by the third meaning attached to *deinotēs*, mastery of all styles and when to use them). These two kinds of *deinotēs* correspond roughly to the oral and written styles that Aristotle distinguishes in

[36] William K. Wimsatt and Cleanth Brooks, *Literary Criticism* (1957), 342.

[37] See Trimpi, "HASD," 65; and Edinger, *Samuel Johnson*, 154–56.

Rhetoric, 3.12.[38] In oral, deliberative oratory, speakers must perform on a grand scale, raising the passions of the audience by emphasizing the importance of the topic at hand rather than drawing attention to their own ingenuity. In epideixis, where orators are writing in an atmosphere of leisure for a sophisticated audience that has read numerous treatments of the same topic and is unlikely to forgive inattention to detail, extreme precision and originality carry the day.

To explain the different levels of refinement appropriate in different kinds of oratory, Aristotle compares the spoken styles of deliberative and forensic oratory to different kinds of paintings:

> The deliberative style is exactly like a rough sketch (*skiagraphia*), for the greater the crowd, the further off is the point of view; wherefore in both too much refinement is a superfluity and even a disadvantage. But the forensic style is more finished, and more so before a single judge, because there is least opportunity of employing rhetorical devices, since the mind more readily takes in at a glance what belongs to the subject and what is foreign to it; there is no discussion, so the judgement is clear. . . . where action is most effective, there the style is least finished. . . . (*Rhetoric,* 3.12.5)

(Aristotle's contrast here between deliberative and forensic oratory implicitly holds all the more true for the contrast between deliberative and epideictic oratory, since he immediately goes on to say that epideictic is still more finished than forensic.)

Wesley Trimpi has shown that Aristotle's rhetorical analogy underlies a variety of later analogies between the literary and visual arts that juxtapose a rough grandeur to meticulous detail: particularly important for the later reception of admirable style is Horace's comparison *ut pictura poesis* in lines 361–90 of the *Art of Poetry.*[39] Horace's comparison, which follows a group of lines in which he makes allowance for some errors in long works of great scope, such as the Homeric epics, contains three terms:

[38] My discussion of the two kinds of *deinotēs* in relation to Aristotle's distinction between oral and written styles relies on Wesley Trimpi's investigations of this distinction and its aftermath in "MHP"; "HASD"; and *Muses,* 100–102.

[39] On the intersections between the literary and visual arts in the Renaissance, see also Rensselaer W. Lee, *Ut Pictura Poesis* (1967); and Jean H. Hagstrum, *The Sister Arts* (1958), 57–128. On the question of mannerism in various arts see Mirollo, *Mannerism and Renaissance Poetry;* and John Shearman, *Mannerism* (1967).

Ut pictura poesis: erit quae, si propius stes,
te capiat magis, et quaedam, si longius abstes.
haec amat obscurum, volet haec sub luce videri,
haec placuit semel, haec deciens repetita placebit.

A poem is like a picture: one strikes your fancy more, the nearer you
stand; another, the farther away. This courts the shade, that will wish
to be seen in the light, and dreads not the critic insight of the judge.
This pleased but once; that, though ten times called for, will always
please.

One style of poem or painting is more effective up close and in the
shade rather than in the full light of the sun, and pleases once; another
is more effective at a distance and in full sunlight, and pleases always.
Trimpi notes that even the earliest commentators on Horace tended to
mix up these three terms of comparison, and that critics have used
Horace's lines to defend whatever point of view they happen to hold
regarding either poetry or painting ("MHP," 24–25). When applying
Horace's terms of comparison to epigrammatic style, neoclassical critics
are no more consistent than the early scholiasts. Yet, as examination of
the overlap between Horace's *ut pictura poesis* and several passages in
On the Sublime reveals, the rhetorical background for Horace's comparison illuminates why neoclassical critics rejected admirable style. Quintilian's Latin terminology supplied the arsenal for the attacks carried
out by Samuel Johnson in the *Life of Cowley* and Alexander Pope in the
Essay on Criticism, but Horace and "Longinus" supplied the battle plan.
   Yet even English critics who aligned "Longinus" with Horace and
Quintilian could not simply dismiss admirable style, particularly because "Longinus" defends boldness and creates confusion over the relationship between passion and figurative language. Horace does not express a preference for either the work best seen at a distance or the work
best seen up close, but "Longinus" champions the noble but faulty work
over that which is precise and correct but not sublime. "Correctness
escapes censure: greatness earns admiration as well (*to mega de kai
thaumazetai*)" (36.1). He champions Homer, Plato, and Demosthenes,
despite their faults, against more correct but less ambitious authors, and
prefers the Colossus, monstrously ungainly when seen up close, to Poly-
cleitus' well-proportioned statue of a spearman (32.8–36.4). "Longinus"
here lays the groundwork for the clash between the Schools of Sense and
Taste in the seventeenth and eighteenth centuries, a battle which pro-

vided one of the rare contexts in neoclassical criticism where epigrammatic brevity received at least fitful praise.

As J. E. Spingarn explains in the preface to *Critical Essays of the Seventeenth Century*, even before Boileau's translation of *On the Sublime* appeared in 1674 some English critics had begun to rebel against the recent tendency to reject any work that was not faultless. By 1687, when John Sedley wrote the preface to *Bellamira*, this revolt against "French" correctness was in full career: "I have taken my Idea of Poetry more from the Latin than the French, and had rather be accus'd of some Irregularities than tire my Reader or Audience with a smooth, even stream of insipid words and accidents, such as one can neither like nor find fault with."[40] So much for Denham's Thamesian ideal. Samuel Johnson's often-repeated preference for Shakespearean grandeur over Addisonian correctness—in contrast to Voltaire's indictment of Shakespeare for his wildness and irregularity—reveals the continuing influence of this "Longinian" scale of value, and helps to explain why Johnson could have at least temporarily preferred a bold epigrammatic style in letters to a milder style modeled on the sonnet.

After 1674, then, preference for the bold, sublime work became neoclassical orthodoxy, although critics routinely included a disclaimer that avoidable faults were not to be tolerated.[41] Here they followed Horace and "Longinus," with significant consequences for admirable style. Although they abide some faults in ambitious works, both Horace and "Longinus" expect some writers to justify all excesses as inevitable detours on the path to excellence. Horace tries to preempt this move by noting that he weeps when Homer nods (358–59); "Longinus" weeps too

---

[40] *Critical Essays*, 1:xcviii n2; see 1:lxxvi–ci; as Spingarn makes clear, however, French critics also contributed to the development of the School of Taste, which preferred works that contained a kind of excellence not explicable by reference to rules, a *je ne sais quoi*.

[41] See for example Hume, "Of the Standard of Taste":

To check the sallies of the imagination and to reduce every expression to geometrical truth and exactness would be the most contrary to the laws of criticism, because it would produce a work which by universal experience has been found the most insipid and disagreeable. But though poetry can never submit to exact truth, it must be confined by rules of art. . . . If some negligent or irregular writers have pleased, they have not pleased by their transgressions of rule or order, but in spite of those transgressions. They have possessed other beauties, which were conformable to just criticism, and the force of those beauties has been able to over power censure, and give the mind a satisfaction superior to the disgust arising from the blemishes. (*Eighteenth-Century Critical Essays*, ed. Scott Elledge (1961) 2:814–15)

(*On the Sublime,* 33.4), and offers a more thorough repudiation of the "noble failure":

> For often when they [Asiatic orators] think themselves inspired, their supposed ecstasy is merely childish folly (*pollachou gar enthousian heautois dokountes ou bakcheuousin alla paizousin*). Speaking generally, tumidity seems one of the hardest faults to guard against. For all who aim at grandeur, in trying to avoid the charge of being feeble and arid, fall somehow into this fault, pinning their faith to the maxim that 'to miss a high aim is to fail without shame.' Tumours are bad things whether in books or bodies, those empty inflations, void of sincerity, as likely as not producing the opposite to the effect intended. (3.4)[42]

"Longinus" offers this general criticism after examining such particular examples of tumidity as Gorgias' comparison of vultures to "living sepulchres." Such comparisons, as noted in chapter 1, are for "Longinus" pseudotragic; they "make for confusion rather than intensity (*dedeinōtai*)," and when examined "in the light of day" they nose-dive "from the terrible to the ridiculous" (3.1–2).

This disclaimer against faulty but ambitious styles allowed critics to attack bold strong lines without exposing themselves to the charge of being overly interested in correctness. The ambitious metaphors and rough, epigrammatic brevity of strong lines could only with difficulty be seen as excessively correct; they could, however be seen as misguided attempts at sublimity. And they were: Meric Casaubon, in his *Treatise of Enthusiasme* (first printed in 1655), explicitly equates "strong lines" with affected tumidity. "*Longinus*," he says, has several passages concerning enthusiasm: "As when he saith, speaking of that kind of language, which when I was a Boy in the University, was called *strong lines; pollachu gar enthousian heautois dokountes, ou bakcheuousin, alla paizousin. Many men,* saith he, *whilst they strain their wits to find somewhat that is very extraordinary, and may relish of some rapture, or Enthousiasme; they plainly rave,* [or, *play the fools,*] *and not ravish.*"[43]

[42] See Trimpi, "MHP," 18n26, and "HASD," 33n6.

[43] Meric Casaubon, *A Treatise Concerning Enthousiasme,* 2nd. ed. (1656; 1970), 189. As George Williamson has shown, critiques of "enthusiasm" after 1649 often link it with melancholy and with a private religious fervor, juxtaposed to publicly affirmed reason, that is politically dangerous (*Seventeenth Century Contexts,* 205–39). Especially after the Restoration, he shows, recent history was adduced as empirical proof of the disruptive power of extravagant wit. For the somewhat coordinate treatment of Cromwell and other revolutionary leaders as dissembling Machiavels, see Victoria Kahn, *Machiavellian Rhetoric* (1994), esp. 3–5, 132–65.

Strong lines, Casaubon asserts, are not sublime but affected: implicitly they deserve none of the leniency "Longinus" extends to the Colossus and Homer.

Poems featuring strong lines were rarely colossal. The growing insistence on wonder in sixteenth-century criticism—an insistence maintained, as in the case of Grasso's critique of Terence's plain style in comedy, even in the teeth of standard expectations for genres—led lyric poets to pursue this traditional goal of epic and tragedy through extraordinary style. Later critics, with renewed interest in keeping genres distinct, and in keeping the "lesser" genres in their place, would not excuse this kind of transgression of decorum.[44] In the *Idler* essays by Joshua Reynolds, this concern for judging according to the dictates of particular genres—of poetry or of painting—is especially clear. In *Idler* no. 79, Reynolds lectures the viewer not to expect in the grand style of Michelangelo ("the Homer of painting") the "minute exactness in the detail" found in the Dutch and Venetian styles; in *Idler*, 76 he says that "what may be an excellence in a lower class of painting becomes a blemish in a higher; as the quick, sprightly turn, which is the life and beauty of epigrammatic compositions, would but ill suit with the majesty of heroic poetry."[45]

The only big fish in the small lyric pond is the ode, as Abraham Cowley explains when introducing his own odes in the preface to his *Works* (1656). Significantly, he positions them after the lyrics of *The Miscellanies* and *The Mistress*, and before his epic, *Davideis*:

> For as for the *Pindarick Odes* . . . I am in great doubt whether they will be understood by most *Readers*; nay, even by very many who are well enough acquainted with the common Roads, and ordinary Tracks of *Poesie*. They either are, or at least were meant to be, of that kind of *Stile* which *Dion. Halicarnassus* calls, *Megalophues kai hēdu meta deinotētos*, and which he attributes to *Alcaeus*: The digressions are many, and sudden, and sometimes long, according to the fashion of all *Lyriques*, and of *Pindar* above all men living. The *Figures* are unusual

---

[44] "Longinus" facilitates this attempt to disassociate epigrammatic style from sublimity by criticizing as "deficient in grandeur . . . those passages which are too close-packed and concise, broken up into tiny fragments and short syllables" (*On the Sublime* 41.3). Such passages, he says, "give the impression of being roughly dovetailed together with close-set pins"; they are the opposite of the overly smooth passages Quintilian describes, quoting Cicero, as "a *tesselated pavement of phrases nicely dovetailed together in intricate patterns*" (*Institutio*, 9.4.113): see Trimpi, "HASD," 41–43. "Longinus" also belittles extremely concise, "absolutely short sentences" as "the small change of literature" (42.1).

[45] *Eighteenth-Century Critical Essays*, 2:831.

and *bold*, even to *Temeritie*, and such as I durst not have to do withal
in any other kind of *Poetry*: The *numbers* are various and irregular,
and sometimes (especially some of the long ones) seem harsh and un-
couth. (In *Poems*, 11)

All lyrics may have license to digress, but for Cowley only the ode has
license to use the harshness and obscurity of admirable style; Cowley,
as Tayler notes, "compresses" a passage from the surviving fragment of
Dionysius of Halicarnassus's *On Imitation* (or *De veterum scriptorum
censura*), 2.8: "naturally grand, with brevity, charm, and force."[46] As one
whom Johnson heaped with Donne as a metaphysical wit, Cowley's de-
murral is all the more telling of how the increasing concern with strict
prescriptions for genres worked against admirable style.

When Dryden defends bold figures in "The Author's Apology for Heroic Poetry and Poetic License" (1677), the view that wonder belongs
only in epic or tragedy seems increasingly standard. If Tasso less than a
century earlier was anxious to argue that wonder belonged *especially* to
heroic poetry, Dryden is anxious to argue that wonderful style belongs
there *at least*. Drawing on "Longinus," Horace, and various modern authorities, Dryden insists that epic poets in particular are licensed to fly.
His examples, however, reveal that he still finds lyric wit excusable: he
approves the "strength" of images in Cowley's *Odes* and in other lyric
poems (*Essays*, 1:186). Even "the severest writers of the severest age"—
Virgil and Horace—"have made frequent use of the hardest metaphors,
and of the strongest hyperboles" (1:183).[47] By citing examples from Virgil's *Eclogues* and *Georgics* as well as the *Aeneid*, and Horace's description of the death of Cleopatra (*Odes*, 1.37.26), Dryden extends poetic
license beyond the epic. He follows the trend, however, in handling the
subject, rather than style alone, as the most legitimate cause of poetic
sublimity: "sublime subjects ought to be adorned with the sublimest,
and consequently often with the most figurative expressions" (1:190).
Like most neoclassical critics, Dryden generally adopts his notion of
"sublime subjects" from "Longinus," finding strange and obscure language most appropriate in descriptions of heroes, gods, epic battles, vast

---

[46] I have translated the full phrase from *Dionysii Halicarnasei*, vol. 6.2, ed. Hermann Usener and Ludwig Radermacher (1965); see also *Literary Criticism*, ed. Tayler,
304n5. Dionysius here explicitly links qualities that other authors, Demetrius above
all, take more pains to separate: Alcaeus functions as one of his examples of a mixed
style. In *Rambler* no. 158 Samuel Johnson attacks the idea that lyrics have special
license to digress.

[47] Dryden also aligns in one paragraph the use of bold figures and roughness, both of
which passion excuses or hides (1:185–86).

regions, and powerful forces in nature. He defends, for example, the hyperbole Cowley uses in *Davideis* when describing "Goliah":

> The valley, now, this monster seem'd to fill;
> And we, methought, look'd up to him from our hill.[48]

Here "the two words, *seemed* and *methought*, have mollified the figure; and yet if they had not been there, the fright of the Israelites might have excused their belief of the giant's stature" (1:185). Dryden establishes an implicit order that would become increasingly explicit, especially in Addison and Dennis: "wit" or sublime style is best justified by a grand subject, or by grand passion (in this case epic terror); it is least justified when pursued as an end in itself.[49]

Dryden at least hesitates before restricting wonderful style to epic; others leap. In the essay *Of Poetry* (1690), Sir William Temple anticipates Reynolds' juxtaposition of epic to epigram, grand canvas to intricate miniature. Lyric genres scarcely fulfill his definition of poetry, as he laments when complaining that poets after Ariosto, Tasso, and Spenser abandoned epic (he is apparently ignorant of Davenant, Cowley, and Milton):

> The Wits of the Age soon left off such bold Adventures, and turned to other Veins, as if, not worthy to sit down at the Feast, they contented themselves with the Scraps, with Songs and Sonnets, with Odes and Elegies, with Satyrs and Panegyricks . . . wanting either Genius or Application for Nobler or more Laborious Productions, as *Painters* that cannot Succeed in great Pieces turn to Miniature. (in *Critical Essays*, ed. Spingarn, 3:99)[50]

Modern poetry, he continues, has mined two veins of false gold: ridicule (including but not restricted to satire) and "certain *Fairyes* in the old Regions of Poetry, called *Epigrams*, which seldom reached above the Stature of Two or Four or Six Lines, and which, Being so short, were all turned upon Conceit, or some sharp Hits of Fancy or Wit" (3:100). Sam-

---

[48] Samuel Johnson, too, quotes approvingly from Cowley's description of Goliah—a passage describing his spear as "the trunk . . . of a lofty tree, / Which nature meant some tall ship's mast should be"—and notes that Milton borrowed the image when describing Satan's spear (*Paradise Lost* 1.292): see *Lives*, 1:58.

[49] Cf. *Essays*, 2:166–72; and (for example) Joseph Addison, John Dennis, Joseph Trapp, and Alexander Pope on sublimity, especially epic sublimity, in *Eighteenth-Century Critical Essays* 1:44–71 (esp. 61–64), 100–42, 229–50, and 257–300.

[50] Cf. 3:82, 3:310, and Addison's derisive reference in *Spectator* no. 160 to having "heard many a little Sonneteer [in the general sense of a poet of short lyrics] called a *fine Genius*" (2:126).

uel Werenfels comes down equally hard on the epigram in *A Disserta-tion concerning Meteors of Stile, or False Sublimity* (1711). He offers a general attack on the lack of decorum exhibited by poets who "make *Tityrus* talk in a Pastoral, like *Aeneas* in the Epopee," but reserves spe-cial scorn for "*Ausonius's* Epigram on the Death of *Dido*," which he (or the anonymous translator of his text from Latin to English) translates:

> Poor *Dido* ne'er a happy Husband try'd:
> When the first dy'd, she fled; and when this fled, she dy'd.

His commentary could apply equally well to the epigrams by Donne examined in the introduction, and to his "Niobe":

> Nothing can be more delicate, and yet nothing can be
> less sublime: for he that reads this will not pity the
> Death of *Dido*, but admire the Wit of the Poet; and the
> Beauty of the Antithesis, and the apt turn on the
> words, *fugere* and *perire*, *fly* and *die*, have no other
> effect on us than to make us forget her. St *Augustin*,
> who could not read the Death of *Dido*, in *Virgil's*
> Fourth Æneid, without Tears, wou'd certainly never
> have moisten'd his Eyes at this Epigram.

Wit fails the test of passion here, and wonder fails to be its own excuse. For Werenfels, deliberately strange style is as obsolete as the wonder cabinet, as he makes explicit: "they form a Stile at last, which is just like a Cabinet that is design'd to hold only the Wonders and Curiositys of Nature and Art."[51]

   Werenfels' critique of the epigram on Dido as producing admiration but no passion presages Samuel Johnson's similar complaints through-out the *Life of Cowley*. In his approach to the English authors he found most sublime—Milton and Shakespeare—Johnson's pejorative view of small genres is also notable. His refusal to appreciate "Lycidas" is most famous, but he has limited praise for all of Milton's minor poems, or is at least eager to set them aside to consider *Paradise Lost* (*Lives*, 1:162–70); when Hannah More expressed surprise that "the poet who wrote *Paradise Lost* should write such poor sonnets," Johnson is reputed to have replied, "Milton, Madam, was a genius that could cut a Colossus from a rock, but could not carve heads upon cherry-stones" (1:163n1).

---

[51] *A Dissertation Concerning Meteors of Stile, or False Sublimity*, intro. Edward Tomarken (1980), 206, 214–15, 210.

Johnson of course praises Milton and Shakespeare to the skies for choosing subjects and events of sublimely universal importance; he clips their wings for all instances of admirable style, particularly equivocation, which he finds especially bothersome in Milton's "Lycidas" and throughout Shakespeare.[52] Johnson could tolerate quibbles in what he sees as the colossal corpus of Shakespeare, but not in the small works that resemble Horace's painting that pleases best when the observer is close.

The second and third terms of Horace's comparison, as read through the spectacles of "Longinus" and Quintilian, provided even more ammunition: "This courts the shade, that will wish to be seen in the light, and dreads not the critic insight of the judge. This pleased but once; that, though ten times called for, will always please" (*Art of Poetry*, 363–64). In his second term, Horace does not express a preference either for the work that loves darkness or for that which seeks the sunlight. In the rhetorical tradition, however, where agonistic style was likened to the activity of the soldier, fighting in the open light amid heat and dust, and the epideictic style of the Sophists and the schools of declamation was likened to exercise in the shaded leisure of the gymnasium, to say that a style could not stand the light was to damn it.[53] Scholastic style shrinks from the light of the sun, which represents both the active sphere and the sharp critical scrutiny that would make its artifice noticeable.

Loving the shade, such style fears the public, critical spotlight that would dim the dazzle of its own lights (*lumina*). Following Cicero (*De Oratore*, 3.101–3), Quintilian warns that an overload of *lumina* or *sententiae*, however brilliant, will produce only confusion (*Institutio*, 8.5.25–29; cf. 2.12.7, 12.10.73–78):

> In pictures a definite outline is required to throw objects into relief, and consequently artists who include a number of objects in the same design separate them by intervals sufficient to prevent one casting a shadow on the other. Further, this form of display breaks up our speeches into a number of detached sentences; every *reflexion* (*sententia*) is isolated, and consequently a fresh start is necessary after each. . . . Further, the colour, though bright enough, has no unity, but consists of a number of variegated splashes. . . . Wherefore, although these ornaments may seem to stand out with a certain glitter of their own, they are rather to be compared to sparks flashing through the smoke than to the actual brilliance of flame: they are, in fact, invisible when

[52] See *Lives*, 1:165 and the *Preface to Shakespeare*, in *Works* 7:73–74.
[53] See Trimpi, "MHP," 8–17, and "HASD," 32–49, 68–71; Shuger, *Sacred Rhetoric*, 14–28; and Edinger, *Samuel Johnson*, 146–48.

the language is of uniform splendour, just as the stars are invisible in the light of day.[54]

Both Pope in the *Essay on Criticism* (especially lines 311–17) and Johnson in the *Life of Cowley* draw on Quintilian's attack when they contrast the prismatic, fragmented flash of accumulated conceits with the sun's steady glare; for both Pope and Johnson, as for Horace and Quintilian, design is crucial, and a fragmented representation cannot convey the gestalt of an experience.

"Longinus" seems to indict a style that seeks the shade both when describing forced comparisons as declining "from the terrible to the ridiculous" in the light of day (3.1) and when offering his own comparison of the verbal and the visual (17.1–3). Yet, as in the case of boldness, "Longinus" provides equivocal testimony, supporting both the attacks on admirable wit and a possible defense of it; his handling of the relationship of figures to passion both opens and closes doors for wit. Investigating this relationship was one of the primary interests of neoclassical critics. Drawing on the insistence by Cicero, Horace (*si vis me flere* . . .; "if you would have me weep, . . ."), and "Longinus" himself that an impassioned speaker is a moving speaker, they initiated what M. H. Abrams describes as the transition from mimetic and pragmatic theories of poetry to the expressive theory popular in the nineteenth century.[55] "Longinus," as Abrams and William Edinger have shown, was unique in treating metaphor as the natural language of the passions, but is inconsistent in connecting metaphor to sublimity (17–18, 29, 32).[56] Whereas he treats figures in 17.1–3 and 32.4 as effective only when concealed by a passion that is implicitly distinct from them, he treats metaphor elsewhere as *precisely* the expression of passion in the speaker (32.2 and 32.4) and the cause of emotion in the audience (29.2). "Longinus" does not seem especially concerned to decide whether figurative language causes passion or is an effect of it, probably because for him it can be both.[57]

[54] See Trimpi, "HASD," 65. Edmund Burke, however, finds crowded images especially sublime: see *A Philosophical Enquiry*, esp. 58–64, 78–79.

[55] See M. H. Abrams, *Mirror*, 70–78. Abrams explodes the easy equation of neoclassical criticism with rationalism: "The assertion that eighteenth-century critics read by reason alone is gross calumny. Readers of no age have demanded more, or more violent, emotion from poetry, and not only the sentimentalists, but the most judicial readers as well" (*Mirror*, 71); see also Steven Shankman, *Pope's* Iliad (1983).

[56] See Abrams, *Mirror*, 73; and Edinger, *Samuel Johnson*, 115–17.

[57] Ultimately, as the author of a rhetorical treatise, he is more interested in effects than causes; however thrilled he may be by a speaker's enthusiastic expression of emotion, he concentrates on the pragmatic, on how style affects an audience.

To avoid attracting suspicion, he says, speakers must disguise the artifice of their rhetorical figures under the bright cover of passion or sublimity (17.2–3):

> Much in the same way that dimmer lights vanish in the surrounding radiance of the sun, so the all-embracing atmosphere of grandeur obscures the rhetorical devices (*rhētorikēs sophismata*). We see something of the same kind in painting. Though the high lights and shadows lie side by side in the same plane, yet the high lights spring to the eye and seem not only to stand out but to be much nearer. So it is in writing. What is sublime and moving lies nearer to our hearts, and thus, partly from a natural affinity, partly from brilliance of effect, it always strikes the eye long before the figures. . . .

Rhetorical figures belong in the shade, hidden by the art that conceals art, if they are to have their effect; sublimity—here passion—is on the other hand equivalent to the sun: its darkness bright provides the distraction even the best verbal magician needs.[58] Later, noting that Aristotle and Theophrastus advise speakers to throw in "as it were" when risking a particularly strained metaphor, he encourages them also to cover figures with "strong and timely emotion and genuine sublimity" (32.4).[59] Emotion and sublimity "by their nature sweep everything along in the forward surge of their current, or rather they positively demand bold imagery as essential to their effect, and do not give the hearer time to examine how many metaphors there are, because he shares the excitement of the speaker." Here he blurs together two distinguishable defenses of the daring metaphors of admirable style: that they are expressions of passion, or that their tenuous connections pass unnoticed by readers swept away by enthusiasm.

Because both forms of *deinotēs*—the forceful and the sophistic—employ bold metaphors, and because neoclassical critics tended to classify before evaluating, their judgment concerning the compatibility of compressed metaphor with strong emotion largely determined their attitude

---

[58] On the theme of *ars celare artem* in *On the Sublime* and other rhetorical treatises, see D. A. Russell's edition of "Longinus," *On the Sublime* (1964), 132; and Trimpi, "MHP," 12n18. Sublimity disarms criticism of daring metaphors just as, according to Samuel Johnson, the precociousness of Congreve's "efforts of early genius" insures that "whatever objections may be made either to his comick or tragick excellence . . . are lost at once in the blaze of admiration" (*Lives*, 2:219; cf. 1:2–4). See Paul K. Alkon, "Johnson's Conception of Admiration," *Philological Quarterly* 48 (1969): 66.

[59] Those who describe "Longinus" as Romantic routinely overlook his use of words such as "timely (*eukaira*)" when he describes heightened emotions.

toward admirable style. If they had fully accepted the premise that bold metaphors embody passion, and not focused instead on figures as crowded and affected, they might have characterized admirable style as sublime, on the model of the most forceful or *deinoi* orators, rather than sophistically affected, on the model of Gorgias and other *deinoi* Sophists.

They did not. When Samuel Johnson argued in the *Life of Cowley* that metaphysical conceits were neither sublime nor pathetic, he was following the lead of Dryden, William Walsh, and John Dennis.[60] Taking special aim at admirable style in love poetry, Walsh in the preface to *Letters and Poems, Amorous and Gallant* (1692) claims that unlike Ancient love poets, the Moderns "fill their Verses with Thoughts that are surprizing and glittering, but not tender, passionate, or natural to a Man in Love." Moderns have mistaken the purpose of love poetry, which he takes "not to be the getting Fame or Admiration from the World, but the obtaining the Love of their Mistress." Here the neoclassical emphases on passion and on the requirements of specific genres gang up on witty poetry initially designed more to impress a male coterie and a courtly audience than to pitch sincere woo. In order "to make her love you," a male poet should "convince her that you love her," which "is certainly not to be done by forc'd Conceits, far fetch'd Similes, and shining Points; but by a true and lively Representation of the Pains and Thoughts attending such a Passion." To cap his argument, he simply quotes Horace's familiar lines "*Si vis me flere, dolendum est / Primum ipsi tibi. . . .*"[61]

Charles Gildon came to the defense of conceits, insisting in his *Miscellaneous Letters and Essays* (1694) that to win a mistress's love a poet *should* provoke admiration: "*Admiration* is the only just, and unquestionable Parent of Love; for the Senses or the Mind must be first won with some Perfection, either real or imaginary. Whatever therefore can ravish Fame from the envious censorious World, may justly be suppos'd able to give *Admiration* to a Mistress." Using "Admiration" in its modern sense of respectful love but with still a hint of its connection to rapture, Gildon claims it is entirely compatible with the ultimate goal of love poetry, as are *sententiae*: "*Similes*, fine *Thoughts*, and *shining Points*, if they be just, and good, must certainly give a greater Idea of any Pain, than a bare and unpolished Rhime, without Beauty or Grace. *This*

---

[60] See Edinger, *Samuel Johnson*, 116–18; and Williamson, *Proper Wit*, 108–23.

[61] In *Miscellany Poems*, 4:336–37; later he says that Donne, Waller, Suckling, and Cowley, although in turn witty, gallant, gay, and a genius, all lacked "that Softness, Tenderness, and Violence of Passion, which the Ancients thought most proper for Love Verses" (4:338–39).

gives us a *weak*, a *faint*, an *unmoving* View of the Pain; *That* sets it close to us, magnifies and enlarges it."[62] Gildon's argument shows that metaphors could still be seen as amplifying passion, but few of his contemporaries agreed; as Williamson says, he seems to have been "arguing a lost cause in outmoded terms."[63]

John Dennis, for example, extends Walsh's ban on glittering style to heroic and dramatic poetry, insisting in his *Remarks on . . . Prince Arthur* (1696) that a poet "is oblig'd always to speak to the Heart." Therefore, he says, "Point and Conceit, and all that they call Wit, is to be for ever banish'd from true Poetry; because he who uses it, speaks to the Head alone."[64] Dryden's critique of metaphor is even more pertinent, for two reasons: he draws on "Longinus" to reject the Longinian view of metaphor as the natural language of passion, and like Cowley he grows critical after the Restoration of a style he had used in his youth (most notably in "Upon the Death of the Lord Hastings"). A year after Walsh, Dryden criticizes Donne because he "affects the metaphysics, not only in his satires, but in his amorous verses, where nature only should reign" (*A Discourse Concerning the Original and Progress of Satire* [1693]).[65] In the *Preface to Troilus and Cressida* (1679), he had argued that authors must work passion up gradually and should avoid "pointed wit, and sentences affected out of season; these are nothing of kin to the violence of passion: no man is at leisure to make sentences and similes, when his soul is in an agony." "It is not that I would explode the use of metaphors from passion," Dryden continues, "for Longinus thinks 'em necessary to raise it: but to use 'em at every word, to say nothing without a metaphor, a simile, an image, or description, is, I doubt, to smell a little too strongly of the buskin."[66] Dryden's phrase "smell . . . of the

---

[62] In *Literary Criticism*, ed. Tayler, 403. Again, it is notable that the culprits needing defense include Edmund Waller and Abraham Cowley, which suggests that modern literary historians too sharply juxtapose the "easy" poets to Donne. Grierson's inclusion of Suckling and Davenant in the first edition of *Metaphysical Lyrics* (1921) indicates, as Alastair Fowler notes, that "his idea of it [metaphysical poetry] was wider than ours" (*Metaphysical Lyrics* (1995), viii). See also Johnson, *Lives*, 1:22; and Marotti, *Manuscript, Print*, 155.

[63] *Proper Wit*, 112.

[64] *The Critical Works of John Dennis*, ed. Edward Niles Hooker (1939), 1:127.

[65] In Dryden, *Essays*, 2:19. Dryden attacks strong lines more fiercely in his "Dedication of The Spanish Friar" (1681: "in the heightenings of Poetry, the strength and vehemence of figures should be suited to the occasion, the subject, and the persons. All beyond this is monstrous: 'tis out of Nature, 'tis an excrescence, and not a living part of Poetry" (1:247).

[66] Ibid., 1:223. The gradual, accumulative method of amplification that Dryden encourages in drama resembles that which "Longinus" attributes to Cicero in oratory, and compares unfavorably with the more abrupt method of Demosthenes (*On the*

buskin" echoes other critiques of affected style as "smelling of the lamp"; for Dryden such style exhibits what "Longinus" describes as "puerility (*meirakiōdes*)," or "the academic attitude, where over-elaboration ends in frigid failure" (*On the Sublime*, 3.4). Despite the high status that "Longinus" himself accords metaphor, then, Dryden, like Meric Casaubon, uses "Longinus" to treat strong lines as affected, as sophistic not sublime.[67]

The final term in Horace's comparison—"This pleased but once; that, though ten times called for, will always please"—harmonizes with the second when critics describe admirable style as composed of little lights unequal in intensity or duration to the splendor of the sun. They repeatedly deny the claim that Anthony Bacon had made for Tacitean obscurity, that "the seconde reading over will please thee more than the first, and the third then the second" (*The Ende of Nero*, ¶3r). In rejecting wit's wonder as ephemeral, Samuel Johnson in particular undercuts the justification it derives from philosophy, theology, and rhetoric: that obscurity teaches by provoking inquiry. By comparing the admiration produced by metaphysical style to that produced by the novel and strange rather than the profound—by separating "admiration" from "rational admiration"—Johnson places metaphysical poetry into the category of Horace's poem and painting that please only once.

Critics of wit often align the second and third terms in Horace's analogy with the contrast Quintilian offers between the little lights of sententious style and the sun's grand, enduring splendor. Well before Pope or Johnson describe wit's effect as prismatic, John Sheffield, Earl of Musgrave, chops wielders of wit down from hidden gods into wavers of sparklers:

Sublime, 12). After alluding to the critique by "Longinus" of pseudotragic comparisons in Aeschylus, Dryden uses *occupatio* to insinuate that Shakespeare errs likewise: "I will not say of so great a poet, that he distinguished not the blown puffy style from true sublimity ; but . . . the fury of his fancy often transported him beyond the bounds of judgment, either in coining of new words and phrases, or racking words which were in use, into the violence of a catachresis" (1:224).

[67] Thomas Warton claims in "Observations on the *Fairy Queen*" (1754) that after Spenser "allegory began to decline, and by degrees gave place to a species of poetry whose images were of the metaphysical and abstracted kind." He attributes this "fashion" to "the predominant studies of the time, in which the disquisitions of school divinity and the perplexed subtilities of philosophical disputation became the principal pursuits of the learned" (*Eighteenth-Century Critical Essays*, 2:781). Two decades before Johnson wrote the *Life of Cowley*, Warton had already combined Dryden's criticism of Donne because he "affects the metaphysics" and "perplexes" his readers with Bacon's attack on scholastic method for its "digladiation about subtilities."

> 'Tis not a Flash of Fancy which sometimes
> Dasling our Minds, sets off the slightest Rimes;
> Bright as a blaze, but in a moment done;
> True Wit is everlasting, like the Sun,
> Which though sometimes beneath a cloud retir'd,
> Breaks out again, and is by all admir'd.[68]

Dryden's *Dedication of the Aeneis* (1697) similarly juxtaposes the stay-
ing power of true wit—found in works where judgment controls imagination—to that of quick wit.[69] "Judicious" works win loyalty from
"souls of the highest rank, and truest understanding," an elite superior
both to "mob readers" who "like nothing but the husk and rind of wit,"
preferring "a quibble, a conceit, an epigram before solid sense and elegant expression," and to "warm young men, who are not yet arrived so
far as to discern the difference betwixt fustian, or ostentatious sentences, and the true sublime." Authors winning approval from the highest souls "can never lose it, because they never give it blindly." "For
this reason," Dryden concludes:

> A well-weighed judicious poem, which at first appearance gains no
> more upon the world than to be just received, and rather not blamed
> than much applauded, insinuates itself by insensible degrees into the
> liking of the reader: the more he studies it, the more it grows upon
> him; every time he takes it up, he discovers some new graces in it.
> And whereas poems which are produced by the vigour of imagination
> only have a gloss upon them at first which time wears off, the works
> of judgment are like the diamond; the more they are polished, the
> more lustre they receive. Such is the difference betwixt Virgil's *Aeneis*
> and Marini's [sic] *Adone.*

Marino, of course, is the poet of the marvelous whom Johnson accuses
in the *Life of Cowley* of being a foreign model for English metaphysical
style.[70]

For Johnson, similarly, the metaphysicals, though at times capable of
producing "admiration," "never attempted that comprehension and ex-

---

[68] *An Essay on Poetry* (1682), in *Critical Essays*, 2:286; W. Lee Ustick and Hoyt H.
Hudson attribute this poem to George Villiers, second Duke of Buckingham: see
"Wit, 'Mixt Wit,' and the Bee in Amber," *Huntington Library Bulletin* 8 (1935): 105–
6.

[69] See Ustick and Hudson, "Wit," 114.

[70] Dryden, *Essays*, 2:223, 2:225; cf. 1:221; on the style, influence, and reputation of
Marino see Mirollo, *Poet of the Marvelous.*

panse of thought which at once fills the whole mind, and of which the first effect is sudden astonishment, and the second rational admiration" (*Lives*, 1:20–21).[71] Johnson's comment derives from a passage in "Longinus" concerning the duration of wonder:

> The true sublime, by some virtue of its nature, elevates us. . . . If, then, a man of sense, well-versed in literature, after hearing a passage several times finds that it does not affect him with a sense of sublimity, and does not leave behind in his mind more food for thought than the mere words at first suggest, but rather that on careful consideration it sinks in his esteem, then it cannot really be the true sublime, if its effect does not outlast the moment of utterance. (*On the Sublime*, 7.2–3)

"Food for thought" is exactly what the poets Johnson labels "metaphysical" believed they were providing through the brief, obscure lines they wrote in emulation of the *suspiciones* of ancient rhetoric. They did not satisfy Johnson's appetite.

Johnson routinely uses both "wonder" and "admiration" as terms for the brief pleasure evoked by strangeness, as Paul Alkon and William Edinger have shown; he defines "wonder," for example, as "the effect of novelty upon ignorance" (*Lives*, 2:303).[72] The metaphysicals, who he says "fail to give delight, by their desire of exciting admiration," sometimes produce lines that are "improper and vitious" through "a voluntary deviation from nature in pursuit of something new and strange" (*Lives*, 1:35). Admiration based on the unnatural, as he says when analyzing the burlesque in the *Life of Butler*, is doomed: "All disproportion is unnatural; and from what is unnatural we can derive only the pleasure which novelty produces. We admire it awhile as a strange thing; but, when it is no longer strange, we perceive its deformity. It is a kind of artifice, which by frequent repetition detects itself; and the

---

[71] Cf. Johnson's explanation of Shakespeare's lasting appeal in the *Preface to Shakespeare* (*Works*, 7:61–62).

[72] See Alkon, "Johnson's Conception of Admiration" and Edinger, *Samuel Johnson*, 152–53. Johnson criticizes Dryden's *Absalom and Achitophel*, for example, because it has "little imagery or description, and a long poem of mere sentiments easily becomes tedious; though all the parts are forcible and every line kindles new rapture, the reader, if not relieved by the interposition of something that soothes the fancy, grows weary of admiration, and defers the rest" (*Lives*, 1:437). As Alkon notes (68), Johnson includes among his definitions of "sentiment" "a striking sentence in a composition." Johnson similarly admits that Pope's *Essay on Man* "abounded in splendid amplifications and sparkling sentences, which were read and admired," but admired only "for a time" (*Lives*, 3:164). A work that consists of *sententiae* without relief, lights without background, soon cloys.

reader, learning in time what he is to expect, lays down his book" (*Lives*, 1:218).[73] The strange, as Aristotle says, is admirable; but only, Johnson adds, until it too becomes familiar. By classifying metaphysical style as unnatural, novel, monstrous, Johnson and others imply that it can please only until its forms of strangeness become predictable, its deviations a new norm.

Admirable wit's failure "to give delight" is strike three. Out of tune with influential accounts of intellection, passion, and pleasure, wonderful style loses its primary defense, its protean ability to present itself as fulfilling the three primary goals poetry had borrowed from rhetoric: teaching, moving, and delighting. Having outlived the social circumstances that made indulgence in it so appealing, and made self-representation as a quick wit both necessary and dangerous, admirable style could not outlive the critical assault that began to be directed at it early in the century, and intensified. Critics who viewed strong lines through a composite lens provided by Horace, "Longinus," and Quintilian saw the *deinotēs* of the Sophists, not the *deinotēs* that transports the audience. According to these critics, poems written in imitation of the Sophists' style would, obscure themselves, love the shade (*oscurum*), prefer to avoid critical inquiry, and please once, briefly. Because their poems lacked the grandeur of tragedy and epic, lyric poets were forced to give back the thunder they had stolen.

As the continuing employment of Modernist techniques in various arts even at the end of the century that gave birth to them shows, styles often come more quickly than they go. Free verse has already reigned longer, and come to seem more natural, than strong lines or metaphysi-

---

[73] See Alkon, "Johnson's Conception of Admiration," 73. William Drummond of Hawthornden, in the letter to Dr. Arthur Johnston labeling contemporary poetry "metaphysical," declares that any possible "new *Idea* like *Poesy*" that the new poets could create "may (indeed) be something like unto *Poesy*, but it is no more *Poesy* than a Monster is a Man. Monsters breed Admiration at the First, but have ever some strange Loathsomeness in them at last" (*Literary Criticism*, ed. Tayler, 216). Dryden, who like Drummond found conceited style to be scholastic, states that "the union of two contraries may as well produce a monster as a miracle" (ibid., 16; cf. 340–41). Those who find conceited style monstrous see deformity in its lack of unity and proportion: the whole is sacrificed for the parts, which are themselves exaggerated. They often draw on the opening of the *Art of Poetry*, where Horace ridicules a painter who would choose "to join a human head to the neck of a horse, and to spread feathers of many a hue over limbs picked up now here now there, so that what at the top is a lovely woman ends below in a black and ugly fish." "Quite like such pictures," he insists, "would be a book, whose idle fancies shall be shaped like a sick man's dreams, so that neither head nor foot can be assigned to a single shape" (1–10). Like his concluding portrait of the mad poet who thinks himself inspired by furor poeticus, Horace's opening comparison sticks a pin in those who claim artistic license excuses all structural deficiencies.

cal wit did. Far-fetched metaphors had the longest vogue, in part because they were so adaptable to devotional verse re-presenting the Christian mysteries, and in part because no courtly culture seems able to operate without hyperbole. Roughness disappeared more quickly, falling to the combined force of the increasingly cosmopolitan tone at court (as reflected in the classical proportions of Inigo Jones's designs), the pacifism of James, and the banning of satire, the lyric genre that most tolerated harshness, abruptness, and brevity. Equivocation and quick wit became increasingly suspect early in the Stuart era, and the kind of self-display with which they were connected became less and less necessary because of the expansion of titles and the constriction of courtly duties (at least nominally) under absolutism.

In a sense, admirable lyric wit was the flamboyant finale of courtier poetry, its flameout before extinction. If the rise of absolutism seems merely coincident with the fall of witty wonder, it is worth remembering that more than a style disappeared in the middle of the seventeenth century, that the methods of the new mechanistic philosophy were brought to bear on more than the natural landscape: both poetry and politics became substantially more professional over the course of the century, and the courtier-poet, reflecting dread majesty at a third remove, became obsolete. It takes less than metaphysical wit, that is, to yoke three developments: print lost its stigma, Hoby's translation of the *Courtier* lost its audience, and lyric poets lost their claim on the strange and admirable, their ability to insinuate themselves into power.

Bibliography

Primary Texts

Ad C. Herennium: de ratione dicendi (Rhetorica ad Herennium). Trans. Harry Caplan. Loeb Classical Library. Cambridge: Harvard University Press, 1954.

Addison, Joseph. *The Spectator*. 5 vols. Ed. Donald F. Bond. Oxford: Clarendon Press, 1965.

Advice to a Son: Precepts of Lord Burghley, Sir Walter Raleigh, and Francis Osborne. Ed. Louis B. Wright. Ithaca: Cornell University Press, 1962.

Albertus Magnus. *Opera Omnia*. Vol. 6. Ed. Augustus Borgnet. Paris: Apud Ludovicum Vives, Bibliopolam Editorem, 1890.

Andrewes, Lancelot. *The Works of Lancelot Andrewes*. 11 vols. Library of Anglo-Catholic Theology. 1841–54. New York: AMS, 1967.

Anton, Robert. *Vices Anotomie, Scourged and Corrected in New Satires*. London, 1617.

Aquinas, Thomas. *Basic Writings of Saint Thomas Aquinas*. 2 vols. Ed. Anton C. Pegis. New York: Random House, 1945.

——. *Summa Theologiae*. London: Blackfriars, 1963–75.

Aristotle. *The "Art" of Rhetoric*. Trans. J. H. Freese. Loeb Classical Library. Cambridge: Harvard University Press, 1926.

——. *The Complete Works of Aristotle: The Revised Oxford Translation*. 2 vols. Ed. Jonathan Barnes. Princeton: Princeton University Press, 1984.

——. *On the Soul*. Trans. W. S. Hett. Loeb Classical Library. Cambridge: Harvard University Press, 1964.

——. *The Poetics.* Trans. W. Hamilton Fyfe. Loeb Classical Library. Rev. ed. Cambridge: Harvard University Press, 1932.

Ascham, Roger. *The Schoolmaster* (1570). Ed. Lawrence V. Ryan. Folger Documents of Tudor and Stuart Civilization 13. Charlottesville: University Press of Virginia, 1967.

Aubrey, John. *Aubrey's Brief Lives.* Ed. Oliver Lawson Dick. London: Secker and Warburg, 1950.

Augustine, Aurelius. *The Confessions of Saint Augustine.* Trans. Edward B. Pusey, D.D. New York: Collier, 1961.

——. *De Utilitate Credendi. A Library of Fathers of the Holy Catholic Church* 22. Ed. John Henry Parker. London: Rivington, 1847.

——. *De Utilitate Credendi. Patrologiae Cursus Completus* 42. Ed. J.-P. Migne. Paris: Migne, 1845.

——. *Epistulae. Corpus Scriptorum Ecclesiasticorum Latinorum* 33. Ed. Alois Goldbacher. 1895. New York: Johnson Reprint, 1970.

——. *Letters.* Vol. 2. Trans. Sister Wilfrid Parsons. New York: Fathers of the Church, 1953.

——. *On Christian Doctrine.* Trans. D. W. Robertson, Jr. Indianapolis: Bobbs-Merrill, 1958.

Bacon, Francis. *The Works of Francis Bacon.* 14 vols. Ed. James Spedding et al. 1857–74. Stuttgart: Friedrich Frommann, 1963.

Boccalini, Traiano. *The New-Found Politicke.* London, 1626. [Translation of *Ragguagli di Parnasso* (Venice, 1612).]

Boileau-Despréaux, Nicolas. *The Art of Poetry.* In *Critical Theory Since Plato,* ed. Hazard Adams. 258–71. New York: Harcourt Brace Jovanovich, 1971.

A Book of "Characters." Ed. and Trans. Richard Aldington. London: Routledge, 1924.

Breton, Nicholas. *The Court and Country.* London, 1618.

——. *Melancholike Humours.* 1600. Ed. G. B. Harrison. London: Scholartis, 1929.

Bright, Thomas. *A Treatise of Melancholie.* 1586. New York: Columbia University Press, 1940.

Browne, Sir Thomas. *Religio Medici.* In *Selected Writings.* Ed. Sir Geoffrey Keynes. Chicago: University of Chicago Press, 1968.

Burke, Edmund. *A Philosophical Enquiry into the Origin of Our Ideas of the Sublime and Beautiful.* Ed. James T. Boulton. 1958. Notre Dame: University of Notre Dame Press, 1968.

Burton, Robert. *The Anatomy of Melancholy.* Ed. Holbrook Jackson. 1932. New York: Vintage, 1977.

Cartwright, William. *Comedies, Tragi-Comedies, With other Poems.* London, 1651.

Casaubon, Meric. *A Treatise Concerning Enthusiasme.* 2nd. ed. 1656. Gainesville, Fla.: Scholars' Facsimiles, 1970.

Castiglione, Baldassare. *The Book of the Courtier.* Trans. Sir Thomas Hoby. 1561. New York: Dutton, 1975.

Cicero, M. Tullius. *De Inventione, De Optimo Genere Oratorum, Topica.* Trans. H. M. Hubbell. Loeb Classical Library. Cambridge: Harvard University Press, 1949.

——. *Orator.* In *Brutus, Orator.* Trans. G. L. Hendrickson and H. M. Hubbell. Loeb Classical Library. Rev. ed. Cambridge: Harvard University Press, 1962.

——. *De Oratore.* 2 vols. Trans. E. W. Sutton and H. Rackham. Loeb Classical Library. Cambridge: Harvard University Press, 1942.

——. *De Partitione Oratoria.* Trans. H. Rackham. Loeb Classical Library. Cambridge: Harvard University Press, 1942.

Clash, The. "Death or Glory." *London Calling.* LP. CBS (U.K.), 1979.

Clement of Alexandria. *Les Stromates.* Vol. 2. Trans. Claude Mondesert, S.J. Sources Chrétiennes 38. Paris: Editions du Cerf, 1954.

——. *The Stromata, or Miscellanies. The Ante-Nicene Fathers.* Vol. 2. Ed. The Rev. Alexander Roberts and James Donaldson. American ed. Grand Rapids, Mich.: Eerdmans, 1951.

Cleveland, John. *The Poems of John Cleveland.* Ed. Brian Morris and Eleanor Withington. Oxford: Oxford University Press, 1967.

The "Conceited Newes" of Sir Thomas Overbury and His Friends. A Facsimile Reproduction of the Ninth Impression of 1616 of *Sir Thomas Overbury His Wife.* Ed. James E. Savage. Gainesville, Fla.: Scholars' Facsimiles, 1968.

Cowley, Abraham. *Poems.* Ed. A. R. Waller. Cambridge: Cambridge University Press, 1905.

Critical Essays of the Seventeenth Century. Ed. J. E. Spingarn. 3 vols. 1908–9. Bloomington: Indiana University Press, 1957.

Critical Theory Since Plato. Ed. Hazard Adams. New York: Harcourt, 1971.

Cusanus, Nicholas. *Nicholas of Cusa on Learned Ignorance.* Trans. Jasper Hopkins. 2d. ed. Minnneapolis: Banning, 1981.

——. *Nicholas of Cusa's Dialectical Mysticism.* Trans. Jasper Hopkins. Minneapolis: Banning, 1985.

Davenant, William. *Madagascar; With Other Poems.* London, 1638.

Dekker, Thomas. *The Dramatic Works of Thomas Dekker.* Vol. 2. Ed. Fredson Bowers. Cambridge: Cambridge University Press, 1964.

Demetrius. *Demetrius On Style.* Ed. and trans. W. Rhys Roberts. 1902. Hildesheim: Georg Olms, 1962.

——. *On Style.* Trans. W. Rhys Roberts. Loeb Classical Library. Rev. ed. Cambridge: Harvard University Press, 1932.

Dennis, John. *The Critical Works of John Dennis.* 2 vols. Ed. Edward Niles Hooker. Baltimore: Johns Hopkins University Press, 1939.

Descartes, René. *The Passions of the Soul.* Trans. Stephen Voss. Indianapolis: Hackett, 1989.

Dionysius of Halicarnassus. *The Critical Essays.* Trans. Stephen Usher. 2 vols. Loeb Classical Library. Cambridge: Harvard University Press, 1974–85.

——. *Dionysii Halicarnasei*. Vol. 6.2. Ed. Hermann Usener and Ludwig Radermacher. 1929. Stuttgart: Teubner, 1965.

Donne, John. *Devotions Upon Emergent Occasions*. Ann Arbor: University of Michigan Press, 1959.

——. *The Divine Poems*. Ed. Helen Gardner. 2nd ed. Oxford: Clarendon Press, 1978.

——. *The Elegies and the Songs and Sonnets*. Ed. Helen Gardner. Oxford: Clarendon Press, 1965.

——. *The Epithalamions, Anniversaries, and Epicedes*. Ed. W. Milgate. Oxford: Clarendon Press, 1978.

——. *Essays in Divinity*. Ed. Evelyn M Simpson. Oxford: Oxford University Press, 1952.

——. *Ignatius His Conclave*. Ed. T. S. Healy, S.J. Oxford: Oxford University Press, 1969.

——. *The Satires, Epigrams and Verse Letters*. Ed. W. Milgate. Oxford: Clarendon Press, 1967.

——. *The Sermons of John Donne*. 10 vols. Ed. Evelyn M. Simpson and George R. Potter. Berkeley: University of California Press, 1953–62.

Dryden, John. *Essays of John Dryden*. 2 vols. Ed. W. P. Ker. Oxford: Clarendon Press, 1900.

——. *The Works of John Dryden*. Vol. 1. Ed. E. N. Hooker and H. T. Swedenborg, Jr. Berkeley: University of California Press, 1956.

Eighteenth-Century Critical Essays. Ed. Scott Elledge. 2 vols. Ithaca: Cornell University Press, 1961.

Elizabethan Critical Essays. Ed. G. G. Smith. 2 vols. Oxford: Oxford University Press, 1904.

Elyot, Sir Thomas. *The Book Named the Governor*. Ed. S. E. Lehmberg. London: Dent, 1962.

——. *The Castel of Helth*. 1541. New York: Scholars' Facsimiles, n.d.

English Literary Criticism: The Renaissance. Ed. O. B. Hardison, Jr. New York: Meredith, 1963.

Fracastoro, Girolamo. *Naugerius, sive De Poetica Dialogus*. Trans. Ruth Kelso. *University of Illinois Studies in Language and Literature* 9 (1924): 1–88 [318–404].

Gorgias. "Encomium of Helen." In *Ancilla to the Pre-Socratic Philosophers*, ed. Kathleen Freeman. 131–33. Cambridge: Harvard University Press, 1948.

Greene, Robert. *The Life and Complete Works in Prose and Verse of Robert Greene, M.A.* Vol. 5. Ed. Alexander B. Grosart. London, 1883.

Greville, Fulke [First Lord Brooke]. *Poems and Dramas of Fulke Greville, First Lord Brooke*. 2 vols. Ed. Geoffrey Bullough. New York: Oxford University Press, 1945.

Guazzo, Stefano. *The Civile Conversation of M. Steeven Guazzo*. Books 1–3. Trans. George Pettie 1581. Book 4. Trans. Bartholomew Young 1586. 2d ed. 2 vols. Ed. Edward Sullivan. London: Constable, 1925.

Hall, Joseph. *The Collected Poems of Joseph Hall.* Ed. Arnold Davenport. Liverpool: University Press of Liverpool, 1949.

Harington, John. *Nugae Antiquae.* Vol. 2. Ed. Thomas Park. 1804. New York: AMS Press, 1966.

Herbert, George. *The English Poems of George Herbert.* Ed. C. A. Patrides. London: Dent, 1974.

Lord Herbert of Cherbury, Edward Herbert. *The Poems English and Latin of Edward, Lord Herbert of Cherbury.* Ed. G. C. Moore Smith. Oxford: Clarendon Press, 1923.

Hermogenes. *Hermogenes' On Types of Style.* Trans. Cecil W. Wooten. Chapel Hill: University of North Carolina Press, 1987.

Horace. *Satires, Epistles and Ars Poetica.* Trans. H. Rushton Fairclough. Loeb Classical Library. Rev. ed. Cambridge: Harvard University Press, 1929.

Hoskyns, John. *Directions for Speech and Style, by John Hoskins.* Ed. Hoyt H. Hudson. Princeton: Princeton University Press, 1935.

——. *The Life, Letters, and Writings of John Hoskyns 1566–1638.* Ed. Louise Brown Osborn. 1930. Hamden, Conn.: Archon, 1973.

Huarte, Juan. *Examen De Ingenios: The Examination of Mens Wits.* Trans. Richard Carew. 1594. Ed. Carmen Rogers. Gainesville, Fla.: Scholars' Facsimiles, 1959.

Hume, David. *A Treatise of Human Nature.* Ed. L. A. Selby-Bigge. 2d ed. Rev. Ph. H. Nidditch. Oxford: Clarendon Press, 1978.

Isocrates. *Isocrates.* 3 vols. Trans. George Norlin and LaRue Van Hook. Loeb Classical Library. Cambridge: Harvard University Press, 1928–45.

James I. *The Political Works of James I.* Ed. Charles Howard McIlwain. 1918. New York: Russell & Russell, 1965.

Johnson, Robert. *Essaies, or, Rather Imperfect Offers.* 1607. Ed. Robert Hood Bowers. Gainesville, Fla.: Scholars' Facsimiles, 1955.

Johnson, Samuel. *Lives of the English Poets.* Ed. George Birkbeck Hill. 3 vols. Oxford: Clarendon Press, 1905.

——. *The Yale Edition of the Works of Samuel Johnson.* Gen. ed. John H. Middendorf. New Haven: Yale University Press, 1958–.

Jonson, Ben. *Ben Jonson.* 11 vols. Ed. C. H. Herford, and Percy and Evelyn Simpson. Oxford: Clarendon Press, 1925–52.

——. *Ben Jonson.* Ed. Ian Donaldson. Oxford Authors Series. Oxford: Oxford University Press, 1985.

Juvenal. *Juvenal and Persius.* Trans. G. G. Ramsay. Loeb Classical Library. Rev. ed. Cambridge: Harvard University Press, 1940.

Kant, Immanuel. *Kritik der Urteilskraft.* Ed. Karl Vorländer. 1924. Hamburg: Meiner, 1968.

——. *The Critique of Judgment.* Trans. James Creed Meredith. 1928. Oxford: Oxford University Press, 1957.

Keats, John. *John Keats.* Ed. Elizabeth Cook. Oxford: Oxford University Press, 1994.

Laurentius, M. Andreas. *A Discourse of the Preservation of the Sight: of Melancolike Diseases; of Rheumes, and of Old Age.* Trans. Richard Surphlet. 1599. Shakespeare Association Facsimiles 15. Oxford: Oxford University Press, 1938.

Literary Criticism: Plato to Dryden. Ed. Allan H. Gilbert. 1940. Detroit: Wayne State University Press, 1962.

Literary Criticism of Seventeenth-Century England. Ed. Edward W. Tayler. New York: Knopf, 1967.

Lodge, Thomas. *The Complete Works of Thomas Lodge.* Vol. 4. 1883. New York: Johnson Reprint, 1966.

"Longinus." *On the Sublime.* Trans. W. Hamilton Fyfe. Loeb Classical Library. Rev. ed. Cambridge: Harvard University Press, 1932.

——. *On the Sublime.* Ed. D. A. Russell. Oxford: Clarendon Press, 1964.

Marlowe, Christopher. *The Complete Plays.* Ed. J. B. Steane. Harmondsworth: Penguin, 1969.

Marston, John. *The Poems of John Marston.* Ed. Arnold Davenport. Liverpool: Liverpool University Press, 1961.

——. *The Selected Plays of John Marston.* Ed. MacDonald P. Jackson and Michael Neill. Cambridge: Cambridge University Press, 1986.

Marvell, Andrew. *Andrew Marvell: The Complete Poems.* Ed. Elizabeth Story Donno. Harmondsworth: Penguin, 1972.

Metaphysical Lyrics and Poems of the Seventeenth Century: Donne to Butler. Ed Herbert J. C. Grierson. Rev. Alastair Fowler. New York: Oxford University Press, 1995.

Milton, John. *Complete Poems and Major Prose.* Ed. Merritt Y. Hughes. Indianapolis: Odyssey, 1957.

——. *Complete Prose Works of John Milton, vol. 2: 1643–1648.* Ed. Ernest Sirluck. New Haven: Yale University Press, 1959.

——. *The Works of John Milton.* Gen. Ed. Frank Allen Patterson. Vol. 3, Part 1. New York: Columbia University Press, 1931.

Montaigne, Michel de. *The Essayes of Montaigne.* Trans. John Florio. 1603. New York: Modern Library, 1933.

Peacham, Henry. *The Garden of Eloquence.* 1577. English Linguistics 1500–1800, no. 267. Menston, Eng.: Scolar Press, 1971.

Philostratus. *The Life of Apollonius of Tyana.* Vol. 2. Trans. F. C. Conybeare. Loeb Classical Library. Rev. ed. Cambridge: Harvard University Press, 1950.

Plato. *The Collected Dialogues of Plato.* Ed. Edith Hamilton and Huntington Cairns. Bollingen Series 71. Princeton: Princeton University Press, 1963.

——. *Opera.* Vol. 4. Scriptorum Classicorum Bibliotheca Oxoniensis. Oxford: Clarendon Press, 1905.

——. *Plato's Euthyphro, Apology of Socrates, and Crito.* Ed. John Burnet. Oxford: Clarendon Press, 1924.

——. *Plato's Theory of Knowledge (The Theaetetus and the Sophist of Plato).* Trans. Francis M. Cornford. 1934. Indianapolis: Bobbs-Merrill, 1957.

Plotinus. *Plotinus: The Enneads*. Trans. Stephen MacKenna, rev. S. B. Page. London: Farber, 1962.

Plutarch. *The Philosophie, commonlie called, The Morals*. Trans. Philemon Holland. London, 1603.

Le Prince d'Amour. London, 1660. [Microfilm].

Pseudo-Dionysius. *Pseudo-Dionysius: The Complete Works*. Trans. Colm Luibheid. Classics of Western Spirituality. New York: Paulist Press, 1987.

Puttenham, George. *The Arte of English Poesie*. Ed. Gladys Doidge Willcock and Alice Walker. Cambridge: Cambridge University Press, 1936.

Quarles, Francis. *Argalus and Parthenia*. London, 1647.

Quintilian. *Institutio Oratoria*. 4 vols. Trans. H. E. Butler. Loeb Classical Library. Cambridge: Harvard University Press, 1920–21.

Rainolde, Richard. *The Foundation of Rhetoric*. 1563. English Linguistics 1500–1800, no. 347. Menston, Eng.: Scolar Press, 1972.

Rankins, William. *Seven Satires*. 1598. Ed. A. Davenport. London: University Press of Liverpool, 1948.

Reynolds, Sir Joshua. *Discourses on Art*. Introduction by Robert R. Wark. 1959. New York: Collier, 1966.

Rudyerd, Sir Benjamin. *Memoirs of Sir Bejamin Rudyerd, Knt., Containing His Speeches and Poems*. Ed. James Alexander Manning. London: T & W Boone, 1841.

Seneca, Lucius Annaeus. *Ad Lucilium Epistulae Morales*. 3 vols. Trans. Richard M. Gummere. Loeb Classical Library. Cambridge: Harvard University Press, 1917–25.

——. *Moral Essays*. Vol. 2. Trans. John W. Basore. Loeb Classical Library. Cambridge: Harvard University Press, 1979.

——. *The Workes of Lucius Annaeus Seneca, Both Moral and Naturall*. Trans. Thomas Lodge. London, 1614.

Shakespeare, William. *The Complete Pelican Shakespeare: The Comedies and the Romances*. Gen. ed. Alfred Harbage. Rev. ed. 1969. Harmondsworth: Penguin, 1981.

——. *A Midsummer Night's Dream*. Ed. R. A. Foakes. The New Cambridge Shakespeare. Cambridge: Cambridge University Press, 1984.

——. *The Riverside Shakespeare*. Ed. G. Blakemore Evans et al. Boston: Houghton Mifflin, 1974.

Sidney, Sir Philip. *A Defence of Poetry*. Ed. J. A. Van Dorsten. 1966. Oxford: Oxford University Press, 1971.

Tacitus, Cornelius. *The Ende of Nero and Beginning of Galba. Fower Bookes of the Histories of Cornelius Tacitus. The Life of Agricola*. Trans. Sir Henry Savile. *The Annales of Cornelius Tacitus. The description of Germanie*. Trans. Richard Greneway. London, 1598.

Tasso, Torquato. *Discourses on the Heroic Poem*. Trans. Mariella Cavalchini and Irene Samuel. Oxford: Clarendon Press, 1973.

——. _Scritti Sull'Arte Poetica_. Ed. Ettore Mazzali. 1959. 2 vols. Torino: Einaudi, 1977.
The Three Parnassus Plays (1598–1601). Ed. J. B. Leishman. London: Ivor Nicholson & Watson, 1949.
Vaughan, Henry. _The Complete Poems_. Ed. Alan Rudrum. 1976. New Haven: Yale University Press, 1981.
Walkington, Thomas. _The Optick Glasse of Humours_. 1631. Ed. John A. Popplestone and Marion White McPherson. Delmar, N.Y.: Scholars' Facsimiles, 1981.
Walsh, William. "Preface to _Letters and Poems, Amorous and Gallant_." _Miscellany Poems_. [Attributed to John Dryden] Vol. 4: 335–342. Ed. Jacob Tonson. London, 1716.
Watson, William. _A Decacordon of Ten Quodlibeticall Questions_. 1602. Ed. D. M. Rogers. English Recusant Literature 197. London: Scolar, 1974.
Werenfels, Samuel. _A Dissertation Concerning Meteors of Stile, or False Sublimity_ (1711). Intro. Edward Tomarken. Augustan Reprint Society Publication 199. Los Angeles: Augustan Reprint Society, 1980.
Wilson, Thomas. _The Arte of Rhetorique_. London, 1553.
Wright, Thomas. _The Passions of the Minde in Generall_. 1604. Ed. Thomas O. Sloan. Urbana: University of Illinois Press, 1971.

✳ ✳ ✳ ✳ ✳ ✳ ✳ ✳ ✳ ✳ ✳ ✳ ✳ ✳ ✳ ✳ ✳ ✳ ✳ ✳

Secondary Texts

Abrams, M. H. _The Mirror and the Lamp: Romantic Theory and the Critical Tradition_. London: Oxford University Press, 1953.
Alkon, Paul K. "Johnson's Conception of Admiration." _Philological Quarterly_ 48 (1969): 59–81.
Altman, Joel. _The Tudor Play of Mind_. Berkeley: University of California Press, 1978.
Amussen, Susan. _An Ordered Society: Gender and Class in Early Modern England_. Oxford: Blackwell, 1988.
Anglo, Sydney. "More Machiavellian than Machiavel." In _John Donne: Essays in Celebration_, ed. A. J. Smith, 349–84. London: Methuen, 1973.
Armstrong, Alan. "The Apprenticeship of John Donne: Ovid and the _Elegies_." _ELH_ 44 (1977): 419–42.
Atkins, J. W. H. _English Literary Criticism: 17th and 18th Centuries_. New York: Barnes & Noble, 1966.
——. _Literary Criticism in Antiquity_. 2 vols. 1934. Gloucester: Peter Smith, 1961.
Auerbach, Erich. _Literary Language and Its Public in Late Latin Antiq-_

uity and in the Middle Ages. Trans. Ralph Manheim. Bollingen Series 74. New York: Pantheon, 1965.

——. *Mimesis: The Representation of Reality in Western Literature.* Trans. Willard R. Trask. Princeton: Princeton University Press, 1953.

——. *Scenes from the Drama of European Literature.* 1959. Gloucester: Peter Smith, 1973.

Babb, Lawrence. *The Elizabethan Malady: A Study of Melancholia in English Literature from 1580 to 1642.* East Lansing: Michigan State College Press, 1951.

Bald, R. C. *John Donne: A Life.* Oxford: Oxford University Press, 1970.

Baumlin, James S. *John Donne and the Rhetorics of Renaissance Discourse.* Columbia: University of Missouri Press, 1991.

Beaurline, L. A. "Dudley North's Criticism of Metaphysical Poetry." *Huntington Library Quarterly* 25 (1962): 299–313.

Benjamin, Edwin B. "Bacon and Tacitus." *Classical Philology* 60 (1965): 102–10.

Bethell, S. L. "The Nature of Metaphysical Wit." In *Discussions of John Donne,* ed. Frank Kermode. Boston: Heath, 1962.

Biester, James. "Gender and Style in Seventeenth-Century Commendatory Verse." *Studies in English Literature, 1500–1900* 33 (1993): 507–22.

Bireley, Robert, S.J. *The Counter-Reformation Prince: Anti-Machiavellianism or Catholic Statecraft in Early Modern Europe.* Chapel Hill: University of North Carolina Press, 1990.

Bland, D. S. "Rhetoric and the Law in Sixteenth-Century England." *Studies in Philology* 54 (1957): 498–508.

Bourdieu, Pierre. *Outline of a Theory of Practice.* Trans. Richard Nice. Cambridge: Cambridge University Press, 1977.

Bradford, Alan T. "Stuart Absolutism and the 'Utility' of Tacitus." *Huntington Library Quarterly* 46 (1983): 127–55.

Bundy, Murray W. "'Invention' and 'Imagination' in the Renaissance." *Journal of English and Germanic Philology* 29 (1930): 535–45.

——. *The Theory of Imagination in Classical and Medieval Thought.* University of Illinois Studies in Language and Literature 12 and 13 (1927): 183–471.

Caplan, Harry. *Of Eloquence: Studies in Ancient and Medieval Rhetoric.* Ed. Anne King and Helen North. Ithaca: Cornell University Press, 1970.

Charlton, Kenneth. "Liberal Education and the Inns of Court in the Sixteenth Century." *British Journal of Educational Studies* 9 (1960): 25–38.

Coddon, Karin S. "'Suche Strange Desygns': Madness, Subjectivity, and Treason in *Hamlet* and Elizabethan Culture." *Renaissance Drama* n.s. 20 (1989): 51–75.

Colie, Rosalie L. *Paradoxia Epidemica: The Renaissance Tradition of Paradox.* Princeton: Princeton University Press, 1966.

Colish, Marcia L. *The Mirror of Language.* New Haven: Yale University Press, 1968.
——. "St. Augustine's Rhetoric of Silence Revisited." *Augustinian Studies* 9 (1978): 15–24.
Cook, Elizabeth. *Seeing Through Words.* New Haven: Yale University Press, 1986.
Cooper, Thomas. *Thesaurus Linguae Romanae et Brittanicae.* 1565. Menston, Eng.: Scolar, 1969.
Coulter, James A. *The Literary Microcosm: Theories of Interpretation of the Later Neoplatonists.* Columbia Studies in the Classical Tradition 2. Leiden: E. J. Brill, 1976.
Crane, W. G. *Wit and Rhetoric in the Renaissance.* New York: Columbia University Press, 1937.
Croll, Morris W. *"Attic" and Baroque Prose Style.* Ed. J. Max Patrick and R. O. Evans with John M. Wallace. Princeton: Princeton University Press, 1966.
Cunliffe, Richard John. *A Lexicon of the Homeric Dialect.* 1924. Norman: University of Oklahoma Press, 1963.
Cunningham, J. V. *The Collected Essays of J. V. Cunningham.* Chicago: Swallow, 1976.
Curtius, Ernst Robert. *European Literature and the Latin Middle Ages.* Trans. Willard R. Trask. Bollingen Series 36. 1953. Princeton: Princeton University Press, 1973.
Daniells, Roy. "English Baroque and Deliberate Obscurity." *Journal of Aesthetics and Art Criticism* 5 (1946): 115–21.
Dime, Gregory T. "The Difference between 'Strong Lines' and 'Metaphysical Poetry.'" *Studies in English Literature, 1500–1900* 26 (1986): 47–57.
Ebeling, Heinrich, Ed. *Lexicon Homericum.* 2 vols. 1885. Hildesheim: Georg Olms, 1963.
Eden, Kathy. "Hermeneutics and the Ancient Rhetorical Tradition." *Rhetorica* 5 (1987): 59–86.
——. *Poetic and Legal Fiction in the Aristotelian Tradition.* Princeton: Princeton University Press, 1986.
——. "The Rhetorical Tradition and Augustinian Hermeneutics in *De doctrina christiana.*" *Rhetorica* 8 (1990): 45–63.
Edinger, William. *Samuel Johnson and Poetic Style.* Chicago: University of Chicago Press, 1977.
Elledge, Scott. "The Background and Development in English Criticism of the Theories of Generality and Particularity." *PMLA* 62 (1947): 147–82.
——. "Cowley's Ode 'Of Wit' and Longinus on the Sublime: A Study of One Definition of the Word 'Wit.'" *Modern Language Quarterly* 9 (1948): 185–98.
Elliott, Robert C. *The Power of Satire: Magic, Ritual, Art.* Princeton: Princeton University Press, 1960.

Ernesti, Io. Christ. Theoph. *Lexicon Technologiae Graecorum Rhetori-cae*. 1795. Hildesheim: Georg Olms, 1962.
——. *Lexicon Technologiae Latinorum Rhetoricae*. 1797. Hildesheim: Georg Olms, 1962.
Fink, Zera S. "Jaques and the Malcontent Traveler." *Philological Quarterly* 14 (1935): 237–52.
Finkelpearl, Philip J. *John Marston of the Middle Temple*. Cambridge: Harvard University Press, 1969.
Fish, Stanley. "Masculine Persuasive Force: Donne and Verbal Power." In *Soliciting Interpretation: Literary Theory and Seventeenth-Century English Poetry*, ed. Elizabeth D. Harvey and Katharine Eisaman Maus, 223–52. Chicago: University of Chicago Press, 1990.
Franklin, Julian H. *Constitutionalism and Resistance in the Sixteenth Century*. New York: Pegasus Press, 1969.
Freeman, Kathleen. *Ancilla to the Pre-Socratic Philosophers*. Cambridge: Harvard University Press, 1948.
Freud, Sigmund. *The Standard Edition of the Complete Psychological Works of Sigmund Freud*. Trans. James Strachey et al. Vol. 11. London: Hogarth, 1957.
Fuhrmann, Manfred. "Obscuritas (Das Problem der Dunkelheit in der rhetorischen und literarästhetischen Theorie der Antike)." *Immanente Ästhetik: Ästhetische Reflexion*, ed. Wolfgang Iser, 47–72. Munich: Fink, 1966.
Galyon, Linda. "Puttenham's *Enargeia* and *Energeia*: New Twists for Old Terms." *Philological Quarterly* 60 (1981): 29–40.
Gardner, Helen, Ed. Introduction. *The Metaphysical Poets*. Rev. ed. Harmondsworth: Penguin, 1966.
Gilman, Ernest B. *The Curious Perspective: Literary and Pictorial Wit in the Seventeenth Century*. New Haven: Yale University Press, 1978.
Ginzburg, Carlo. "High and Low: The Theme of Forbidden Knowledge in the Sixteenth and Seventeenth Centuries." *Past and Present* 73 (November 1976): 28–41.
Goldberg, Jonathan. *James I and the Politics of Literature*. 1983. Stanford: Stanford University Press, 1989.
Gombrich, E. H. *Symbolic Images: Studies in the Art of the Renaissance II*. Chicago: University of Chicago Press, 1972.
Gordon, D. J. *The Renaissance Imagination*. Ed. Stephen Orgel. Berkeley: University of California Press, 1975.
Gray, Hanna H. "Renaissance Humanism: The Pursuit of Eloquence." In *Renaissance Essays*, ed. Paul Oskar Kristeller and Philip Wiener, 199–217. New York: Harper, 1968.
Greenblatt, Stephen. *Learning to Curse: Essays in Early Modern Culture*. New York: Routledge, 1990.
——. *Marvelous Possessions: The Wonder of the New World*. Berkeley: University of California Press, 1991.

——. *Renaissance Self-Fashioning: From More to Shakespeare.* Chicago: University of Chicago Press, 1980.

——. *Shakespearean Negotiations: The Circulation of Social Energy in Renaissance England.* Berkeley: University of California Press, 1988.

Grube, G. M. A. *A Greek Critic: Demetrius on Style.* Phoenix Supplementary Volume 4. Toronto: University of Toronto Press, 1961.

Hagstrum, Jean H. *The Sister Arts: The Tradition of Literary Pictorialism and English Poetry from Dryden to Gray.* Chicago: University of Chicago Press, 1958.

Hardin, Richard F. "The Early Poetry of the Gunpowder Plot: Myth in the Making." *English Literary Renaissance* 22 (1992): 62–79.

Hardison, O. B., Jr. *The Enduring Monument: A Study of the Idea of Praise in Renaissance Literary Theory and Practice.* 1962. Westport, Conn.: Greenwood, 1973.

Harvey, Elizabeth D., and Katherine Eisaman Maus, Eds. *Soliciting Interpretation: Literary Theory and Seventeenth-Century English Poetry.* Chicago: University of Chicago Press, 1990.

Hathaway, Baxter. *Marvels and Commonplaces: Renaissance Literary Criticism.* New York: Random House, 1968.

Helgerson, Richard. *Self-Crowned Laureates: Spenser, Jonson, Milton, and the Literary System.* Berkeley: University of California Press, 1983.

Hendrickson, G. L. "The Origin and Meaning of the Ancient Characters of Style." *American Journal of Philology* 26 (1905): 249–90.

Hepburn, R. W. *"Wonder" and Other Essays: Eight Studies in Aesthetics and Neighbouring Fields.* Edinburgh: Edinburgh University Press, 1984.

Herrick, Marvin T. *Comic Theory in the Sixteenth Century.* 1950. Urbana: University of Illinois Press, 1964.

——. "Some Neglected Sources of *Admiratio.*" *Modern Language Notes* 62 (1947): 222–26.

Hester, M. Thomas. *Kinde Pitty and Brave Scorn: John Donne's Satyres.* Durham: Duke University Press, 1982.

Hirst, Derek. *Authority and Conflict: England, 1603–1658.* Cambridge: Harvard University Press, 1986.

Huntley, Frank L. "*Macbeth* and the Background of Jesuitical Equivocation." *PMLA* 79 (1964): 390–400.

Jackson, B. Darrell. "The Theory of Signs in St. Augustine's *De Doctrina Christiana.*" In *Augustine: A Collection of Critical Essays,* ed. R. A. Markus, 92–147. Modern Studies in Philosophy. New York: Anchor, 1972.

Janko, Richard. *Aristotle on Comedy: Towards a Reconstruction of Poetics II.* London: Duckworth, 1984.

Javitch, Daniel. "The Impure Motives of Elizabethan Poetry." *Genre* 15 (1982): 225–38.

——. *Poetry and Courtliness in Renaissance England.* Princeton: Princeton University Press, 1978.

——. "Rival Arts of Conduct in Elizabethan England: Guazzo's *Civile*

Conversation and Castiglione's *Courtier.*" *Yearbook of Italian Studies* 1 (1971): 178–98.

Johnson, W. R. *The Idea of Lyric: Lyric Modes in Ancient and Modern Poetry.* Berkeley: University of California Press, 1982.

Jordan, William J. "Aristotle's Concept of Metaphor in Rhetoric." In *Aristotle: The Classical Heritage of Rhetoric,* ed. Keith V. Erickson, 235–50. Metuchen, N.J.: Scarecrow, 1974.

Kahn, Victoria. *Machiavellian Rhetoric: From the Counter-Reformation to Milton.* Princeton: Princeton University Press, 1994.

Kantorowicz, Ernst H. *Selected Studies.* Locust Valley, N.Y.: Augustin, 1965.

Kegl, Rosemary. *The Rhetoric of Concealment: Figuring Gender and Class in Renaissance Literature.* Ithaca: Cornell University Press, 1994.

Kemp, Martin. "From 'Mimesis' to 'Fantasia': The Quattrocento Vocabulary of Creation, Inspiration, and Genius in the Visual Arts." *Viator* 8 (1977): 347–405.

Kenseth, Joy, Ed. *The Age of the Marvelous.* Hanover, N.H.: Hood Museum of Art, Dartmouth College, 1991.

Kernan, Alvin. *The Cankered Muse: Satire of the English Renaissance.* New Haven: Yale University Press, 1959.

Klause, John L. "Donne and the Wonderful." *English Literary Renaissance* 17 (1987): 41–66.

Klibansky, Raymond, Erwin Panofsky, and Fritz Saxl. *Saturn and Melancholy.* New York: Basic Books, 1964.

Knafla, Louis A. "The Law Studies of an Elizabethan Student." *Huntington Library Quarterly* 32 (1969): 221–40.

Knights, L. C. *Drama and Society in the Age of Jonson.* 1937. New York: W. W. Norton, 1968.

——. *Further Explorations.* Stanford: Stanford University Press, 1965.

Kristeller, Paul Oskar. "Rhetoric in Medieval and Renaissance Culture." In *Renaissance Eloquence.* Ed. James J. Murphy. Berkeley: University of California Press, 1983.

Kustas, George L. *Studies in Byzantine Rhetoric.* Analecta Vlatadon 17. Thessalonica, 1973.

Lanham, Richard A. *The Motives of Eloquence: Literary Rhetoric in the Renaissance.* New Haven: Yale University Press, 1976.

Laporte, Valerie Dorothy. "John Donne and the Esoteric Tradition." Ph.D. diss. Columbia University, 1986.

Lausberg, Heinrich. *Handbuch der Literarischen Rhetorik.* 2 vols. Munich: Max Hueber, 1960.

Lee, Rensselaer W. *Ut Pictura Poesis: The Humanistic Theory of Painting.* New York: W. W. Norton, 1967.

Le Goff, Jacques. *The Medieval Imagination.* Trans. Arthur Goldhammer. Chicago: University of Chicago Press, 1988.

Lesky, Albin. *A History of Greek Literature.* Trans. James Willis and Cornelis de Heer. New York: Crowell, 1966.

Levy, F. J. "Francis Bacon and the Style of Politics." In *Renaissance Historicism: Selections from* English Literary Renaissance, ed. Arthur F. Kinney and Dan S. Collins, 146–67. Amherst: University of Massachusetts Press, 1987.

Lewalski, Barbara Kiefer. *Donne's* Anniversaries *and the Poetry of Praise: The Creation of a Symbolic Mode.* Princeton: Princeton University Press, 1973.

——. *Protestant Poetics and the Seventeenth-Century Religious Lyric.* Princeton: Princeton University Press, 1979.

Liddell, Henry George, and Robert Scott. *A Greek-English Lexicon.* Rev. Sir Henry Stuart Jones, supplement ed. E. A. Barber. Oxford University Press, 1968.

Lipking, Joanna Brizdle. "Traditions of the *Facetiae* and Their Influence in Tudor England." Ph.D. diss. Columbia University, 1970.

Lovejoy, Arthur O. *Essays in the History of Ideas.* 1948. New York: Capricorn, 1960.

Lyons, Bridget Gellert. *Voices of Melancholy: Studies in Literary Treatments of Melancholy in Renaissance England.* New York: W. W. Norton, 1975.

Lytle, Guy Fitch, and Stephen Orgel, Eds. *Patronage in the Renaissance.* Princeton: Princeton University Press, 1981.

MacCaffrey, Wallace T. "Place and Patronage in Elizabethan Politics." In *Elizabethan Government and Society,* ed. S. T. Bindoff et al., 95–126. London: Athlone, 1961.

Malloch, A. E. "The Techniques and Function of the Renaissance Paradox." *Studies in Philology* 53 (1956): 191–203.

Markus, R. A., Ed. *Augustine: A Collection of Critical Essays.* Modern Studies in Philosophy. New York: Anchor, 1972.

——. "St. Augustine on Signs." In *Augustine: A Collection of Critical Essays,* ed. R. A. Markus, 61–91. Modern Studies in Philosophy. New York: Anchor, 1972.

Marotti, Arthur F. "John Donne and the Rewards of Patronage." In *Patronage in the Renaissance,* ed. Guy Fitch Lytle and Stephen Orgel, 207–34. Princeton: Princeton University Press, 1981.

——. *John Donne, Coterie Poet.* Madison: University of Wisconsin Press, 1986.

——. *Manuscript, Print, and the English Renaissance Lyric.* Ithaca: Cornell University Press, 1995.

Marrou, Henri-Irénée. *Saint Augustin et la fin de la culture antique.* Paris: E. de Boccard, 1938.

Mazzeo, Joseph A. *Renaissance and Seventeenth-Century Studies.* New York: Columbia University Press, 1964.

Medine, Peter E. "Isaac Casaubon's *Prolegomena* to the *Satires* of Persius: An Introduction, Text, and Translation," *English Literary Renaissance* 6 (1976): 271–98.

Miner, Earl. *The Cavalier Mode from Jonson to Cotton.* Princeton: Princeton University Press, 1971.

——. *The Metaphysical Mode from Donne to Cowley.* Princeton: Princeton University Press, 1969.

Mirollo, James V. *Mannerism and Renaissance Poetry.* New Haven: Yale University Press, 1984.

——. *The Poet of the Marvelous: Giambattista Marino.* New York: Columbia University Press, 1963.

Monfasani, John. "The Byzantine Rhetorical Tradition and the Renaissance." In *Renaissance Eloquence,* ed. James J. Murphy, 174–87. Berkeley: University of California Press, 1983.

Monk, Samuel H. *The Sublime: A Study of Critical Theories in XVIII-Century England.* New York: MLA, 1935.

Mullaney, Steven. "Lying Like Truth: Riddle, Representation and Treason in Renaissance England." *ELH* 47 (1980): 32–47.

——. *The Place of the Stage: License, Play, and Power in Renaissance England.* Chicago: University of Chicago Press, 1988.

——. "Strange Things, Gross Terms, Curious Customs: The Rehearsal of Cultures in the Late Renaissance." In *Representing the English Renaissance,* ed. Stephen Greenblatt, 65–92. Berkeley: University of California Press, 1988.

Nahm, Milton C. "The Theological Background of the Theory of the Artist as Creator." *Journal of the History of Ideas* 7 (1947): 363–72.

Neale, J. E. *The Age of Catherine de Medici and Essays in Elizabethan History.* London: Cape, 1963.

Neely, Carol Thomas. "Did Madness Have a Renaissance?" *Renaissance Quarterly* 20 (1991): 766–88.

Nicolson, Marjorie Hope. *Newton Demands the Muse: Newton's Opticks and the Eighteenth Century Poets.* Princeton: Princeton University Press, 1946.

O Hehir, Brendan. *Expans'd Hieroglyphicks: A Study of Sir John Denham's Cooper's Hill with a Critical Edition of the Poem.* Berkeley: University of California Press, 1969.

O'Meara, Dominic J., ed. *Neoplatonism and Christian Thought.* Studies in Neoplatonism: Ancient and Modern 3. Albany: State University of New York Press, 1982.

Orgel, Stephen. *The Illusion of Power: Political Theater in the English Renaissance.* Berkeley: University of California Press, 1975.

——. "The Poetics of Incomprehensibility." *Shakespeare Quarterly* 42 (1991): 431–37.

Osborn, James M. *Young Philip Sidney, 1572–1577.* New Haven: Yale University Press, 1972.

Oxford Latin Dictionary. Ed. P. G. W. Glare. Oxford: Clarendon Press, 1968–82.

Panofsky, Erwin. "Artist, Scientist, Genius: Notes on the 'Renaissance-Dämmerung.'" *The Renaissance.* New York: Harper, 1962.

——. *Idea: A Concept in Art Theory.* Trans. Joseph J. S. Peake. New York: Harper, 1968.

Park, Katharine, and Lorraine J. Daston. "Unnatural Conceptions: The Study of Monsters in Sixteenth- and Seventeeth-Century France and England." *Past and Present* 92 (1981): 20–54.

Parry, Graham. *The Golden Age Restor'd: The Culture of the Stuart Court, 1603–42.* New York: St. Martin's Press, 1981.

Patterson, Annabel M. "All Donne." In *Soliciting Interpretation: Literary Theory and Seventeenth-Century English Poetry*, ed. Elizabeth D. Harvey and Katharine Eisaman Maus, 37–67. Chicago: University of Chicago Press, 1990.

——. *Hermogenes and the Renaissance.* Princeton: Princeton University Press, 1970.

Peck, Linda Levy. "Court Patronage and Government Policy: The Jacobean Dilemma." In *Patronage in the Renaissance*, ed. Guy Fitch Lytle and Stephen Orgel, 27–46. Princeton: Princeton University Press, 1981.

——, ed. *The Mental World of the Jacobean Court.* Cambridge: Cambridge University Press, 1991.

Pépin, Jean. "Saint Augustin et la fonction protreptique de l'allégorie." *Recherches Augustiniennes* 1 (1958): 243–86.

Platt, Peter G. "'Not before either known or dreamt of': Francesco Patrizi and the Power of Wonder in Renaissance Poetics." *Review of English Studies* n.s. 43 (1992): 387–94.

——. *Reason Diminished: Shakespeare and the Marvelous.* Lincoln: University of Nebraska Press, forthcoming.

Plett, Heinrich F. "Aesthetic Constituents in the Courtly Culture of Renaissance England." *New Literary History* 14 (1983): 597–621.

Pocock, J. G. A. "Texts as Events: Reflections on the History of Political Thought." In *Politics of Discourse: The Literature and History of Seventeenth-Century England*, ed. Kevin Sharpe and Steven N. Zwicker, 21–34. Berkeley: University of California Press, 1987.

——. *Virtue, Commerce, and History: Essays in Political Thought and History, Chiefly in the Eighteenth Century.* Cambridge: Cambridge University Press, 1985.

Praz, Mario. *Machiavelli and the Elizabethans.* 1928. Folcroft, Penn.: Folcroft, 1973.

——. *Studies in Seventeenth-Century Imagery.* 2d ed. 1964. Sussidi Eruditi 16. Rome: Edizioni di Storia e Litteratura, 1975.

Prescott, Anne Lake. "Humanism in the Tudor Jestbook." *Moreana* 24 (1987): 5–16.

Prest, Wilfred R. *The Inns of Court under Elizabeth I and the Early Stuarts, 1590–1640.* Totowa, N.J.: Rowman and Littlefield, 1972.

Pye, Christopher. "The Sovereign, the Theater, and the Kingdome of Darknesse: Hobbes and the Spectacle of Power." In *Representing the English Renaissance*, ed. Stephen Greenblatt, 279–301. Berkeley: University of California Press, 1988.

Quadlbauer, Franz. "Die genera dicendi bis auf Plinius d.J." *Wiener Studien* 71 (1958): 55–111.

Quinn, Dennis. "Donne and the Wane of Wonder." *ELH* 36 (1969): 626–47.

Rebhorn, Wayne A. *Courtly Performances: Masking and Festivity in Castiglione's* Book of the Courtier. Detroit: Wayne State University Press, 1978.

——. *Foxes and Lions: Machiavelli's Confidence Men*. Ithaca: Cornell University Press, 1988.

Robinson, Forrest G. *The Shape of Things Known: Sidney's Apology in Its Philosophical Tradition*. Cambridge: Harvard University Press, 1972.

Salmon, J. H. M. "Seneca and Tacitus in Jacobean England." In *The Mental World of the Jacobean Court*, ed. Linda Levy Peck, 169–88. Cambridge: Cambridge University Press, 1991.

Saunders, J. W. "The Social Situation of Seventeenth-Century Poetry." In *Metaphysical Poetry*, ed. Malcolm Bradbury and David Palmer, 236–59. Bloomington: Indiana University Press, 1971.

——. "The Stigma of Print: A Note on the Social Bases of Tudor Poetry." *Essays in Criticism* 1 (1951): 139–64.

Schellhase, Kenneth C. *Tacitus in Renaissance Political Thought*. Chicago: University of Chicago Press, 1976.

Schenkeveld, Dirk Marie. *Studies in Demetrius on Style*. Amsterdam: Hakkert, 1964.

Schoeck, R. J. "O Altitudo! Sir Thomas Browne, Scriptures, and Renaissance Tradition." *English Language Notes* 19 (1982): 402–8.

Scott, Inez Gertrude. *The Grand Style in the Satires of Juvenal*. Northampton: Smith College Classical Studies 8, 1927.

Selden, Raman. *English Verse Satire 1590–1765*. London: Allen and Unwin, 1978.

Shankman, Steven. *Pope's Iliad: Homer in the Age of Passion*. Princeton: Princeton University Press, 1983.

Shapiro, I. A. "The 'Mermaid Club.'" *Modern Language Review* 45.1 (1950): 6–17.

Shapiro, James. *Rival Playwrights: Marlowe, Jonson, Shakespeare*. New York: Columbia University Press, 1991.

Sharp, Robert Lathrop. *From Donne to Dryden*. Chapel Hill: University of North Carolina Press, 1940.

——. "Some Light on Metaphysical Obscurity and Roughness." *Studies in Philology* 31 (1934): 497–518.

Sharpe, Kevin. *Criticism and Compliment: The Politics of Literature in the England of Charles I*. Cambridge: Cambridge University Press, 1987.

Sharpe, Kevin, and Steven N. Zwicker, eds. *Politics of Discourse: The Literature and History of Seventeenth-Century England*. Berkeley: University of California Press, 1987.

Shawcross, John T., ed. *The Complete Poetry of John Donne*. New York: Anchor, 1967.

Shearman, John. *Mannerism*. Harmondsworth: Penguin, 1967.
Sheavyn, Phoebe. *The Literary Profession in the Elizabethan Age*. 2d ed. Rev. J. W. Saunders. New York: Barnes & Noble, 1967.
Shuger, Debora K. *Habits of Thought in the English Renaissance: Religion, Politics, and the Dominant Culture*. Berkeley: University of California Press, 1990.
——. *Sacred Rhetoric: The Christian Grand Style in the Renaissance*. Princeton: Princeton University Press, 1988.
Skinner, Quentin. *The Foundations of Modern Political Thought: Volume One: The Renaissance*. Cambridge: Cambridge University Press, 1978.
Smith, A. J., ed. *John Donne: The Critical Heritage*. London: Routledge, 1975.
——, ed. *John Donne: Essays in Celebration*. London: Methuen, 1972.
——. *Metaphysical Wit*. Cambridge: Cambridge University Press, 1991.
Smuts, R. Malcolm. *Court Culture and the Origins of a Royalist Tradition in Early Stuart England*. Philadelphia: University of Pennsylvania Press, 1987.
——. "The Political Failure of Stuart Cultural Patronage." In *Patronage in the Renaissance*, ed. Guy Fitch Lytle and Stephen Orgel, 165–87. Princeton: Princeton University Press, 1981.
Snell, Bruno. *The Discovery of the Mind in Greek Philosophy and Literature*. Trans. T. G. Rosenmeyer. 1953. New York: Dover, 1982.
Solmsen, Friedrich. "The Aristotelian Tradition in Ancient Rhetoric." *American Journal of Philology* 62 (1941): 35–50, 169–90.
Spencer, Theodore. "The Elizabethan Malcontent." In *Joseph Quincy Adams Memorial Studies*, ed. James G. McManaway et al., 523–35. Washington, D.C.: Folger Library, 1948.
Stein, Arnold. "Donne's Obscurity and the Elizabethan Tradition." *ELH* 13 (1946): 98–118.
Stevens, Paul. "Subversion and Wonder in Milton's Epitaph 'On Shakespeare,'" *English Literary Renaissance* 19 (1989): 375–88.
Stone, Lawrence. *The Crisis of the Aristocracy, 1558–1641*. Oxford: Oxford University Press, 1965.
Sullivan, Ernest W., II. *The Influence of John Donne: His Uncollected Seventeenth-Century Printed Verse*. Columbia: University of Missouri Press, 1993.
Summers, David. *The Language of Sense: Renaissance Naturalism and the Rise of Aesthetics*. Cambridge: Cambridge University Press, 1987.
——. *Michelangelo and the Language of Art*. Princeton: Princeton University Press, 1981.
Tayler, Edward W. *Donne's Idea of a Woman*. New York: Columbia University Press, 1991.
——. *Milton's Poetry: Its Development in Time*. Pittsburgh: Duquesne University Press, 1979.
Tenney, Mary F. "Tacitus in the Politics of Early Stuart England." *The Classical Journal* 37 (1941): 151–63.

Thomson, Patricia. "Donne and the Poetry of Patronage: The *Verse Letters*." In *John Donne: Essays in Celebration*, ed. A. J. Smith, 308–23. London: Methuen, 1972.

——. "The Literature of Patronage, 1580–1630." *Essays in Criticism* 2 (1952): 267–84.

——. "The Patronage of Letters under Elizabeth and James I." *English* 7 (1949): 278–82.

Tigerstedt, E. N. "*Furor Poeticus*: Poetic Inspiration in Greek Literature before Democritus and Plato." *Journal of the History of Ideas* 31 (1970): 163–78.

Trimpi, Wesley. *Ben Jonson's Poems: A Study of the Plain Style*. Stanford: Stanford University Press, 1962.

——. "Horace's 'Ut Pictura Poesis': The Argument for Stylistic Decorum." *Traditio* 34 (1978): 29–73.

——. "The Meaning of Horace's *Ut Pictura Poesis*." *Journal of the Warburg and Courtauld Institutes* 36 (1973): 1–34.

——. *Muses of One Mind: The Literary Analysis of Experience and Its Continuity*. Princeton: Princeton University Press, 1983.

Tuve, Rosemond. *Elizabethan and Metaphysical Imagery: Renaissance Poetic and Twentieth-Century Critics*. Chicago: University of Chicago Press, 1947.

Ustick, W. Lee, and Hoyt H. Hudson. "Wit, 'Mixt Wit,' and the Bee in Amber." *Huntington Library Bulletin* 8 (1935): 103–30.

Van Hook, J. W. "'Concupiscence of Witt': The Metaphysical Conceit in Baroque Poetics." *Modern Philology* 84 (1986): 24–38.

Voit, Ludwig. *Deinotēs: ein antiker Stilbegriff*. Leipzig: Dieterich'sche Verlagsbuchhandlung, 1934.

Wall, John N., Jr., and Terry Bunce Burgin. "'This sermon . . . upon the Gun-powder day': The *Book of Homilies* of 1547 and Donne's Sermon in Commemoration of Guy Fawkes' Day, 1622." *South Atlantic Review* 49 (1984): 19–29.

Wallerstein, Ruth. *Studies in Seventeenth-Century Poetic*. 1950. Madison: University of Wisconsin Press, 1965.

Wanamaker, Melissa C. *Discordia Concors: The Wit of Metaphysical Poetry*. National University Publications: Literary Criticism Series. Port Washington, N.Y.: Kennikat, 1975.

Weinberg, Bernard. "Demetrius Phalereus." In *Catalogous Translationum et Commentariorum: Mediaeval and Renaissance Latin Translations and Commentaries*, vol. 2, ed. P. O. Kristeller, 27–41. Washington, D.C.: Catholic University Press, 1971.

——. *A History of Literary Criticism in the Italian Renaissance*. 2 vols. Chicago: University of Chicago Press, 1961.

Whigham, Frank. *Ambition and Privilege: The Social Tropes of Elizabethan Courtesy Theory*. Berkeley: University of California Press, 1984.

——. "Interpretation at Court: Courtesy and the Performer-Audience Dialectic." *New Literary History* 14 (1983): 623–39.

Whitfield, J. H. "Livy, Tacitus." In *Classical Influences on European Culture A.D. 1500–1700*, ed. R. R. Bolgar, 281–93. Cambridge: Cambridge University Press, 1976.

Williamson, George. *The Proper Wit of Poetry*. London: Faber, 1961.

———. *The Senecan Amble: Prose Form from Bacon to Collier*. 1951. Chicago: University of Chicago Press, 1966.

———. *Seventeenth-Century Contexts*. London: Faber, 1960.

Wilson, F. P. "Some Notes on Authors and Patrons in Tudor and Stuart Times." In *Joseph Quincy Adams Memorial Studies*, ed. James G. McManaway et al., 553–61. Washington, D.C.: Folger Library, 1948.

Wimsatt, William K., and Cleanth Brooks. *Literary Criticism: A Short History*. New York: Knopf, 1957.

Wind, Edgar. *Pagan Mysteries in the Renaissance*. Rev. and enl. ed. New York: W. W. Norton, 1968.

Index